THE
Light and Easy
COOKBOOK

Other cookbooks by Barbara Gibbons:

THE INTERNATIONAL SLIM GOURMET

THE SLIM GOURMET

THE YEAR-ROUND TURKEY

THE
Light and Easy
COOKBOOK

Barbara Gibbons

MACMILLAN PUBLISHING CO., INC.
New York

COLLIER MACMILLAN PUBLISHERS
London

Copyright © 1980 by Barbara Gibbons

All rights reserved. No part of this book may be reproduced or transmitted in any form or by any means, electronic or mechanical, including photocopying, recording or by any information storage and retrieval system, without permission in writing from the Publisher.

Macmillan Publishing Co., Inc.
866 Third Avenue, New York, N.Y. 10022
Collier Macmillan Canada, Ltd.

Library of Congress Cataloging in Publication Data
Gibbons, Barbara.
The light and easy cookbook.
Includes index.
1. Cookery.   2. Low-calorie diet—Recipes.
I. Title.
TX715.G42   641.5'55   80-18310
ISBN 0-02-543120-X

10   9   8   7   6   5   4   3   2   1

Designed by Jack Meserole

Printed in the United States of America

ACKNOWLEDGMENTS

The recipes may be "light and easy," but putting together a cookbook is heavy work that needs lots of help. I'd like to express my grateful appreciation to Jeanne Fredericks, and to editor Toni Lopopolo and all the other people at Macmillan who worked so hard at getting it togther, getting it right—and getting it done! This book wouldn't have been possible without the dedicated assistance of my friend and co-worker, home economist Dorothea Fast, and the conscientious care of secretaries Moira McKaig and Alvina Ostrowski. And last but by no means least, I'd like to say thanks to all the information people in the food field who provided quick answers, often on short notice and at odd hours.

CONTENTS

The "Light" Revolution
Is Under Way

Up until now, Americans have adopted a style of eating and cooking that is simply too fattening, too "heavy"—too calorie-laden—for the way we live. Our food—no longer in the hands of home cooks, but corporate food producers and fast-food franchisers—supplies too many calories and too little appetite satisfaction.

This generation has come to rely on a style of eating that *induces* hunger. A generation ago Americans ate "three squares" a day. Today, the typical American picks and snacks and nibbles from morning until night . . . and may have as many as twenty food encounters in one day, much of it "junk" food. The devitalized, empty-caloried fast-food that makes up such a large part of our daily menu may seem "light" in appetite satisfaction—that's why we need to eat so much of it—but it's actually heavy in calories.

Our calorie-heavy "thorn of plenty" has created a nation of overweights. Obesity and fat-inducing eating habits are related to our major diseases: heart attacks, cancer, stroke, and diabetes. In that respect, excess pounds is our number one health problem and unneeded calories our most dangerous food additive.

THE
Light and Easy
COOKBOOK

1

Shedding Some Light on

the "Light" Revolution

The Hidden High Price of Eat-Out, Take-Home, Thaw-and-Serve Convenience Meals

If you're like most Americans, you're caught on the horns of a dining dilemma: eating wisely and well or eating in a hurry. If you're like most *busy* Americans, a lack of time generally dictates the latter choice. And because most Americans have so little time, fast-food franchises and convenience industries now thrive.

Remember in the old war movies how draft notices usually arrived while the family was sitting around the dining table—a quaint custom that most Americans joined in at least twice a day. Back in 1940, Mother spent an average of five hours a day preparing family meals, from real foods with real ingredients. But by the end of the 1970s most women between the ages of twenty-five and fifty-four were working outside the home. Instead of "three squares," Americans ate whenever and wherever it was convenient. Mealtime gave way to "snacktime," and the average amount of time that family members spent eating together had shrunk to twenty minutes. More than one out of three food dollars was going to fast-food places, snack bars, restaurants, and cafeterias. The seventh largest food advertiser in America was McDonald's!

In the space of one generation, Americans became meal buyers as opposed to meal makers. And although fast-foods seem inexpensive compared with "slow" foods prepared from scratch or leisurely enjoyed in better restaurants, the kinds of foods Americans have come to rely on are actually a poor bargain. Fast-food meals often deliver relatively little in nutrition, taste, and enjoyment for what they actually cost in both cash *and* calories. Designed to be shoveled in as quickly as possible, fast-foods cram us with calories without satisfying either our appetites or our hunger, a chief reason why overweight has become a major American health problem.

Today, the majority of us weigh more than we should or more than we want. America's leading diseases are related to our calorie-rich diet of too many refined fats, starches, and sugars and too few whole grains, fruits, and vegetables.

The Diet Delusion

With many of us unhappy about our weight, it's no wonder that dieting has become the rage. Americans are sold "fast" diets and quick-weight-loss schemes in the same way that they have been sold fast-foods. Advertising has conditioned us to expect an instant, packaged, no-work solution for every problem, and overweight is no exception. What Americans bought was the promise that excess pounds could simply melt away. Despite a better than 90 percent failure rate on diets, the populace remained unshakably convinced that the next fourteen-day miracle fad—the next best-selling diet book, the next pill or potion— would finally do what all the other easy schemes had failed to do.

While some Americans did indeed lose weight, virtually all of them gained it back. Typical dieters viewed their diet as something to "go on"—and then "go off"—when the scale descended to the magic number. What they failed to grasp was the inevitable fact that once you go off a diet, you go back to the weight you used to be. And often more!

REAL FOOD AND DIET FOOD   During the ritual of dieting, Americans abstained from "real" (usual) food and ate "diet" ("unreal") foods that were carefully segregated into a special section of the supermarket—a penitent's ghetto of mock milk-shake meals and chemical desserts. The diet foods themselves were clearly punitive: often unattractively packaged, overpriced, bland, and boring. Most items aimed at reaching all possible markets at once. They were low-calorie, low-sugar, low-salt, low-cholesterol, low-fat, low-carbohydrate . . . and low-taste! "Regular" people didn't eat diet foods, only dieters did.

Then, in the late 1970s, the diet fad reached its ultimate expression: fasting, augmented by a foul-tasting "protein-sparing" mucilage-like liquid that promised to prevent the body from consuming its own organs. Some people went months without solid food and lost enormous amounts of weight. Some of them also died.

Is Eating Dangerous to Your Health?

If *not* eating was dangerous, eating seemed even more so. Throughout the 1970s, consumers were assaulted with reports of danger on the end of the fork. It seemed as if every week another food was declared suspect, toxic, carcinogenic, or potentially life-shortening in one way or another. We were told to avoid sugar *and* sugar substitutes, eggs *and* egg substitutes, butter *and* margarine. Meat was full of fat; fish was full of mercury. With hot dogs and hamburgers you could take your pick of things to worry about: high calorie count, fat content, cholesterol, synthetic hormones, salt, meat extenders, nitrosamines, rodent hairs, and insect parts. Meanwhile the cost of eating leapfrogged. Prices escalated so rapidly that supermarket clerks were hard-pressed to find room on cans and boxes to stamp the latest increases.

Food became a federal case: the United States Senate Subcommittee on Nutrition, chaired by George McGovern of South Dakota, was formed to investigate the American menu and come up with recommendations for a saner way of eating. Its recommendations seemed harmless: less red meat; more poultry and seafood; fewer refined carbohydrates; more whole grains, fruits, and vegetables; less sugar and cholesterol-laden foods; only enough calories to sustain a desirable weight. The suggestions were viewed as potentially harmful to so many segments of the food industry, however, that a battle was shortly under way.

Bureaucrats, the medical establishment, legislators, nutritionists, consumer advocates, industry partisans, and the press have become embroiled in a debate over a national food policy to promote a healthier, slimmer, and less suicidal way of eating. But even though the food industry succeeded in weakening the original recommendations, the net effect of all this attention was healthy. All but the most oblivious consumers were forced to reexamine their long-entrenched shopping and eating habits.

By the end of the 1970s there were changes in the wind. From a crosscurrent of countertrends, a new "light" approach to food had begun to emerge. It grew from a diversity of movements—fitness, vegetarianism, gardening, conservation, health foods, back-to-nature, travel, home entertaining, gourmet cooking, holistic medicine, Women's Liberation, and the aspirations of the "me" generation. Americans were beginning to demand more and less of their daily bread: more nutrition, taste, flavor, sustenance, and appetite-appeasement, and fewer calories, less fat, less sugar, and less chemical contamination.

Some people were actually baking their own bread. Do-it-yourself kitchen gadgetry became big business, not only bread-making equipment but pasta machines, crêpe makers, slow cookers, fast cookers, and fancy-priced food processors. The fashionable kitchen was no longer a Formica cubbyhole, but a quaint clutter of copper pots, hanging plants, bleached butcher-block counters, and real wood shelves displaying real ingredients. Or it became a no-nonsense "high tech" food-making headquarters modeled after professional kitchens, with restaurant pots hung on wall grids or stacked on stainless steel wire racks.

The occupants of these new kitchens were no longer sex-stereotyped. Women's Lib consciousness-raising had made it okay for men to take an interest in their daily bread. In some cases it was mandatory . . . they cooked while their wives worked! Or they had no wives. By the late 1970s the typical TV sitcom-type suburban family—Mom, Dad, Sonny, and Sis—was more the exception than the rule. The actual household was just fractionally over two people. Because every American home no longer necessarily had its own full-time, live-in chief cook, maid, and bottle washer, the need for speed in the kitchen was paramount. What Americans really wanted was food that was both fast and nonfattening, convenient but not calorie-laden: food that could be economical, nutritious, and delicious as well.

It was the beer company, Miller Brewing, that came up with the right word and the right marketing approach to sell the American public on what it was looking for in drink as well as food. There had been low-calorie and diet beers before, but they were never commercially successful. In late summer 1973, Miller began test-marketing what was ultimately to become a history-making advertising campaign; the product was its calorie-reduced "Lite" beer. The new slogan, "Everything you want in a beer and less," answered the hopes of many consumers. "Lite" was an instant success. Moreover, Miller's marketing strategy didn't go unnoticed by food makers. Predictably, there followed all sorts of "lite" or "light" products, foods as well as beers. Miller lost a legal attempt to keep the word "lite" for itself, and soon it, or "light," was on its way to becoming the food word of the 1980s . . . what "natural" had been in the early 1970s.

By the end of the 1970s, following Miller's lead, there were some twenty lower-calorie brews on the market, with counts that ranged from 70 to 137 a 12-ounce can (compared with 150 for regular brews). Some vintners followed suit with "light" wines at a lower alcohol content: 8 or 9 percent (compared with 11 or 12 percent for most table wines). Some soda bottlers began to relabel their diet drinks as "light."

The revolution moved into the supermarkets. There were "light" margarines with a calorie count per tablespoon midway between regular margarine (100 calories) and diet margarine (50 calories). Some had cut the fat content by adding yogurt. There were "light" jams and jellies, preserves, and marmalades, so-called because they contained only half the calories and more fruit than conventional spreads. Dessert lovers could find "light" cakes and pies to soothe their sweet tooth. Some were made with less sugar and no fat, some were sweetened with fruit sugar (. . . and some were simply a rip-off, with no real calorie savings!). There were "light" cake and frosting mixes, cheeses, salad dressings, cereals, breads, and soups.

But, as often happens, some food manufacturers took advantage of the gullible. Just as all health foods aren't necessarily healthful, neither are all "light" foods low in calories. Trading on the implication of lightened calorie counts, some food makers simply relabeled or repackaged products without actually reducing fattening ingredients or lowering calories. The word "light," after all, can mean anything: color, texture, weight, or whatever the manufacturer chooses. (Consumers should take "light" claims lightly and look for calorie verification on the label.)

Inevitably, the "light idea" has now spread to home cooking. No longer the special province of dieters, waistline watchers, and those with special health problems, eating right and cooking light are common concerns of Americans on every level. "Gourmet" cooks are mastering a new kind of French cooking: the lighter, less calorié-laden "cuisine nouvelle" and "cuisine minceur." Ethnic cooks are experimenting with adaptations and alterations of traditional favorites to capture foreign flavor with fewer calories. Entertaining cooks are creating imaginative menus based on today's fashionable foods: fresh fruits and vegetables, exotic grains, lean seafood, poultry, and veal. Budget-minded cooks are scrutinizing labels, newly aware of nutrition and wary of false bargains that provide more calories than sustenance.

And cooks-in-a-hurry—which includes most of us—are looking for ways to shortcut time and trouble as well as calories without sacrificing taste and nutrition.

If that describes you, you're the person for whom this book was written.

2

Who Says "Fast" Foods

Have to Be Fattening?

TODAY, eating both wisely and well is easier than ever, if you know how. No matter how busy you are, you don't have to rely on eat-out or take-home "fast-foods" or thaw-and-serve, heat-and-eat convenience meals. You don't have to spend a lot of time and money cooking special foods or shopping in health food, gourmet, or "import shoppes," either!

Today, weight-wary shoppers are in the *majority,* so you'll find an ever-increasing variety of choices on hand, right in your own neighborhood supermarket. With today's growing interest in health and fitness, supermarkets have responded by offering shoppers more—and better—choices. You'll find a wider selection of fresh fruits and vegetables all year long; more lean meats, seafood, and poultry; and a growing variety of lower-caloried alternatives to products that are normally fattening.

While it's become fashionable to knock American food, it's unfair to focus only on the convenience mixes, fast-food outlets, fabricated junk foods, and devitalized snacks and ignore the bountiful harvest of healthy whole foods also available, in convenient forms, in almost any American supermarket. Not only do we have freedom of choice, we have the widest choice in the world. While the French, Italian, and Chinese are primarily limited to French, Italian, and Chinese foods, Americans have the whole world's cuisines to choose from. We can make our "Italian food" fattening or nonfattening, fast or fancy . . . a literal translation or a loose adaptation. While our supermarkets may be guilty of displaying high-profit, low-nutrition processed foods, the same supermarkets also offer a worldwide harvest of fresh fruits and vegetables, lean meat, poultry, seafood, herbs, spices, and seasonings, plus lighter, low-fat, part-skim, and sugarless alternatives to the more fattening ingredients. With little time and trouble, most Americans can find whatever they want, including the ingredients for light and easy meals.

The "Light" Answer

WHAT'S THE LIGHT IDEA? The "Light Idea" is to select ingredients that maximize the pleasure and satisfaction of every dish while avoiding or minimizing "empty-calorie" ingredients that promote overeating, hunger, and weight gain.

WHAT ARE "EMPTY-CALORIE" INGREDIENTS AND HOW DO THEY PROMOTE HUNGER AND WEIGHT GAIN? "Empty-calorie" ingredients are the foods that provide calories with little redeeming nutritional or appetite-satisfying value. Empty-calorie foods are low in vitamins, minerals, lean proteins, or the natural fiber that provides bulk.

Fat and sugar are the prime examples of empty-calorie ingredients that make fast-foods and convenience products fattening while offering little in nutritional value. Because many convenience foods are so nutritionally unsatisfactory, it's easy to use up half your daily "calorie allotment" on a fast meal or snack . . . and still be hungry! Fat offers no flavor satisfaction, and fast-foods and snacks that are high in sugar (or refined starches) can actually *promote* hunger instead of satisfying it. That's because sugar can cause your blood sugar level to soar, then plummet, leaving you with a shaky, hungry feeling that can only be eliminated by another snack.

WHAT INGREDIENTS MAXIMIZE DINING PLEASURE AND APPETITE SATISFACTION? Foods that are both flavorful and filling are what we need to satisfy both our hunger and the desire for dining pleasure. Neither flavor nor bulk is necessarily high in calories. The notion that everything that "tastes good" is "fattening" is simply not true! "Tasting good" depends on flavor. Many of the most flavorful foods and seasonings are low-calorie . . . some are no-calorie. Consider such flavorful favorites as shrimp and lobster, peaches and tomatoes . . . or peppers, garlic, mint, oregano, cinnamon, hot mustard, lemon juice, and horseradish! Many high-calorie ingredients, on the other hand, are bland or even tasteless. Fat and flour, for example. What "flavor" do we get from sugar? Sugar provides one-dimensional sweetness, whereas fresh fruit provides flavor, nutrition, and fiber along with sweetness.

About Calorie Counts and Serving Sizes

At the end of every recipe in this book is an indication of the number of servings and the calorie count of each serving. For this book to be most useful, it's important for the reader to understand how serving sizes and calorie counts have been calculated.

I have computed calorie counts on the basis of U.S. Department of Agriculture data for standard and generic ingredients: cornflakes, apples, oranges, and medium heads of lettuce, for example. However, many of the foods brought home in your grocery bag are not the staples and basics for which government calorie counts are available. In the last decade hundreds of new food products have come on the market. With all the fresh emphasis on "light" eating, many new low-fat and low-sugar low-calorie alternatives have become available, further complicating calorie counts.

Here is how I have handled it: In the case of food products for which USDA calorie data are not available, I have used calorie counts provided by the manufacturers of the most widely available brands. If there is a calorie difference between two competing brands that sell equally well on a national basis, I struck an average between the two.

All calorie counts have been rounded off to the nearest "five." If the computation yielded a count of 348, for example, the calories are listed as "350 per serving." (All calorie counts, after all, are approximations, since one peach or peapod is never identical to the next.)

Having tallied the calories for all the ingredients in a recipe, I then divided the total by the number of servings in order to arrive at the calories per portion. Here we run into the question of what constitutes a serving size. Consider, for example, the variance between a steakhouse steak and one served on an airline meal.

In listing serving sizes I have attempted to follow the standard practices of the food industry, allowing, for instance, half-cup or 100-gram (roughly 3½ ounce) portions of such items as cooked vegetables, puddings, and side dishes. Main course dishes containing protein foods—meat, poultry, seafood, etc.—have been computed to allow between 15 and 20 grams of protein per serving, or about the amount you would find in 3½ to 5 ounces of meat. If a recipe in this book serves four, "a serving" is obviously one-quarter of the total. If you eat half of a four-serving recipe yourself, then the calorie count for your double helping is double!

A final caution regarding calorie counts: note carefully the ingredient listings. If a recipe calls for one pound fat-trimmed lean beef round, the calorie count will not be the same if you substitute ordinary hamburger. If you use regular mayonnaise (100 calories a tablespoon) and the recipe called for low-fat mayonnaise (40 calories), you have added an extra 60 calories for each tablespoon. And speaking of tablespoons, teaspoons, and cups, both the recipes and the calorie counts were arrived at by using level measurements. A rounded teaspoon is more like a teaspoon and a half. A heaping teaspoon can be closer to a tablespoon!

"Light and Easy" Cooking Doesn't Mean You Shortcut Taste . . . Or Appetite Satisfaction!

In fact, just the reverse is true. If you have to be calorie-careful, you know that the desire for satisfying meals can eventually outweigh even the strongest resolve to be slim. Sooner or later even the most figure-conscious cook will abandon a Spartan regimen that denies the pleasure of satisfying meals. My "light and easy" recipes are designed to satisfy the desire for foods that taste and look "rich and fattening" (even though they aren't!). "Light and easy" meals are meant to be filling and appetite-satisfying as well as appealing.

3

The "Light and Easy"-Minded

Cook's Kitchen

Isn't it ironic that efficiency apartments always have such inefficient kitchens? Supposedly aimed at busy people with insufficient time to food-shop, many apartments are actually equipped with "eat-out" kitchens: tiny refrigerators, a freezer that holds little else but ice cubes, and such a dearth of storage space that the harried occupants have to stop at the market any night they plan to eat at home!

In this chapter I offer some food for thought on equipping your kitchen, no matter how small it may be, to make light of culinary chores.

Finding Storage Space

You don't have to move or remodel to expand your kitchen. Reorganizing (or sometimes just organizing) cabinet space can create room where there wasn't any.

Short on space? Begin by clearing the kitchen of everything that isn't used regularly. The turkey platter, corn popper, clam steamer, and ice-cream machine can be stored in the hall closet, attic, or garage. (If you have no attic, garage, or closet space to spare, you may need to rethink your need for a corn popper or clam steamer! You can steam clams and pop corn in *any* big pot.)

Consider the following space-saving hints:

- Shallow metal shelves added to the inside of cabinet and closet doors can accommodate many cans, jars, and bottles.
- A restaurant-style pot rack from a kitchen supply store can be ceiling-mounted to hang pans and utensils presently taking up drawer space.
- Empty walls can be covered with wire grids or peg board for spice racks and/or utensils.
- Empty space between cabinet tops and the ceiling can be put to use to display those attractive but infrequently utilized platters, trays, and casseroles. Baskets can hide smaller items needed only occasionally.
- If you've stocked up on your favorite brand of canned tuna or crushed pineapple at a sensational price, there's no law that says it has to be stored in the kitchen. In a pinch you can put spare space to work as an annex pantry—under the bed, for example, in slide-out plastic dishpans used as drawers.
- Another way to liberate cabinet space and simplify meal making is to keep frequently used appliances on the countertop rather than behind cabinet doors. If you have to haul out your blender before you can use it, you may be less inclined to do so. Meanwhile, it's taking up valuable interior space.
- If counter work space is at a premium, buy a chopping block that you can prop partway over the sink or stove as an annex counter.
- Consider replacing your kitchen table with one that's counter height. Better yet, replace it with a bar that has covered shelves beneath . . . more storage space!

And if (or when) you move into new quarters, keep in mind that the busier you are, the more entitled you are to a kitchen that makes light work of cooking!

Choosing and Using Your Refrigerator

It's not necessarily true that smaller households require smaller refrigerators. Working people who grocery-shop only two or three times a month may have *more* need for a big refrigerator than the six-child household with a full-time homemaker who shops frequently.

Because fresh fruits and vegetables are such an important part of the light cook's cuisine, ample refrigerator space is doubly important. Besides size in a refrigerator, look for flexibility of interior space: shelves that can be removed or rearranged to accommodate special and seasonal needs—a leftover turkey, for example, or a watermelon.

If your kitchen layout leaves no room for the refrigerator you'd like, consider adding a small spare one elsewhere. Some "executive" office refrigerators are designed so that they won't be out of place in a den or a dining room. A spare refrigerator can be kept in the basement, under the stairs, in the attic, or in the garage. (Remember, however, that an empty refrigerator is a safety hazard to children; store it in such a way that the door can't be opened.) A second-hand refrigerator can be a bargain, but be sure that it works before you buy it. Check that both the insulation and door gasket are in good condition.

Freezer Space

More than anything else a well-stocked freezer can save you from having to rely on fattening fast-foods! To be a "deep" freezer it must be capable of maintaining zero-degree cold. The ice-cube compartment of a one-door apartment-size refrigerator is not a "deep" freezer because its temperature range is much higher, twenty to thirty degrees.

In selecting a freezer, you have many alternatives to consider: (1) Should it be a top-loading chest freezer or a front-loading free-standing freezer? (2) Should it be part of a combination refrigerator-freezer? (3) If so, should the freezer section be on the top, on the bottom, or on the side? (4) Should you pay extra for an ice-cube maker or the frost-free feature? (5) How big should it be?

Here are some thoughts on these questions to help you decide.

If you have the space, a combination refrigerator-freezer *that provides sufficient freezer space* is generally the most convenient and economical solution for most households. Many "light and easy"-minded cooks may find, however, that the combinations offer proportionally too little freezer space and too much refrigerator room. Before you decide, be sure to check all the brands available through retail and catalog stores to see how competing makes compare on refrigerator-freezer space ratios.

Now, because you will be opening the freezer door less often than the refrigerator door, a bottom-loading freezer is more convenient than a top-loading one. (A few years ago bottom-loading combinations all but disappeared from appliance stores, but manufacturers have now begun making them again.) An on-the-side design may seem to be the best compromise. However, in the smaller models the freezer section is so narrow that it may not accommodate bulky items easily, if at all.

Frost-free freezers cost more than freezers that need periodic defrosting. Frost free may seem like a desirable feature but it dries out and dehydrates all but the most carefully wrapped foods. For that reason most foods will remain in better condition in a conventional freezer. If you opt for a combination refrigerator-freezer, an on-the-side, or a model with an ice-cube maker, you may *have* to take the frost-free feature whether you want it or not. If so, plan to take extra care with the wrapping of foods.

An ice-cube maker is a marvelous convenience that's particularly appreciated in households that entertain a lot. On the other hand, you lose about two cubic feet of freezer space to have that mechanism. An endless supply of ice also invites youngsters to open and reopen the freezer door, thereby raising the interior temperature and increasing operating costs.

How big a freezer? Even if space isn't a consideration, rapidly escalating energy costs are. The bigger the freezer, the more it costs to buy and operate. What's more, a half-empty freezer costs more to run than a full one.

Ovens and Ranges

If you're lucky enough to be remodeling, here are some features you'll want to keep in mind.

- Self-cleaning and self-starting ovens are obvious advantages to a busy cook.
- A rotisserie is an enjoyable and important feature to the calorie-careful. (With a built-in one you'll definitely want an oven that doesn't need scouring.)
- The choice between a gas or an electric oven and stove may be determined less by personal preference than by the ease of providing a gas line or current and by the relative utility costs in your area.
- A microwave oven is certainly handy to have, but built-ins and combination units are expensive and countertop units hog counter space. Once you have one, though, you'll never want to be without it. A microwave oven is wonderful for thawing or reheating pre-

pared foods in moist sauces. It makes short work of a lot of kitchen chores: softening gelatin, warming leftovers, heating filled omelets, reheating soups and stews. But a microwave oven can't replace other cooking appliances. Many meat, poultry, and seafood dishes are better prepared on top of the range, under the broiler, or in the oven. Unless the microwave oven has a browning unit, meat does not brown desirably, nor will the quality, moistness, and tenderness of the meat be equal when compared with other cooking techniques. Though a microwave oven cooks small quantities of food in less time, large quantities take proportionally longer. Therefore, it may not save you any time at all if you attempt to cook a big roast or large casserole. It is also necessary to open the door and turn foods frequently, or stir them often, to assure even cooking, so microwave meals aren't as attention-free as you may think! To eliminate the need for constant turning of food, there are units that feature a revolving turntable. Because microwave ovens are most efficient when used for small quantities of food—and take a lot of room—you might consider a smaller model.

Pots and Pans

The most important feature the "light and easy"-minded cook should look for in cookware is a nonstick finish that will eliminate or minimize the need for added fat. Today's no-stick coatings on pots and pans are much sturdier than in the past and can hold up under tougher handling and heavier use. Follow the manufacturer's directions: Before using new pans, preseason them with a light coating of oil. Avoid using sharp utensils and abrasive cleansers. Once a nonstick finish becomes scratched and pitted and fails to perform without oil or shortening, replace it.

Mixers, Blenders, and Food Processors

Some of the jobs these handy helpers do overlap . . . but not exactly. If your space and budget are unlimited, you'll want to have them all. If not, you'll have to make a choice.

ELECTRIC MIXER   This appliance can beat egg whites, cream, and evaporated skim milk stiff. That's a job that none of the other machines can do as effectively. It can also do a better job of mashing potatoes and other softened vegetables and beating air into cake batters. A portable, hand-held mixer can be used in different bowls; a stationary mixer on a stand cannot. The stationary mixer is usually more expensive, but it has a stronger motor and is more versatile. Moreover, most can be equipped with attachments for slicing, grating, shredding, grinding, and dough kneading, making them very versatile indeed.

BLENDER   As its name implies, a blender does a superior job of blending and liquefying ingredients, a job that a mixer cannot do and that most moderately priced food processors can do only in small quantities because of their smaller containers and limited speed. Depending on the brand, power, speed, flexibility, and container size, a blender can also purée, crush ice, rough-chop, coarse-grind, or finely powder certain foods, but not as easily or precisely as a food processor. A blender can even blend batters, but not with the same finesse of a mixer because it won't incorporate as much air. A blender is unequaled, however, at making shakes, beverages, puddings, cheesecakes, and custard mixtures.

FOOD PROCESSOR   This appliance can perform the widest variety of functions with relative ease and convenience. It can slice, chop, shred, or julienne vegetables or other foods; grind raw meats; chop nuts; and blend mixtures either coarse or smooth. You can use it to make short work of salads, stuffings, spreads, sauces, dressings, doughs, dips, batters, and burgers. About the only thing most food processors can't do is beat cream and egg whites really stiff, though some newer models claim they can with a "whip" attachment. Prices range from several hundred dollars for top-of-the-line imports and professional extra-capacity models to forty dollars or less for American versions on sale at discount outlets. In the main, the budget-priced domestic copies perform all the same functions of the standard imports.

COMBINATIONS   If you are equipping a kitchen and have none of the above, you'll want to investigate investing in a multi-function unit that combines all these features in a single appliance.

Slow Cookers/Fast Cookers

Slow cookers were an instant success after being introduced in the early 1970s. They promised a workable solution to cooks who are away all day. Thermostat-controlled to provide an even temperature just below the boiling point, the slow cooker turns budget cuts of meat into tender stew in eight or ten hours, while leaving any vegetables in the pot relatively firm and well textured. With a slow cooker, you can prepare a meal before leaving for work in the morning, turn it on, and come home at night to a ready dinner.

Disadvantages? Because ingredients vary and the cooking time is so elongated, you can never be certain whether a combination dish will take six or eight or ten hours, or maybe even longer. And if you want to brown the meat or thicken the liquid into a gravy or simmer it down into a sauce, your one-pot dinner will actually require other pots. Finally, fatty meats and poultry, such as chuck or duck, create a high-calorie meal because the fat has nowhere to go.

If you decide on a slow cooker, look for one with a separate submersible crockery liner that can go into the dishpan or dishwasher for easy cleaning. A range of temperature settings is also important; it allows you to fast-cook when necessary.

Fast cookers, or pressure cookers, go to the other extreme and cut cooking time to one-third or less. With a pressure cooker you can make a pot roast in an hour, spaghetti sauce in twenty minutes, chicken in fifteen minutes, and vegetables in a matter of seconds. Where speed is concerned, it's sort of a poor man's microwave oven. In fact it can cook a large quantity of food faster than a microwave. You can brown foods over high heat in it, you can simmer down ingredients to make sauces in it, and you can use it as a heavy stockpot or a steamer or for pressure canning.

The pressure cooker is not a new appliance. It was the rage in the 1930s primarily because of its ability to tender-cook budget meats. Then it fell into disfavor, partly because a rising economy had brought with it a disinterest in budget meals and partly because of reports that it could explode. But in the past half-century the design has been updated several times. In a test report in 1973 *Consumer Reports* stated that contemporary pressure cookers were so well designed fear of explosion need not be a deterrent from buying one. Current models incorporate safety-locking lids that can't be opened, even intentionally, until the pressure is reduced.

Today the biggest danger of a pressure cooker is in overcooking foods. If you forget to set a timer, it cooks so quickly that it can easily turn beef into strings or vegetables into mush. And if you fail to add enough liquid to the pot, you can't peek in to see it boil away, burning dinner and leaving you with quite a clean-up challenge.

Today's pressure cookers come in a variety of sizes from a handy two-and-one-half-quart capacity to a six-quart size. (Pressure canners are even larger.) Available in stainless steel, polished, or color-coated aluminum, they come in stovetop and all-electric submergible models. As of this writing, only the all-electric ones come with a nonstick coating—a definite asset for the "light and easy"-minded cook!

Other Single-Purpose Appliances

Those who worry that marriage may be going out of style need only look at the proliferation of "shower-gift" kitchen gadgetry to be reassured that some aspects of traditional coupling are still healthy and well! In the past five years or so appliance manufacturers have come up with special-purpose gadgets to perform nearly every kitchen function you can think of, and some you may never have thought of . . . until somebody gave you a gadget to do it. Many of these single-purpose gimmicks really don't do a better job than multipurpose equipment. What they are designed to do is provide an answer for the gift shopper who has to buy a present for the person "who has everything" (else).

Unless you're a person who has room for everything—and few of us are—you'll want to think long and hard about cluttering up your kitchen with one-purpose gadgets. After all, you can make crêpes in a nonstick skillet or omelet pan. A broiler or fry pan does a better job with hamburgers or hot dogs than single-purpose "cookers" supposedly designed for them. Grilled sandwiches can be made on a nonstick skillet. Pizza can be cooked in the oven; you don't need a pizza maker. Peanut butter can be made in a blender or food processor instead of a peanut butter machine. Yogurt can be made in a Thermos bottle or in any warm place.

Still, some one-purpose appliances may be worth owning if they do a better job. Here are some ideas:

ELECTRIC ICE-CREAM MAKER   This appliance can make light work of such calorie savers as homemade low-fat, low-sugar ice milk and frozen yogurts. There are two types: those that work *outside* the freezer and require ice cubes and those that work *inside* the freezer and are powered through a special flat electric cord that allows the freezer door to close over it. The latter is more convenient if you have a large enough freezer.

HOT-AIR POPCORN POPPER   This machine makes homemade popcorn, a relatively nonfattening, high-fiber snack compared to other nibbles. Today's hot-air popcorn poppers allow you to pop popcorn with no oil or fat whatsoever.

ELECTRIC SLICERS   This gadget allows you to make deli-thin cuts of very lean meats and roasts that might be considered tough if not sliced sliver-thin. If counter area is limited, look for a fold-up model, which takes up only a few inches of space when not in use.

AN ALL-SEASON BARBECUE WITH PERMANENT COALS   Such an appliance makes it easy to enjoy light-calorie cookouts (or cook-ins, any time of year!). Some cook tops even come equipped with permanent coals for barbecuing in the kitchen. But a portable gas or electric barbecue is far more versatile and can be found in a variety of sizes and price ranges. The larger ones include the option of a motorized rotisserie.

MORE NECESSITIES AND NICETIES   If you have to be calorie conscious (and who doesn't) you really need your own department of weights and measures. It can be as simple and inexpensive as a postal scale, as charming as an antique greengrocer's scale, or a sleek, modern fold-up scale that's light on counterspace requirements. Whichever you choose, a kitchen scale is absolutely necessary for portion control.

- *Measuring cups* and spoons are necessary for determining quantities and are equally important for portion control.
- An *egg separator* is slit so that the white of a raw egg slides away from the yolk. It's particularly handy for cholesterol watchers.
- A *bulb-type baster* is intended as an aid for basting roasts with their own pan juices. It has another use for "light and easy"-minded cooks: it can suction away the fat that floats to the surface of soups, sauces, and broths.
- A *fat mop,* another handy defatter, looks like a dish mop, but the mop is made of plastic fibers, which have an affinity for attracting and holding on to grease. It's used to "mop up" fat from soups and stews.
- A *meat thermometer* indicates the internal temperature of a roast. There is no other way to know for sure when a roast, chicken, or turkey is properly done. With the price of meat and poultry what it is today a meat thermometer is a wise investment!
- A *folding steamer*—of perforated stainless steel or a wire basket that adjusts to fit a variety of pots—allows you to steam many foods, particularly vegetables, and is a healthy, flavor-saving way to cook.

4

Super Supermarketing for

One-Stop Shoppers

THE BEST WAY to avoid wasting time, money, and calories is to shop less but better! One well-planned, three-hour supermarket foray every two weeks will take less of your time than several in-and-out errands to pick up forgotten items. The thought-out food provisioning trip can save you cash and calories, too. Here's why: Supermarkets are psychologically engineered to sell you food. Every time you push a cart down those aisles, remind yourself that you are walking through a cunningly devised ambush on your wallet and waistline.

According to a report in the trade publication *Advertising Age* (October 30, 1978), the segment of the population most inclined to eat at fast-food franchises is the same group that tends to buy its food on the same day it's eaten. This group also makes its purchases without much regard to cost and doesn't want to spend more than half an hour preparing a meal.

Here are smart strategies for supermarketing the "light" way.

Pick the Right Time to Go to the Supermarket

Schedule your shopping trips carefully and at regular intervals— once a week, every ten days, twice a month, whatever works best for you. Let your family size, storage space, and refrigeration and freezer space determine the frequency of your shopping trips.

Do your marketing at the most convenient time, when the store is least crowded. Traffic patterns vary from market to market depending on how urban or suburban your area is. Talk to the supermarket manager or the checkout clerks to find out the lightest hours. Try to avoid competing with after-work or Saturday shoppers. Never shop the day before a holiday or long weekend. If you have a nine-to-five job, consider shopping very late at an all-night supermarket, on Saturday night, or very early Sunday morning.

Never, never shop during your meal hour! Don't shop when you're hungry. Research shows that hungry shoppers are the most inclined to make "whim purchases" of items they'd never ordinarily buy.

Make a List and Take It With You

Post a shopping list on your refrigerator door and make a habit of jotting down what you need. Ask other household members to add needed items to it and to note down when something is used up. Save your lists and check them over as a reminder of frequently used items that might be forgotten, such as laundry detergent. Before you complete your list, mentally run through a typical day's meals to note down regularly needed items: breakfast cereals, milk, eggs, breads, spreads, lunch meats, salad dressings, soups, condiments, spices, seasonings and herbs, coffee, tea, and beverages.

Check the Newspaper Ads

Plan your purchases by researching the specials and by checking the newspaper to see if items you ordinarily use are on sale. Comparison-shop before you decide which store gets your business.

Think Through Your Menus

Between this shopping trip and the next, plan your meals based on what's in season, what's in the store, what's on sale, and what keeps and what doesn't. Block out your menus to use perishable foods early in the week: ground meat, seafood, lettuce, and other fruits and vegetables. Build your later-in-the-week meals around frozen meat, fish, chicken, smoked or processed meats, fruits and vegetables that need ripening, canned fruit, frozen vegetables.

Consider meat purchases carefully. Meat, including poultry and seafood, constitutes the single costliest food category on your list, in calories as well as in cash. To save calories, be sure to balance "red" and "white" meats. For every pound of beef you buy, try to buy at least an equivalent pound of poultry and seafood. That way you'll have to plan some meals around these less fattening choices. Plan two or three meals from one large less expensive cut of meat or piece of poultry. Recycle the leftovers into casseroles. Several meals from one roast saves time and energy—yours and the utility company's.

Time or Money: Which Is More Important?

Your time is worth money, and therefore it may be wiser to shop at the most convenient, best-stocked supermarket in your area rather than the one with the cheapest prices if the latter is understaffed or frequently out of needed items. In fact, you may save the most time by shopping regularly at the same efficient supermarket because you are already familiar with its layout.

Should you use food coupons? It's true that "cents-off" coupons cost you money whether you use them or not, so it's wasteful not to use them for needed items. On the other hand, clipping, saving, and sorting them takes time that may actually cost you money. Can you delegate coupon clipping to youngsters or other household members?

Remember, coupons cost you money, and if you use them to buy unneeded or overpriced items, they cost you twice. Trading stamps also cost you money. Ideally, the busy shopper is best off finding a store that offers better prices instead of trading stamps.

Stock Up on Needed Sale Items

The emphasis here is on *needed*. Consider your storage space, especially freezer space. A bulky item at a few cents off—bread, for instance—may not be such a bargain if it takes up so much room in your freezer that you can't take advantage of next week's seafood sale. Small nonperishable items at big savings are always good buys: coffee, for example, or canned tuna.

Beware the bad bargain. Don't fall for the large economy size that will spoil before you can use it up or that will make you feel obliged to eat it all before it goes bad. Avoid inferior brands that nobody will eat, day-old baked goods that will be a week old when you reach the final slice, anything you wouldn't normally have purchased. Beware the ultimate "bad buy": high-calorie, non-nutritious junk foods and snack foods that fatten without filling.

Do It Yourself and Save

You can save money by buying a whole roast, for example, and cutting it into steaks or by boning your own chicken breasts. On the other hand, if you have less time than money, it may pay you to let the store do it while you spend your time showing real estate or selling stocks and bonds! Convenience is a commodity that represents a bargain for some people. There's no need to feel guilty if you opt for frozen ready-to-cook carrots over fresh carrots in need of scraping. Frozen carrots are infinitely better than no carrots. No apologies needed! What the "light and easy"-minded cook wants to avoid is convenience contaminated with excess calories: fish sticks in a heavy coating of grease-soaked breading; carrots in a sticky syrupy sauce. Look for "whole" convenience foods in easy-to-use forms: cabbage that's already shredded for coleslaw, fresh or frozen fish fillets, or frozen ready-to-use chopped green pepper or onion.

Read labels carefully. Wear your glasses, if need be, so that you can scrutinize the fine print. Know that the list of ingredients begins with the components in the order of their predominance. That is, if the first word on the list is sugar, the product contains more sugar than anything else (some breakfast cereals, for example). Remember, the two major calorie contaminants in most products are sugar and fat. These two empty-calorie ingredients take many forms. Sugar can also include sucrose, dextrose, corn syrup solids, fructose, and high-fructose corn syrup. Fat includes vegetable oil—olive, corn, safflower—or *any* oil, shortening, butter, margarine, and lard. Some products contain fat or sugar in several forms so that no one of them predominates the list even though the product is primarily fat or sugar. Check the ingredients on several competing products and try to find an alternative with *no* fat or sugar. Tomato sauce is a good example. By shopping carefully, you can find plain tomato sauce that contains neither fat nor sugar. On the other hand, many brands of spaghetti sauce contain both.

Look for nutrition information, especially the calorie count, and use the information to comparison-shop. Today many brands list nutrition data on their labels. The manufacturers who are "up front" about their products deserve your business; the others don't. (It's a safe assumption that the food maker who keeps his products' calorie count secret probably has good reason to do so!) Nutrition labeling is mandatory, by the way, if a food maker makes any nutritional claim on the label such as lower in fat, higher in polyunsaturates.

And don't be misled by label claims: "light," "natural," "nondairy," "part skim," "no butterfat," "98% fat free," "no saturated fat," "high in polyunsaturates," "sugar free," "dietetic," "no artificial anything." Such hard-sell phrases should trigger your impulse to check further. The bottom line you should be looking for is a low calorie count. Bold-print label claims often tell only part of the story, the selling part, and omit mention of other factors that may inflate the calorie count. For example, nondairy cream substitutes are often high in vegetable fat and have as many calories as cream. Low-fat yogurts can be loaded with sugar. Remember, lots of "natural" foods are high in calories!

Don't believe verbal claims or hand-lettered signs about calorie counts. If the person behind the cheese counter tells you an import is low-calorie or if the proprietor of a "diet shop" or "health food store" posts hand-lettered signs stating that a certain veal sausage or frozen yogurt is nonfattening, ask to see verification of this claim on the label of the bulk container. The salesperson may not be deliberately lying. He or she may simply be misled. No reason why you should be.

The "Light and Easy"–Minded Cook's Glossary of What and What Not to Use or What to Choose Instead

- Apples aren't fattening, less than 100 calories each. To increase appetite satisfaction, eat them with the skin on (more fiber and pectin).
- Applesauce is only 100 calories a cupful, unsweetened, but 232 calories with sugar.
- Avocados are fattening only if you compare them with other fruits and vegetables, not compared with meat, cheese, nuts, snacks, and sweets. Florida avocados are 11 percent fat, 389 calories a pound compared with California avocados at 17 percent fat, 589 calories a pound.
- Bacon is 70 percent fat and 3,016 calories a pound. Choose Canadian bacon at 14 percent fat, 980 calories a pound, or the lean-strip

bacon substitutes made from less fatty smoked pork (about 50 percent leaner)

- Bananas are only 100 calories each and high in potassium, a great source of natural sweetness.
- Beans are virtually fat free and a good source of vegetable protein and fiber, which makes them filling instead of fattening. One cup of cooked kidney beans is only 218 calories and contains 14 grams of protein.
- Bean sprouts are a vegetable that even cellar dwellers can grow, very low in calories, only 37 per cupful of fresh mung bean sprouts.
- Beef rib cuts can be as high as 45 percent fat and 2,014 calories a pound (boneless). Choose fat-trimmed round, 612 calories a pound, or flank steak, 631 calories.
- Beer is 150 calories a 12-ounce can or more for dark imports. Choose "light" beer, but check the calories on the label, which can range from 70 to 137 a can.
- Bologna is 28 percent fat and 86 calories an ounce. Choose turkey bologna at only 55 calories per ounce.
- Bread is less fattening if you choose high-fiber calorie-reduced brands at 50 calories a slice. Pita, French, and Italian breads made without sugar or shortening are relatively low-calorie, too.
- Butter is 100 calories a tablespoon; whipped butter is 67 calories a tablespoon.
- Cake calories? Angel food is the lowest at 269 calories a 3½-ounce serving, followed by sponge cake at 297 calories. Pound cake (473 calories) is one of the highest.
- Candy! The only thing worse than chocolate, 150 calories an ounce, is chocolate-coated nuts, 165. Least fattening? Marshmallows, 90 calories an ounce.
- Cheese calories are highest when you choose cheddar (American) cheese at 1,826 calories a pound. If you must buy cheddar, make it extra sharp! Other natural hard cheeses come close (Swiss, 1,704). Pasteurized processed cheeses are less (1,703 calories a pound for pasteurized processed American). Low-fat or "diet" cheese, around 800 calories a pound.
- Chicken is relatively low in calories. Young broilers and fryers have the least fat and calories and average 382 calories per pound (meat only). Older chickens have proportionally more: 791 calories per pound for roasters; 987 calories per pound for stewing chickens (hens and cocks).

- Cookies—chocolate chip cookies, that is—are the worst, about 2,200 a pound; fig bars the best, 1,624 calories a pound and relatively high fiber.
- Corn is not fattening when unbuttered, only 70 calories an ear; it's appetite satisfying and relatively high in fiber. To increase eating satisfaction, always choose corn on the cob rather than cut corn; it takes longer to eat!
- Corned beef is high-calorie if cut from the brisket, 1,329 calories a pound; not so fattening if cut from the round, only 612 calories a pound.
- Cornstarch and flour are both 29 calories a tablespoon, but cornstarch has nearly double the thickening power of flour, so you use less.
- Cream is 38 percent fat, 53 calories a tablespoon, or 838 calories a cupful (which makes 2 cups, when whipped). Evaporated skim milk is only 200 calories a cupful (or 2 cups, when whipped).
- Eggs are 82 calories each, 65 calories in the yolk, 17 calories in the white. The yolk is where the cholesterol is. You can cut cholesterol as well as calories by using two egg whites in place of one whole egg in most recipes. Low-calorie liquid no-cholesterol substitutes are also available, about 40 calories a quarter cupful (the equivalent of one egg).
- Frankfurters are about 170 calories each (2 ounces). Choose chicken or turkey franks instead, about 133 calories per 2 ounces.
- Fruit, canned, is generally about half the calories when packed in fruit juice instead of syrup.
- Hamburger meat—the higher the price, the lower the calories and fat content. Ground beef that's 30 percent fat contains 1,402 per pound. If you can't afford calories, choose lean fat-trimmed bottom round (612 calories per pound) and have it ground to order.
- Ice cream follows this general rule: The lower the price, the lower the calories. Rich ice cream averages 16 percent butterfat, 222 calories a 3½-ounce serving, while inexpensive ice cream with 10 percent fat is only 193 calories. Even cheaper? Ice milk, 5 percent fat, 152 calories. Ice milk with less than 1 percent fat can be less than 100 calories.
- Jams, jellies, and preserves are all approximately the same, about 54 calories per tablespoon regardless of the flavor. Low-sugar versions are a better choice, 24 calories.
- Lamb's leanest cut is the leg, 590 calories a pound (meat only).

- Liquor calories in gin, rum, vodka, Scotch, and other whiskeys depend on the proof; the higher the proof, the greater the percentage of alcohol and the higher the calorie count. Eighty-proof liquor is 65 calories an ounce, while 100-proof liquor is 83 calories an ounce. You get more liquor flavor for fewer calories if you choose a low-proof gin or golden rum instead of a high-proof flavorless vodka. Wine calories depend on both the sweetness and the alcohol content. The most fattening wine would be a high-alcohol (18 percent) dessert wine, about 140 calories a 3½-ounce glass; the least fattening would be light, dry, low-alcohol wines. Some Portuguese and Italian wines have only 8 or 9 percent alcohol.
- Margarine is 100 calories a tablespoon, just as fattening as butter. Use diet margarine, half the calories.
- Marmalade is slightly less than jam, 51 calories a tablespoon; low-sugar, 24 calories per tablespoon.
- Mayonnaise is 100 calories a tablespoon. Low-fat "imitation" mayonnaise can be 25 to 50 calories a tablespoon.
- Oil, be it salad or cooking, is virtually the same, 100 percent fat, 1,984 calories a cupful—the highest calorie count of any food there is! Despite label claims regarding lightness or polyunsaturates, the only way to cut oil calories is to cut it down . . . or out! Use chopped olives or olive liquid for olive oil flavor; use spray-on lecithin cooking sprays to cook without oil; use nonstick utensils.
- Pancake mix in the form of buckwheat mix has a lower calorie count and more fiber than regular pancake and waffle mix (443 calories per cupful instead of 481 calories per cupful).
- Peanuts have fewer calories if they are defatted (136 per ounce) than if either dry-roasted (300 per ounce) or oil-roasted (320 per ounce). And the less fat, the more peanuts per ounce!
- Pie: strawberry is the least (198 calories a 3½-ounce serving) followed by pumpkin (211). Pecan is the worst, 418. (Home-baked pies can be less if you use only one crust, rolled very thin, and eliminate or cut down drastically on sugar.)
- Pork isn't necessarily fattening. Spareribs, the meat of fatty ones, is 37 percent fat and 1,769 calories a pound. At the other extreme is the fat-trimmed meat of lean fresh ham (leg of pork), only 8 percent fat and 762 calories a pound.
- Potatoes aren't fattening, only about 90 calories each. But french fries are 274 a 3½-ounce serving.
- Rice—instant rice, that is—saves calories as well as time. Made

with boiling water according to the package directions, it is only 180 calories a cupful; regular white rice (cooked) is 225 per cupful; brown rice (cooked) is 176 per cupful.

- Salad dressings, low-calorie versions, are only a fraction of the calories in the regular types. Commercial dressings range between 50 and 100 calories a tablespoon, while the low-calorie ones are only 1 to 30 calories a tablespoon.

- Sausage contains 2,259 calories per pound of pork (50 percent fat before it's cooked and 44 percent fat after). Some beef and veal sausage is almost as fattening, so look for calorie information on the label. Turkey sausage is only 880 calories a pound.

- Spaghetti and macaroni have the same calories, 105 an ounce (dry), despite variations in shape. Egg noodles, however, are 110 calories an ounce. Pasta, cooked to the tender stage, has 25 percent fewer calories than when cooked *al dente,* or firm.

- Soups, the creamed, condensed variety, are often called for in casserole recipes and are relatively high in calories. Cream of mushroom, 331 calories a 10½-ounce can, is 8 percent fat. Cream of asparagus is the least, 161 calories, followed by cream of celery at 215 and cream of chicken at 235.

- Sugar (sucrose) is pure calories, 16 per level teaspoon. Confectioners' and brown sugar have slightly fewer calories per teaspoon, but they also have slightly less sweetening power, so they don't save you anything. You need 20 calories' worth (1¼ teaspoons) to equal the sweetness of 16 calories' worth (1 teaspoon) of granulated sugar.

- Yogurt doesn't always live up to its "light" image. United States government calorie guides list 113 as the count for an 8-ounce container of plain low-fat yogurt. However, actual calorie counts of commercial yogurt are much higher. Most brands of plain low-fat yogurt average around 140 calories a container. Sweetened fruit-flavored low-fat yogurts are considerably higher, averaging around 200 calories per container. Fruit-flavored sweetened whole milk yogurt can be as high as 250 calories!

5

Speedy Skillet

Dinners

A FRY PAN doesn't always mean fat. Today's nonstick finishes allow skillet-easy meals that can be calorie-light with little or no fat added.

The electric skillet—that perennial shower gift—is a particularly handy appliance for "light and easy"-minded cooks. Its large capacity, well-fitting lid, precise temperature control, and attractiveness make it ideal for quick one-dish meals that are low on cleanup and calories. But more importantly, most electric skillets are blessed with a sturdy non-stick interior coating that lets you "fry" without fat.

(Of course you don't need an electric skillet to prepare these speedy dinners. Any large, lidded, nonstick-finish skillet or fry pan will do . . . and be easier to store.)

Fear of Frying

Once the finish of a nonstick skillet deteriorates, it's difficult to brown foods without added fats or oil (125 calories a tablespoon). It's important, therefore, to keep the finish in good condition by avoiding sharp utensils or gritty scouring equipment.

Some other hints include:

Follow the manufacturer's directions for "seasoning" an unused nonstick pan with a light rub of salad oil.

Be careful not to let food become burned on. Should that occur, fill the pan with hot soapy water and let it soak all day or overnight, if necessary, until the crust softens enough for nonabrasive removal.

Use soft plastic, wooden, or specially coated spoons and spatulas. Nothing sharp.

Never, *never* cut up meat in a skillet!

Even though your skillet has a nonstick finish, it's wise to use lecithin cooking sprays for no-fat cooking when you're browning very lean meats and poultry with little natural fat content of their own.

With care, a nonstick skillet can turn out light-and-easy meals several nights a week for years. Eventually, of course, the finish will give way to the point where nonstick cooking is difficult without added fat. That's when it's time to buy a new one. Once your skillet becomes a fuel guzzler, your figure can't afford to keep it!

Follow the light-and-easy techniques for these speedy skillet meals that make the most of nutritious ingredients with the least fat and calories.

YOGURT FLANK STEAK

1¼ lb. lean flank steak
Plain or garlic-seasoned meat
   tenderizer
 1 large onion, thinly sliced
 1 cup fat-skimmed canned beef
   broth
 2 Tbs. minced fresh parsley or 2
   tsp. dried parsley

2 Tbs. catsup
1 tsp. prepared mustard
2 Tbs. dry white wine
½ cup plain low-fat yogurt
2 Tbs. flour

On a cutting board score the steak on both sides with a sharp knife in a crisscross pattern. (Don't score it too deeply.) Sprinkle the steak on both sides with meat tenderizer and let it stand for 20 minutes.

Spray a large nonstick skillet or electric fry pan with cooking spray. Add the steak and sear it quickly on both sides over high heat. Remove the steak to a cutting board.

In the skillet combine onion, broth, parsley, catsup, mustard, and wine and cook the mixture, uncovered, stirring occasionally, about 8 to 10 minutes, until the onion is tender.

Meanwhile, slice the steak against the grain into very thin slices. (It will be very rare, almost raw, in the middle.)

In a small bowl blend the yogurt and flour and stir it into the skillet. Stir in the steak and heat it through; don't overcook it: the steak should still be rare. Don't add salt without tasting. May be served with noodles or rice. Serve the steak with the sauce.

Makes 5 servings, 210 calories each (noodles or rice not included).

INDONESIAN FLANK STEAK

1½ lb. lean flank steak
3 Tbs. soy sauce
2 Tbs. lime juice or lemon juice
¼ cup unsweetened pineapple
  juice
1 cup water
2 large onions, thinly sliced
2 red or green bell peppers,
  seeded and sliced into strips

1 clove garlic, minced
2 tsp. cumin seeds or 1 tsp.
  ground cumin
1 tsp. ground turmeric
½ tsp. cinnamon or apple pie
  spice
3 Tbs. sweetened shredded
  dried coconut

On a cutting board, score the steak on both sides with a sharp knife in a crisscross pattern. Transfer the steak to a plate. In a bowl combine the soy sauce, lime juice, and pineapple juice and pour it over the steak. Roll up the steak, cover it, and let it marinate in the refrigerator for several hours.

Spray a large nonstick skillet or electric fry pan with cooking spray. Add the steak and sear it quickly on both sides over high heat. Remove it to a cutting board.

In the skillet combine the remaining ingredients, except the coconut. Cover the mixture and simmer for 2 minutes. Uncover it and cook until most of the liquid has evaporated and the onions and pepper are tender-crisp.

Meanwhile, slice the steak against the grain into very thin slices. (It will be very rare, almost raw, in the middle.)

Stir the steak into the skillet and cook it, stirring, over moderate heat to the desired degree of doneness. Transfer the steak to a platter and sprinkle it with coconut.

Makes 6 servings, 220 calories each.

STEAK MARENGO

2 tsp. olive oil
1 lb. lean fat-trimmed top round
  steak
1 large onion, thinly sliced
1 clove garlic, finely chopped
1 cup thinly sliced fresh
  mushrooms

½ cup dry white wine
4 ripe tomatoes, peeled and cut
  in wedges
Salt and freshly ground pepper

Spray a large nonstick skillet or electric fry pan with cooking spray. Add the olive oil and meat and sear the meat quickly on both sides over moderate heat. Remove the steak to a cutting board.

In the skillet combine the onion, garlic, and mushrooms and cook them over high heat, stirring, just until they are lightly browned.

Stir in the wine and tomatoes and add salt and pepper to taste. Cook, stirring occasionally, just until the onions are tender-crunchy.

Meanwhile, slice the browned steak into very thin strips. (It will be rare in the middle.) Stir the steak into the skillet and continue to cook the mixture, stirring until the steak is heated through but still rare and the sauce is reduced. Serve the steak with the sauce.

Makes 4 servings, 235 calories each.

MEXICAN STEAK

1 tsp. vegetable oil (optional)
1¼ lb. lean flank steak, cut into 4
  pieces
1 large onion, thinly sliced
2 ripe tomatoes, peeled and
  chopped

½ cup water
1 tsp. chili powder
Garlic salt and pepper

Spray a nonstick skillet with cooking spray or coat it with the vegetable oil. Add the steak and sear it quickly on both sides over moderate heat. Remove the steak to a cutting board.

In the skillet combine the remaining ingredients and bring the liquid to a boil. Then simmer the mixture, uncovered, for 5 minutes.

Add the steak to the skillet and cook it to the desired degree of doneness (about 5 minutes for medium-rare) and add garlic salt and pepper to taste. Serve the steak with the sauce.

Makes 4 servings, 235 calories each.

MEXICALI CHILIBURGER SKILLET

1 lb. lean ground round beef
1 cup chopped onion
1 can (16 oz.) whole tomatoes, coarsely cut up
1 can (8 oz.) plain tomato sauce
1¼ tsp. chili powder (or to taste)
1 tsp. oregano
1 tsp. salt

Pepper to taste
1 can (12 oz.) whole kernel corn with sweet peppers
1 cup uncooked protein-enriched elbow macaroni
½ cup water
½ cup (2 oz.) shredded cheddar or Monterey Jack cheese

Spray a large nonstick skillet or electric fry pan with cooking spray. Brown the beef, breaking it into chunks, over high heat. Discard any fat from the skillet.

Stir in the onion, tomatoes, tomato sauce, and seasonings and heat the mixture to boiling.

Add the undrained corn, uncooked macaroni, and water and bring the mixture to a boil. Cover the skillet and simmer for 15 to 20 minutes, or until the macaroni is tender. Sprinkle on the cheese, cover again, and heat until the cheese is melted.

Makes 8 servings, 230 calories each.

LAMB BOMBAY

¾ cup cider
¾ cup tomato juice
1½ tsp. curry powder (or to taste)
1 onion, sliced
3 ribs celery, thinly sliced
1 green or red bell pepper,
 seeded and diced

2 Tbs. raisins
2 cups diced lean, cooked lamb
2 unpeeled red apples, diced
2 Tbs. defatted peanuts,
 chopped

In a large nonstick skillet or electric fry pan combine the cider, tomato juice, and curry powder. Simmer the mixture, uncovered, for 5 minutes.

Stir in the onion, celery, pepper, and raisins and simmer the mixture, uncovered, over low heat, stirring frequently, until the celery is tender-crunchy and nearly all the liquid is reduced to a thick glaze. Stir in the lamb and apples and cook them only until heated through. Transfer the mixture to a dish and sprinkle it with peanuts.

Makes 4 servings, 210 calories each.

VARIATION

Any lean roast meat or poultry may be substituted for the lamb.

ORIENTAL-STYLE LAMB AND CABBAGE

1 lb. lean lamb cut from the leg
¼ cup imported soy sauce
2 Tbs. dry sherry or dry white
 wine
1 small cabbage (about 1 lb.)

1½ cups tomato juice
2 Tbs. catsup
1 cup water
1 Tbs. cornstarch

On a cutting board trim the lamb and cut it into thin strips, about 2 inches long. In a bowl combine the meat with the soy sauce and sherry. Cover the mixture and refrigerate it all day.

Drain the meat and reserve the marinade. Quarter and core the cabbage and slice it into ½-inch shreds. Slice the shreds in the opposite direction, making 2-inch strips.

Spray a large nonstick skillet or electric fry pan with cooking spray. Saute the lamb over high heat until it is lightly browned and add the cabbage, tomato juice, catsup, reserved marinade, and ½ cup of the water. Cover the mixture and cook it for 4 to 5 minutes until the lamb is cooked through and the cabbage is tender-crunchy. In a small bowl combine the cornstarch with the remaining ½ cup water and stir the mixture into the skillet. Cook over moderate heat, stirring, until the sauce simmers and thickens. Serve the dish immediately.

Makes 4 servings, 215 calories each.

VARIATION

Lean beef or pork may be substituted for the lamb. Per serving there will be 220 calories with beef; 280 calories with pork.

FRUITED LAMB CURRY

1¼ lb. lean lamb steaks, cut from the leg, and cut into 1½-inch cubes	3 Tbs. soy sauce
	2 tsp. curry powder (or to taste)
	2 medium unpeeled red apples, diced
¾ cup (6-oz. can) tomato juice	
¾ cup (6-oz. can) unsweetened pineapple juice	½ cup seedless green grapes, halved
2 onions, sliced	4 Tbs. defatted peanuts

Spray a large nonstick skillet or electric fry pan with cooking spray. Brown the lamb over high heat, stirring constantly, to prevent it from sticking.

Add the tomato juice, pineapple juice, onions, soy sauce, and curry powder and simmer the mixture, uncovered, stirring frequently, for 4 to 5 minutes, until most of the liquid is reduced to a thick glaze.

Stir in the apples and grapes at the last minute to heat them through.

Transfer the curry to a platter and sprinkle with nuts. Serve the curry immediately.

Makes 4 servings, 315 calories each.

VEAL CHOPS NEAPOLITAN

4 lean fat-trimmed veal chops
  (about 1½ lb.), ¾ inch thick
2 tsp. olive oil
1 cup undrained canned
  tomatoes, crushed

1 onion, minced
1 clove garlic, minced (optional)
1 tsp. basil
Salt and pepper
4 tsp. grated Romano cheese

In a nonstick skillet or electric fry pan, brown the chops in the oil over high heat, turning them once. Drain fat from the skillet.

In a bowl, combine the remaining ingredients, except the cheese and salt and pepper. Pour the mixture over the chops. Cover the skillet and simmer over low heat for an hour or more, until the chops are very tender. Uncover the skillet and cook until the sauce is reduced and add salt and pepper to taste. Sprinkle the chops with the cheese.

Makes 4 servings, 320 calories each.

POLYNESIAN PORK

1 lb. lean ground pork, cut from
  the leg
¾ cup unsweetened pineapple
  juice
1 package (10 oz.) frozen
  chopped broccoli

½ cup chopped onion
½ cup combined chopped red
  and green bell peppers, fresh
  or frozen
2 Tbs. soy sauce
1 tsp. cornstarch

Spray a nonstick skillet or electric fry pan with cooking spray. Brown the pork over moderate heat, stirring. Drain the fat from the skillet.

Add the pineapple juice, frozen broccoli, onion, and peppers. Cook the mixture, covered, for 3 minutes. Uncover and cook the mixture, stirring, until the vegetables are tender-crunchy.

In a small bowl combine the soy sauce and cornstarch and stir into the skillet. Cook the mixture, stirring, until it thickens slightly.

Makes 4 servings, 235 calories each.

SPICY PORK AND PEPPERS

1 lb. lean pork, cut from the leg
3 Tbs. soy sauce
1 clove garlic, minced (optional)
1 cup unsweetened pineapple juice
1 cup Bloody Mary–seasoned tomato juice

1 to 2 tsp. curry powder (or to taste)
¾ cup cold water
2 red or green bell peppers, seeded and sliced into strips
1 large Spanish onion, sliced
1 Tbs. cornstarch

Trim the pork and cut it into thin strips. In a glass or ceramic bowl combine it with the soy sauce, garlic, and pineapple juice. Let the mixture marinate, covered, in the refrigerator all day or overnight.

Spray a large nonstick skillet or electric fry pan with cooking spray. Drain the pork and reserve the marinade. Saute the pork over high heat until it changes color. (If necessary, drain fat from the skillet.) Stir in the reserved marinade, tomato juice, curry powder, and ¼ cup of the water. Add the peppers and the onion. Simmer the mixture, covered, for 4 to 5 minutes, until the pork is cooked through and the vegetables are tender-crunchy. In a small bowl combine the cornstarch with the remaining water and stir the mixture into pan. Cook, stirring, until the sauce thickens.

Makes 4 servings, 260 calories each.

HAM STEAK WITH RAISIN-WINE SAUCE

1¼ lb. ready-to-eat ham steak, fat-trimmed
½ cup Sauterne or cream sherry

⅛ tsp. ground cloves
⅛ tsp. cinnamon
3 Tbs. raisins

Spray a nonstick skillet or electric fry pan with cooking spray. Brown the ham for about 3 to 4 minutes each side over high heat. Remove to a heated platter.

Combine the remaining ingredients in the skillet and cook the mixture, stirring, until it is reduced to a few tablespoons. Pour over the ham and serve immediately.

Makes 4 servings, 260 calories each.

SWEET-AND-SOUR PORK

1¼ lb. lean fresh ham steak, cut into 1-inch cubes
2 Tbs. cider vinegar
¼ cup soy sauce
1 can (8 oz.) juice-packed pineapple tidbits, including juice

1 tsp. oil
3 onions, chopped
1 green bell pepper, diced
1 red bell pepper, diced
2 Tbs. catsup
1 tsp. coriander seeds (optional)
2 Tbs. brown sugar

In a glass or ceramic bowl combine the ham with the vinegar, soy sauce, and juice from the pineapple. Let the mixture marinate for 1 hour at room temperature, or for several hours, covered, in the refrigerator.

Spray a large nonstick skillet or electric fry pan with cooking spray and add the oil. Drain the ham and reserve the marinade. Brown the ham quickly over high heat.

Stir in the onions, peppers, catsup, coriander seeds, sugar, and reserved marinade. Simmer the mixture, covered, for 3 minutes. Uncover and simmer the mixture only until the vegetables are tender-crunchy and the liquid is reduced to a thick glaze.

Stir in the pineapple at the last minute and heat through.

Makes 4 servings, 335 calories each.

LIVER AND ONIONS

1 lb. beef liver, thinly sliced into serving pieces
3 Tbs. flour
1 large Spanish onion or 4 medium onions, thinly sliced

¼ cup water
2 Tbs. oil
Salt and pepper to taste

On a shallow plate coat the liver lightly with flour.

In a large nonstick skillet or electric fry pan cook the onion in the water, covered, over moderate heat for 3 minutes. Remove the onion and reserve it.

Spray the skillet with cooking spray and heat 1 tablespoon oil over moderate heat. Add the liver and cook it 2 to 3 minutes, until the underside is brown. Turn the liver, add the remaining oil, and cook for 2 or 3 minutes more. At the last minute, stir in the onion and cook the mixture, stirring, until it is heated through. Add salt and pepper to taste.

Makes 4 servings, 225 calories each.

LOW-FAT TURKEY BURGERS

1 cup high-protein cereal
  flakes, crushed
½ cup skim milk
3 tsp. instant beef bouillon
¼ tsp. sage

3 Tbs. minced onions
1 egg or 2 egg whites or ¼ cup
  liquid no-cholesterol
  substitute
1 lb. ground raw turkey

In a bowl combine the ingredients, mixing in the turkey last. Shape the mixture into 8 patties.

Spray a nonstick skillet or electric fry pan with cooking spray, and pan-fry the patties, turning them once.

Makes 4 servings, 270 calories each, or 260 calories each with egg whites or no-cholesterol substitute.

SPEEDY SZECHUAN CHICKEN

1½ lb. skinless boneless chicken
  breasts, cut into 2-inch cubes
1 Tbs. oil
1 cup Bloody Mary–seasoned
  tomato juice
1 can (8 oz.) juice-packed
  crushed pineapple

3 Tbs. soy sauce
½ cup combined chopped red
  and green bell peppers, fresh
  or frozen
¼ tsp. ground ginger

In a nonstick skillet or electric fry pan combine the chicken and oil and cook the mixture over moderate heat, stirring, 2 to 3 minutes until it is lightly browned.

Add the remaining ingredients and cook, stirring, about 6 to 7 minutes, until the sauce is thick.

Makes 6 servings, 180 calories each.

CURRIED COCONUT CHICKEN AND ZUCCHINI

2 lb. frying chicken, cut into pieces
1 large onion, cut in chunks
1 clove garlic, minced (optional)
4 Tbs. raisins
2 Tbs. lime juice or lemon juice
1 can (10 oz.) chicken broth
1 tsp. ground cumin
1 tsp. curry powder
½ tsp. cinnamon
2 medium zucchini, sliced (or two 10-oz. boxes, defrosted)
4 Tbs. sweetened shredded dried coconut

Spray a nonstick skillet or electric fry pan with cooking spray. Brown the chicken pieces skin side down. Turn them to brown evenly, and drain the fat from the skillet.

Turn the chicken pieces skin side up, add the remaining ingredients, except the zucchini and coconut, and simmer the mixture, covered, over low heat about 30 minutes, until chicken is tender.

Stir in the zucchini and cook the mixture, uncovered, until the zucchini is tender and most of the liquid is evaporated. Sprinkle with coconut just before serving.

Makes 4 servings, 295 calories each.

CHICKEN BARBECUE

2 lb. frying chicken cut into pieces
2 Tbs. water

Light-n-Easy Barbecue Sauce
1 can (10¾ oz.) condensed tomato soup, undiluted
1 cup minced onion
2 Tbs. cider vinegar
¼ cup apple cider
1 Tbs. Worcestershire sauce
¼ tsp. oregano
Pinch of poultry seasoning
Hot pepper sauce (to taste)
Liquid smoke seasoning

Trim the fat from the chicken pieces. Spray a large nonstick skillet or chicken fryer with cooking spray. Put the chicken pieces skin side down in the skillet, add 2 tablespoons water, and cook the chicken, covered, over moderate heat for 2 to 3 minutes. Uncover the skillet and cook the chicken until the moisture evaporates and the chicken begins to brown in its own fat. Turn to brown evenly. Drain the fat from the skillet.

Turn the chicken pieces skin side up. In a bowl make the barbecue sauce and pour it over the chicken. Simmer the mixture, covered, for about 45 minutes, until the chicken is tender.

Makes 4 servings, 270 calories each.

CANTON CHICKEN

1 lb. skinless boneless chicken breasts, cut into 1½-inch cubes
1 tsp. salad oil
1 large onion, thinly sliced
1 red or green bell pepper, seeded and diced
1 cup slant-sliced celery
½ cup dry sherry or dry white wine

1 can (5 oz.) bamboo shoots, rinsed, drained, and sliced
½ cup sliced mushrooms, fresh or canned
1½ cups bean sprouts, fresh or canned, rinsed and drained
1 Tbs. cornstarch
3 Tbs. soy sauce

Spray a large nonstick skillet or electric fry pan with cooking spray. Add the chicken and oil and brown the chicken, over high heat, turning it frequently. Remove chicken from the skillet.

In the skillet combine the onion, pepper, celery, and wine, and simmer the mixture, covered, for 5 minutes.

Uncover and stir in the bamboo shoots, mushrooms, chicken, and bean sprouts. Heat the mixture until it is simmering.

In a small bowl, combine the cornstarch with the soy sauce and stir the mixture into the skillet. Cook until it thickens.

Makes 4 servings, 375 calories each.

TUNA CANTONESE

1 cup thinly sliced celery
1 red or green bell pepper, seeded and thinly sliced
1 10-oz. package frozen whole green beans, defrosted, slant-sliced
½ cup water
2 tsp. cornstarch
3 Tbs. soy sauce
2 cans (7 oz. each) water-packed solid white tuna, drained and flaked
4 oz. canned water chestnuts, drained and sliced

In a nonstick skillet or electric fry pan combine the celery, pepper, green beans, and water and simmer the mixture, covered, for 4 minutes.

In a small bowl combine the cornstarch with the soy sauce and stir into the skillet. Add the tuna and water chestnuts and cook the mixture, stirring, until the sauce simmers and thickens and the tuna is heated through.

Makes 4 servings, 195 calories each.

SKILLET SPAGHETTI AND SEAFOOD MARINARA

1 can (16 oz.) stewed tomatoes
1 can (16 oz.) plain tomato sauce
¾ cup (6-oz. can) tomato-clam juice
1½ cups water
1 onion, finely minced
1½ to 2 tsp. oregano, basil, or pizza seasoning
1 or 2 bay leaves (optional)
6 oz. very thin spaghetti or vermicelli, broken into pieces
¾ lb. fish fillets, fresh or partially defrosted, cut in 1½-inch cubes
1 Tbs. grated Parmesan or Romano cheese

In a large nonstick skillet or electric fry pan combine the tomatoes, tomato sauce, tomato-clam juice, water, onion, and seasonings. Simmer the mixture, covered, for 5 minutes.

Stir in the spaghetti, a little at a time, and simmer, stirring occasionally, for 10 minutes.

Gently stir in the fish cubes and simmer, covered, for about 4 to 5 minutes.

Uncover and simmer until most of the liquid is reduced to a thick sauce and the fish flakes easily, another 3 to 4 minutes. Remove the bay leaves, if necessary. Sprinkle the dish with the cheese.

Makes 4 servings, 315 calories each.

CODFISH CHILI-MACARONI SKILLET

3 cups water
2 cups tomato (or tomato-clam) juice
1 can (6 oz.) tomato paste
1 cup diced green bell pepper
1 cup minced celery
1 cup chopped onion
1 clove garlic, minced (optional)
2 tsp. chili powder (or to taste)
½ tsp. ground cumin (optional)
1 tsp. oregano
1½ cups elbow macaroni (dry)
1 lb. cod fillets or cod steaks, fresh or defrosted, cut in 1½-inch cubes
Salt and pepper to taste
6 slices low-fat American-style cheese, broken up
12 cheese-flavored tortilla chips, broken up (optional)

In a large nonstick skillet or electric fry pan or Dutch oven, combine the first ten ingredients, bring the mixture to a boil, and stir in the macaroni a little at a time to prevent it from sticking. Simmer the mixture, covered tightly and stirring often, until the macaroni is quite tender, about 15 minutes.

Stir in the cod and simmer, uncovered, 5 minutes more, until the sauce is thick and the fish flakes easily. Add salt and pepper to taste. Spoon the mixture onto plates and top each serving with cheese and tortilla chips, if desired.

Makes 6 servings, 280 calories each, or 300 calories each with chips.

JAPANESE FLOUNDER

2 tsp. butter or margarine	2 Tbs. dry white wine
1 lb. flounder or other fish	2 Tbs. soy sauce
fillets, fresh or defrosted	1 Tbs. cornstarch
1 clove garlic, minced	¼ cup water
Pinch of MSG (optional)	2 scallions, slant-sliced

In a nonstick skillet or electric fry pan melt the butter or margarine over moderate heat. Add the fish and cook it for 3 to 4 minutes on each side, until it flakes easily. Remove the fish to a heated platter.

Wipe out the skillet and combine in it the garlic, MSG if desired, wine, and soy sauce. Heat to boiling. In a small bowl combine the cornstarch and water and add to the skillet. Cook over moderate heat, stirring, until the sauce simmers and thickens.

Pour the sauce over the fish and sprinkle it with the scallions.

Makes 4 servings, 125 calories each.

6

Oven-Easy

Meals

THE OVEN is a much more versatile meal maker than most people think. If you're a "light and easy"-minded cook, you know that it can do a lot more than prepare an occasional roast or casserole. You can fast-"fry" foods in the oven with only a fraction of the fat you'd need in a deep fryer. You can prebrown, then slow-cook budget meals, and much more conveniently than in a slow cooker. You can use your oven for set-it-and-forget-it combination dinners. You can moist-bake foods in liquids that gently reduce into self-making sauces. Because of its size, the oven can make several dishes or meals at once. Depending on the thermostat setting and the ingredients and whether or not the food is covered, your oven can "fry," "broil," "barbecue," bake, simmer, stew, or thaw-and-serve—all with a minimum of fat and calories.

Time and Temperature

Even the newest ovens can have temperatures that vary from their thermostat settings by twenty-five or fifty degrees. If that is the case, an oven will consistently turn out foods that are over- or undercooked despite the most careful adherence to recipes. An inexpensive oven thermometer can help you discover thermostat error and allow for it. As mentioned earlier, a meat thermometer is another must. And if your oven isn't equipped with a clock that can be set to buzz or otherwise alert you after a desired time has elapsed, then an inexpensive bell timer from a housewares store is another worthwhile purchase. However, even when you're well equipped with gadgets that tell time and temperature, the final equipment every cook needs is judgment and self-confidence. Foods, after all, are as individual as thumbprints. Age, ripeness, and fat and moisture content of individual ingredients vary and can conspire to lengthen or shorten the time a given dish needs to reach its moment of perfection. In fact, the very "moment of perfection" is an individual matter that reflects only your tastes and preferences.

"Fry" in the Oven?

Yes, you *can* "fry" foods in the oven and spare yourself the smoke and spatter, the fuss and fat, the inconvenience and calories of conventional frying. And you can do it with a teaspoon of oil or less, plus only a tablespoon of bread crumbs per serving. You can do it with even the leanest foods: liver, veal, fish, and vegetables. Foods with some fat can be oven-fried with no fat added whatsoever.

THE LIGHT-AND-EASY TECHNIQUE

1. Preheat the oven to 450 or 500 degrees at least 10 minutes before adding the food.
2. Coat the food to be "fried" lightly with salad oil, allowing 4 teaspoons per pound of boneless meat or fillets.
3. Press, roll, or shake the food, a few pieces at a time, in seasoned bread crumbs, cracker crumbs, or flour, allowing 4 tablespoons of crumbs or flour per pound.
4. Use a flat pan with a nonstick surface, such as a baking sheet or shallow roasting pan, and spray it well with cooking spray. (The high temperature required for oven-frying is above the maximum suggested by some cookware manufacturers, and may cause slight warping.)
5. Arrange the food in a single layer with an inch of space between.

6. Put the pan on the middle rack in the oven and cook, turning once, until the food is crisp and cooked through. Exact time depends on the food and its thickness. Total cooking time can be as little as 5 or 6 minutes for very thin fish fillets or as much as 16 or 18 minutes for chops. (Foods that can't be cooked through in that amount of time will require a lower cooking temperature to prevent over-browning.)

Some Variations

Regular mayonnaise or salad dressing or egg-oil or oil-cheese combinations can be used in place of salad oil to add interesting flavors. For example:

A pound of skinless boneless chicken fillets can be breaded by dipping them into a lightly beaten mixture of 1 egg and 2 teaspoons of oil before coating them lightly with seasoned flour, crushed cornflakes, bread crumbs, or cracker meal.

You can give *any* oven-fried food a cheese coating by replacing part of the bread crumbs with grated Parmesan or Romano cheese. Because the cheese provides some of the fat for oven-frying, you can reduce the amount of oil by half.

How to Fry in the Oven Without Fat

Some low-calorie foods have enough natural fat to permit oven-frying with no fat added at all. Chicken with the skin left on is a good example. To oven-fry it, you need only to shake water-moistened pieces with seasoned crumbs in a heavy paper bag. Place them skin side down on a shallow nonstick pan sprayed with cooking spray and oven-fry them in a preheated 400-degree oven, turning once, for 35 to 45 minutes, until the skin is golden-crisp and the chicken is cooked through. Steaks, pork and lamp chops, bluefish, swordfish, fresh tuna, perch, mackerel, herring, and butterfish can generally be oven-fried with only a crumb coating.

In this chapter you'll find many delicious and light ways to use your oven creatively.

OVEN-FRIED CHICKEN

3 chicken breasts, split, or 2 lb.
  frying chicken, cut into pieces
6 Tbs. plain or seasoned bread
  crumbs

½ tsp. onion powder
Salt or celery salt
Pepper
Paprika

Preheat the oven to hot, 400 degrees.

Trim any fat from the chicken and rinse the chicken under cold running water.

Combine the remaining ingredients in a heavy paper bag and add the chicken pieces, a few at a time, shaking until they are lightly coated.

Put the chicken skin side down in one layer in a shallow nonstick pan well sprayed with cooking spray. Put the pan on the middle rack in the oven and bake the chicken, turning it skin side up midway during the cooking, for 35 to 45 minutes.

Make 6 servings, 175 calories each.

⚹ good OVEN-FRIED CHICKEN CORDON BLEU

2 skinless boneless chicken
  breasts, split
4 thin slices (2 oz.) lean cooked
  ham, fat-trimmed
4 thin slices (2 oz.) Swiss
  cheese

¼ cup minced fresh parsley
Salt and pepper
2 Tbs. regular mayonnaise
4 Tbs. bread crumbs

Preheat the oven to very hot, 450 degrees.

With a meat mallet pound the chicken thin. Put a piece of ham and cheese on each piece and sprinkle it with parsley and salt and pepper to taste. Roll up the pieces.

Roll each piece in mayonnaise and then in the crumbs, until it is lightly coated.

Arrange the pieces seam side down on a shallow nonstick pan well sprayed with cooking spray.

Put the pan on the middle rack of the oven and bake the chicken for 20 minutes, or until it is golden and tender.

Makes 4 servings, 240 calories each.

OVEN-FRIED SQUASH

2 medium yellow summer squash or zucchini, thickly sliced
2 Tbs. regular Italian salad dressing or 1 Tbs. salad oil and 1 Tbs. low-calorie Italian salad dressing
3 Tbs. Italian-seasoned bread crumbs
4 tsp. grated Parmesan cheese

Preheat the oven to very hot, 450 degrees.

In a plastic bag combine the squash with the oil and salad dressing, twist the bag closed, and shake it vigorously.

Combine the crumbs and cheese in another plastic bag. Add the squash and shake vigorously.

Arrange the squash in a single layer on a shallow nonstick pan well sprayed with cooking spray. Put the pan on the middle rack of the oven and bake the squash, turning it once, for about 6 to 8 minutes.

Makes 4 servings, 75 calories each.

VARIATION

Substitute 2 small unpeeled eggplants, sliced (cucumber size) for the squash; 85 calories per serving.

OVEN-FRIED LIVER

1 lb. beef or calves' liver, at least ¾ inch thick, sliced into serving pieces
1 Tbs. salad oil
4 Tbs. seasoned bread crumbs
Salt and pepper

Preheat the oven to very hot, 450 degrees.

In a plastic bag sprinkle the oil on the liver and shake the bag to coat the liver evenly.

Combine the crumbs and seasonings in another plastic bag, add the liver, and shake.

Put the liver in one layer in a nonstick pan well sprayed with cooking spray.

Put the pan on the middle rack in the oven and bake the liver for about 8 minutes. Turn after 4 minutes and season to taste. (The liver will be slightly pink in the middle.)

Makes 4 servings, 210 calories each.

OVEN-FRIED ONIONS

1 very large Spanish or
  Bermuda onion, thinly sliced
1 Tbs. salad oil

1 Tbs. water
Salt and pepper

Preheat the oven to very hot, 450 degrees.

In a plastic bag combine the onion and oil and shake the bag to coat the onion evenly.

Put the onions in a shallow layer on a nonstick pan well sprayed with cooking spray, sprinkle on the water, and add salt and pepper to taste.

Put the pan on the middle rack of the oven and bake the onions for 6 to 8 minutes. Turn them once or twice to cook evenly.

Makes 4 servings, 55 calories each.

SPICY SWISS STEAK

¼ cup catsup
1 Tbs. lemon juice
½ cup water
2 tsp. prepared mustard
2 tsp. Worcestershire sauce

2 Tbs. minced onion
Salt, or garlic salt, and pepper
1 tsp. chili powder (or to taste)
1¼ lb. lean top round steak,
  trimmed

Preheat the oven to moderately slow, 300 degrees.

In a bowl combine the first 8 ingredients. In a baking pan pour the mixture over the steak and bake the steak for 1 hour or more until tender. Baste it frequently, adding more water, if needed.

Makes 4 servings, 220 calories each.

SMOTHERED SALISBURY STEAKS

4 onions, sliced
1 lb. lean ground round
2 Tbs. water

1 Tbs. Worcestershire sauce
1 Tbs. soy sauce
1 Tbs. catsup

Preheat the oven to very hot, 450 degrees.

Arrange the onions in a single layer in a shallow nonstick pan well sprayed with cooking spray.

Shape the beef into oval patties and arrange them on the onions.

In a bowl combine the remaining ingredients and pour the mixture over the beef. Bake the mixture in the oven, basting it frequently, until the top is browned. Turn the patties and the onions, basting them frequently, and cook to the desired degree of doneness. To serve, spoon the onions over the patties.

Makes 4 servings, 200 calories each.

LIGHT MEAT LOAF

3 cups high-protein cereal
1 cup skim milk
2 eggs
2 lb. lean ground round
Salt, or garlic salt, and pepper

1 Tbs. Worcestershire sauce
1 cup grated raw carrots
½ cup chopped onion
¼ cup chopped parsley

Preheat the oven to moderate, 350 degrees.

In a bowl combine the cereal and milk, stir in the eggs, and add the remaining ingredients, mixing lightly.

Shape the mixture in a loaf pan. Invert onto a baking pan; remove loaf pan. Bake it for 1 hour.

Makes 10 servings, 185 calories each.

SPANISH RICE MEAT LOAF

2 lb. extra-lean ground round
  (ground to order, if possible)
1 can (15 oz.) Spanish rice
2 eggs or 4 egg whites

2 onions, finely minced
1 tsp. garlic salt
¼ tsp. pepper
1 Tbs. prepared mustard

Preheat the oven to moderate, 350 degrees.

In a bowl combine all the ingredients and shape the mixture into a loaf. Place in a shallow baking pan.

Bake for 1 hour.

Makes 8 servings, 235 calories each, or 220 each with egg whites.

ZESTY BEEF LOAF

2 lb. lean ground round, fat-
trimmed
1 can (8 oz.) plain tomato sauce
1 egg or 2 egg whites
1 Tbs. Worcestershire sauce
½ cup chopped green bell
pepper

3 onions, chopped
¾ cup finely crushed cracker
crumbs or matzoh meal
1 tsp. salt or garlic salt
¼ tsp. pepper

Preheat the oven to moderate, 350 degrees.

In a bowl combine all the ingredients and mix them lightly but thoroughly.

Shape the mixture into a loaf and put it in a roasting pan. Bake the loaf for 1 hour and 15 minutes.

Makes 8 servings, 220 calories each, or 215 each with egg whites.

ROAST BEEF

4 or 5 lb. lean boneless beef
shoulder, fat-trimmed
Meat tenderizer
Onion powder

Garlic powder
1 tsp. dried savory or other
herbs
Salt and pepper

Preheat the oven to slow, 250 degrees.

Sprinkle the beef liberally with meat tenderizer and seasonings, except salt, and prick it in several places with a fork. Put it in a shallow nonstick pan and insert a meat thermometer in the center.

Bake the roast for 4 to 6 hours, until the thermometer registers 140 to 150 degrees.

Remove the roast from the oven immediately and allow it to stand at least 10 to 20 minutes before slicing. Add salt and pepper to taste.

Thinly slice the meat against the grain.

Each 4-oz. serving, lean meat only, 185 calories.

LEMON-BAKED BEEF

1 small onion, thinly sliced
1 clove garlic, chopped
2 lb. lean round steak, fat-
trimmed

½ tsp. oregano
¼ cup lemon juice

Preheat the oven to very slow, 225 degrees.

Arrange the onion and garlic in a nonstick shallow pan just large enough to hold the steak. Add the steak and sprinkle it with oregano and lemon juice.

Bake the steak for 3 hours or more, depending on the thickness, until it is very tender.

(The meat will be well done.)

Makes 6 servings, 210 calories each.

STUFFED BEEF BRACIOLA

1 lb. braciola (lean beef round, sliced thin for rolling)
1 cup shredded part-skim mozzarella cheese
4 Tbs. extra-sharp Romano cheese
2 Tbs. minced onion
1 Tbs. minced parsley or 1 tsp. dried parsley

1 clove minced garlic (optional)
1 tsp. oregano or basil
½ tsp. salt
Pinch of pepper
1 cup plain tomato sauce
½ cup Chianti or other dry red wine or water

Preheat the oven to moderate, 350 degrees.

Lay the beef out flat and sprinkle it with the mozzarella, Romano, onion, parsley, garlic, oregano, salt, and pepper. Roll the beef over the filling, overlapping it, turn the roll over, and put it seam side down in a shallow baking dish just large enough to hold it.

In a bowl combine the tomato sauce with the wine or water and pour the mixture over the roll.

Bake the mixture, uncovered, basting occasionally, for 1 hour. (Add water, if needed.)

Makes 4 servings, 285 calories each.

POULTRY-STUFFED PEPPERS

6 green bell peppers of similar
   size, washed and tops
   removed
3 cups cooked minced chicken
   or turkey white meat
½ cup cooked rice
1 cup chopped onions

Salt and pepper
1 clove garlic, minced (optional)
1 tsp. thyme
1 Tbs. lemon juice
3 cups canned plain tomato
   sauce

Preheat the oven to moderate, 350 degrees.

Seed the peppers.

In a deep bowl combine the poultry, rice, onions, salt, pepper, garlic, thyme, and lemon juice, add 1 cup tomato sauce, and mix well. Divide the filling among the peppers and stand the peppers in a casserole. Pour the remaining tomato sauce over them.

Bake, uncovered, basting them, for about 25 to 30 minutes, until they are tender.

Makes 6 servings, 210 calories each, or 230 each with turkey.

VEAL PARMIGIANA

1 lb. lean veal shoulder,
   trimmed, ground, and shaped
   into 4 patties
1 egg
2 tsp. olive oil
4 Tbs. Italian-seasoned bread
   crumbs

2 cups plain tomato sauce
Salt, or garlic salt, and pepper
1 tsp. basil or oregano
3 oz. part-skim mozzarella
   cheese, shredded

Preheat the oven to very hot, 450 degrees.

Press the patties flat to form cutlets.

In a bowl beat the egg and olive oil together and dip each patty into the mixture. Press into the bread crumbs to coat lightly.

Arrange the patties in a single layer in a nonstick pan and bake them for about 8 to 10 minutes, until they are brown.

In a bowl combine the tomato sauce with the seasonings and pour it over the patties. Bake the dish until the sauce is bubbling. Sprinkle with shredded cheese and return it to the oven until the cheese melts.

Makes 4 servings, 315 calories each.

VARIATION

Substitute 1 lb. raw ground turkey or turkey breakfast sausage for the veal. Makes 4 servings, 375 calories each.

ITALIAN VEAL LOAF

1 can (16 oz.) crushed tomatoes
½ cup combined chopped red and green bell peppers
2 lb. lean ground veal shoulder
2 eggs (or 4 egg whites or ½ cup liquid no-cholesterol substitute)
1 carrot, coarsely shredded
2 onions, finely chopped

1 rib celery, finely minced
½ cup parsley, preferably Italian
1 clove garlic, finely chopped (optional)
1 cup high-protein cereal, crushed
2 tsp. salt
Dash of Tabasco sauce

Preheat the oven to moderate, 350 degrees.

Drain the tomatoes and reserve the juice. In a bowl combine the tomatoes with the remaining ingredients. Toss the mixture lightly and shape it into a loaf.

In a loaf pan bake the mixture, basting it frequently with the reserved tomato juice, for 1 hour and 10 minutes.

Makes 10 servings, 175 calories each, or 165 calories each with egg whites or no-cholesterol substitute.

VARIATION

Substitute 2 lb. raw ground turkey for the veal. Makes 10 servings, 225 calories each.

HAM AND NOODLE BAKE

8 oz. uncooked noodles
1 lb. cooked fat-trimmed ham, cubed (about 3 cups)
1 cup plain low-fat yogurt
1 cup low-fat cottage cheese
1 cup (4 oz.) shredded cheddar cheese
1 small red or green bell pepper, seeded and finely chopped
1 tsp. caraway seeds
1 tsp. instant minced onion
Salt to taste
¼ tsp. garlic powder

Preheat the oven to moderate, 350 degrees.

Cook the noodles according to the package directions and drain them.

In a nonstick two-quart casserole, combine all the ingredients and bake the mixture for 35 to 45 minutes.

Makes 8 servings, 300 calories each.

VARIATION

Omit the cheddar cheese, or substitute low-calorie cheese: 245 calories per serving without cheese, 270 calories per serving with low-calorie cheese.

HAM PATTIES

1 lb. ground cooked ham
1 cup high-protein cereal, crushed
1 egg, lightly beaten
½ cup skim milk
Pinch of black pepper
1 Tbs. prepared mustard
1 cup juice-packed pineapple, crushed
1 tsp. arrowroot or cornstarch

Preheat the oven to moderate, 350 degrees.

In a bowl combine the first 6 ingredients and shape the mixture into 6 patties.

Bake the patties in a nonstick pan for 12 to 15 minutes.

In a bowl stir the pineapple and arrowroot or cornstarch together and pour over patties. Bake an additional 10 minutes.

Makes 6 servings, 180 calories each.

SWISS CHICKEN

1 lb. skinless boneless chicken
breasts, split
1 egg, beaten
1 cup (4 oz.) shredded Swiss
cheese

7 Tbs. Italian-seasoned bread
crumbs
Salt, or garlic salt, and pepper

Preheat the oven to very hot, 450 degrees.

Dip the chicken lightly in beaten egg, the cheese, and then the bread crumbs, until both sides are lightly coated. Season to taste.

Bake the chicken on a shallow nonstick tray well sprayed, turning it once, until it is brown and crisp, about 10 to 12 minutes. (Garnish with lemon, if desired.)

Makes 4 servings, 285 calories each.

JAMAICA CURRIED CHICKEN

2½ lb. frying chicken, cut into
pieces
½ cup thinly sliced scallions or
onions
1 green bell pepper, seeded and
chopped
1 can (6 oz.) tomato paste

1 clove garlic, minced
2 tsp. curry powder
½ tsp. ground allspice
2 cups water
Salt and pepper

Preheat the oven to very hot, 450 degrees.

Trim the fat from the chicken. In a shallow nonstick pan bake the chicken skin side up for 20 to 25 minutes, until the skin is crisp and well rendered of fat. Discard the fat.

In a bowl combine the remaining ingredients and pour the mixture over the chicken. Reduce the heat to moderate, 350 degrees, and bake, basting often, for 25 to 30 minutes or more, until the chicken is tender and the sauce is thick.

Makes 6 servings, 195 calories each.

CHICKEN A L'ORANGE

2 lb. young frying chicken, cut
  into pieces
Salt and pepper
1 cup orange juice

2 tsp. grated orange peel
Pinch of nutmeg
¼ tsp. poultry seasoning

Preheat the oven to very hot, 450 degrees.

Bake the chicken skin side up in a shallow nonstick pan, uncovered, for about 25 minutes, until the skin is crisp and well rendered of fat. Discard the fat.

In a bowl combine the remaining ingredients and pour the mixture over the chicken. Reduce the heat to moderate, 350 degrees, and bake, basting it frequently, for about 25 to 30 minutes, until tender. (Garnish with orange slices, if desired.)

Makes 4 servings, 220 calories each.

INDIAN CHICKEN

3 lb. frying chicken, cut into
  pieces
1 cup plain low-fat yogurt
1½ tsp. salt
1 small clove garlic, crushed

½ tsp. ground cardamom or
  cinnamon
½ tsp. chili powder
¼ tsp. ground ginger
2 tsp. flour

Trim the fat from the chicken.

In a bowl, combine all the remaining ingredients. Let the chicken marinate, covered, in the refrigerator for 4 hours, or overnight.

Preheat the oven to moderate, 325 degrees.

Arrange the chicken skin side up in a nonstick pan.

Spoon the marinade over it and bake, basting it occasionally, for 1¼ to 1½ hours, or until it is tender.

Makes 6 servings, 220 calories each.

PICKLED CHICKEN THIGHS

3 lb. frying chicken thighs
½ cup white or cider vinegar
2 cups cider or apple juice
1 tsp. whole cloves
2 onions, thinly sliced
1 clove garlic, minced (optional)
3 or 4 bay leaves

1 Tbs. salt
¼ tsp. pepper
Pinch of ground allspice
5 Tbs. flour

Combine all the ingredients, except the flour, in a plastic bag. Set the bag in a glass or ceramic bowl and refrigerate it for 12 to 24 hours, turning the thighs occasionally.

Preheat the oven to very hot, 450 degrees.

Drain the chicken and reserve the marinade. Shake up the thighs with the flour in a large paper bag. Arrange the chicken in a single layer in a shallow nonstick pan well sprayed with cooking spray and bake for 35 to 45 minutes, until it is done. Remove the cloves and bay leaves.

Makes 8 servings, 220 calories each. Good hot or cold.

TURKEY THIGH IN TOMATO SAUCE

1 young turkey thigh, boned
1 onion, thinly sliced
1 can (8 oz.) stewed tomatoes,
  well broken up

Salt, or herb-seasoned salt, and
  pepper

Place the turkey thigh skin side up in a small nonstick pan. Broil it for 12 to 15 minutes, just until the skin is crisp. Discard the fat.

Preheat the oven to moderately slow, 300 degrees.

Put the onion under the thigh and pour the tomatoes over it. Season to taste.

Cover the pan tightly with foil and bake for 1½ to 2 hours, until the thigh is tender. Uncover the pan and raise the heat to 450 degrees. Bake, basting frequently, until the sauce is thick.

Makes 5 servings, 290 calories each.

ITALIAN SAUSAGE AND EGGPLANT CASSEROLE

1 lb. turkey sausage
½ lb. lean ground beef or veal
1 tsp. garlic salt
Pinch of pepper
½ tsp. basil
⅓ cup skim milk
1 medium eggplant, pared and cut into 1-inch cubes

2 cups plain tomato sauce
1 small can (2 oz.) mushrooms, stems and pieces
½ tsp. oregano
2 Tbs. Italian-seasoned bread crumbs
8 Tbs. grated Parmesan cheese

In a bowl combine the sausage, ground meat, garlic salt, pepper, basil, and milk and toss the mixture lightly. Shape 12 meatballs and brown them on a rack under the broiler.

Preheat the oven to moderate, 350 degrees.

Combine all the ingredients, except the bread crumbs and cheese, in a casserole. Sprinkle it with bread crumbs and cheese and bake for 30 to 40 minutes or longer, until the eggplant is tender.

Makes 8 servings, 215 calories each.

VARIATION

Substitute 8 tsp. grated extra-sharp Romano cheese for the Parmesan; 195 calories per serving.

SPANISH RICE AND TURKEY LOAF

2 lb. ground turkey or turkey sausage
1 can (15 oz.) Spanish rice
2 eggs, beaten

½ cup minced onion
Garlic salt
¼ tsp. pepper
1 Tbs. prepared mustard

Preheat oven to moderate, 350 degrees.

In a bowl combine all the ingredients, mix them lightly until blended, and shape the mixture into a loaf.

Bake the mixture for 1 hour.

Makes 8 servings, 280 calories each, or 290 each with turkey sausage.

SOLE AND SPINACH CASSEROLE

2 packages (12 oz. each) fresh
spinach, chopped (or two 10-
oz. packages, defrosted)
2 Tbs. minced onion
½ cup skim milk
4 slices low-fat American-style
cheese, shredded

4 sole fillets (4 oz. each), fresh
or defrosted
2 Tbs. lemon juice
Salt and pepper
Paprika

Preheat the oven to moderately hot, 400 degrees.

Cook fresh spinach in a tightly covered pot with no liquid added. (If using frozen spinach, drain it thoroughly.)

Combine the spinach with the onion and spread the mixture in a shallow nonstick pan well sprayed with cooking spray. Add the milk, sprinkle the cheese over the spinach, and arrange the fillets over the cheese in a single layer. Sprinkle the dish with lemon juice, salt and pepper to taste, and paprika. Cover the pan tightly with foil.

Bake for 20 minutes, or until the fish flakes easily.

Makes 4 servings, 180 calories each.

FISH IN FOIL

8 bay leaves, broken up
1 lb. cod steaks or other fish
½ cup lemon juice or dry white
wine

4 tsp. instant minced onion
Paprika (optional)
Salt, or seasoned salt, and pepper
4 tsp. diet margarine

Preheat the oven to very hot, 450 degrees.

Place four sheets of aluminum foil shiny side up and divide the bay leaves among them. Arrange a fish steak in the center of each sheet on top of the bay leaves and sprinkle the fish with the remaining ingredients, except the margarine. Close up the foil loosely.

Bake the packet on a baking sheet (or on a rack in a preheated hooded barbecue grill) for 10 minutes.

Open up the packages, divide the margarine among them, and baste the fish with juices collected in foil. Leave the foil open and bake 4 to 5 minutes more (just until fish flakes easily).

Makes 4 servings, 115 calories each.

FLOUNDER ROLLATINI

3 thin slices part-skim
mozzarella cheese
6 flounder or sole fillets (about
1½ lb.), fresh or defrosted
½ cup chopped fresh
mushrooms
1 Tbs. minced onion

2 Tbs. minced fresh parsley or 1
tsp. dried parsley
Salt and pepper
2 Tbs. low-calorie mayonnaise
4 Tbs. Italian-seasoned bread
crumbs
Paprika

Preheat the oven to moderately high, 425 degrees.

Place ½ cheese slice on each fillet.

In a bowl combine the mushrooms, onion, parsley, salt and pepper to taste with 1 teaspoon mayonnaise. Divide the mixture among the fillets and roll each fillet pinwheel-style.

Spread the rolls with the remaining mayonnaise and roll them in the bread crumbs. Put them seam side down in a shallow baking dish well sprayed with cooking spray. Sprinkle the dish with paprika.

Bake the fillets for 20 minutes, or until the fish is opaque and the bread crumbs are lightly toasted. (Don't overcook.)

Makes 6 servings, 140 calories each.

MEDITERRANEAN BLUEFISH

2 Tbs. lemon juice
¼ cup chopped green bell
pepper
¼ cup chopped onion
1 can (16 oz.) tomatoes,
undrained, well broken up

3 or 4 sprigs of fresh parsley
1 tsp. basil
Salt, or garlic salt, and pepper
1 lb. bluefish fillets

Preheat the oven to very hot, 450 degrees.

In a shallow oven-proof dish combine all the ingredients, except the bluefish. Place the dish in the oven, uncovered, and when the sauce begins to simmer, add the fish in a single layer. Spoon some of the sauce over it and bake, uncovered, basting frequently, for about 12 to 16 minutes, until the fish flakes easily, depending on thickness. (Add water to sauce, if needed.)

Makes 4 servings, 170 calories each.

SEA STEAKS IN YOGURT SAUCE

1½ lb. cod or salmon steaks
1 cup plain low-fat yogurt
1½ Tbs. flour
1 Tbs. grated onion
2 tsp. grated lemon rind
(optional)

Salt
⅛ tsp. paprika
Tabasco sauce to taste

Preheat the oven to moderate, 350 degrees.

Place the fish in a shallow nonstick dish in a single layer. In a bowl combine the remaining ingredients and pour the mixture over the fish.

Bake the dish for 20 to 30 minutes, until the fish flakes easily with a fork.

Makes 4 servings, 180 calories each, or 380 calories each with salmon.

VEAL SPARERIBS IN BARBECUE SAUCE

3 lb. lean fat-trimmed breast of
veal, cut into riblets
1 can (8 oz.) unsweetened
juice-packed crushed
pineapple
2 cups Bloody Mary–seasoned
tomato juice

1 onion, minced
1 bell pepper, minced
1 tsp. liquid smoke seasoning
(optional)

Arrange the riblets in a single layer in a shallow nonstick broiler pan and broil them, close to the heat, turning once, until crisp (about 15 minutes each side). Drain the fat.

Preheat the oven to moderate, 350 degrees.

Combine the riblets with the remaining ingredients in a nonstick roasting pan and bake them, uncovered, until veal is tender and sauce is thick, 1 hour or more. Baste occasionally while baking.

Skim any fat from sauce with a bulb-type baster.

Makes 8 servings, 365 calories each.

7

From Broiler and

Barbecue

COOKOUTS—and cook-ins—are understandably popular with "light and easy"-minded cooks. Broiling is a low-fat way to prepare foods, and it's quick and easy. Smoke adds a special seasoning to ordinary foods like plain hamburger or chicken. What's more, al fresco cooking is festive and fun . . . everybody gets into the act! Making dinner is less likely to be a one-person chore.

Most important, however, broiling or barbecuing decreases fat instead of adding it.

To reap the calorie benefits of broiling, the food itself must be relatively low in fat and calories. And the bastes, marinades, and sauces used must be light as well. There's no advantage to broiled foods if you use high-fat steaks and chops, fatty ground meats, and hot dogs. (Even though broiling or barbecuing melts some of the fat in these high-calorie choices, most of it remains. This is especially true of steaks and hamburgers served rare, the way most people prefer them.)

Why Marinate?

The point of marinades is to tenderize, and the point of bastes and sauces is to prevent the evaporation of moisture, while adding flavor and

(64)

seasoning. Neither oil nor sugar has any ability whatsoever to soften the fibers of less-than-tender meats, so the addition of either to a tenderizing marinade is pointless! Nor do they add any real flavor. Most cooking oil is tasteless and sugar only adds sweetness. As far as keeping foods moist as they cook, *any* fat-free liquid baste can serve that purpose. You don't need oil or sugar.

What are the best ingredients for "light and easy" marinades and basting sauces? For purposes of tenderizing, any acid liquid will do. In fact, it's the acid ingredients in marinades—vinegar, wine, tomato juice, lemon juice, other fruit juices—that do the real work of softening the fibers. These low-cal liquids also add special flavor and impart moistness. Other low-calorie ingredients: Tabasco, Worcestershire sauce, soy sauce, mustard, horseradish, garlic, minced onion, hot pepper, spices, seasonings, and herbs. Fruit juices and fruit purées can add a natural touch of sweetness with no extra sugar needed.

How to Adapt Marinades, Bastes, and Barbecue Sauces for "Light and Easy" Cooking

The first step in lightening a favorite marinade is to omit whatever oil is called for. To keep the volume of liquid the same, simply increase the other liquid ingredients or substitute water for the oil. For example, if a spicy tomato baste calls for a half cupful of oil, you could simply increase the tomato juice called for by a half cupful. Or dilute the other ingredients with a half cup of water.

A popular barbecue shortcut is to use bottled commercial salad dressings as a marinade. With good reason: the bottled dressings contain a balance of herbs and seasonings plus vinegar, which performs the tenderizing function. I've found that the substitution of the low-fat, low-calorie version of the regular commercial bottled dressings works equally well, either diluted with water or combined with other low-calorie ingredients and seasonings.

All-Year Cook-Ins

You can add "cookout" flavor to foods cooked indoors under the broiler by using "light and easy" marinades, flavor-boosting sauces, and moisture-protecting bastes. In fact, they are heartily recommended for lean, low-calorie cuts of meat, poultry, and seafood. The leanest steaks and chops often come from the less tender (and, thankfully, less expensive) cuts, so they can profit from the tenderizing abilities of marinades. Poultry and fish can dry out if not basted with something.

With flavorful marinades and bastes, you'll never hear the complaint that lean, low-calorie foods are bland and boring or lacking in flavor!

STEAK AND MUSHROOM SKEWERS

2 lb. lean fat-trimmed top round
  steak, cut in 1½-inch cubes
1 cup plain low-fat yogurt
2 Tbs. grated onion
Salt

½ tsp. chili powder
¼ tsp. Worcestershire sauce
1 lb. fresh mushrooms
1 tsp. salad oil

In a glass bowl combine the beef with the yogurt, onion, salt, chili powder, and Worcestershire sauce. Let the mixture marinate, covered, for 3 or more hours in the refrigerator.

Thread skewers, alternating beef and mushrooms, and brush them with some marinade and the oil.

Broil or barbecue the skewers 3 to 4 inches from the heat source, turning them occasionally, for 10 minutes or to the desired degree of doneness.

Makes 8 servings, 190 calories each.

BARBECUE BEEF KEBABS IN PACKETS

1 lb. fat-trimmed lean beef
  round steak or arm steak, cut
  into cubes
1 cup any marinade or
  barbecue baste

Skewers
Heavy-duty aluminum foil

To Cook Outdoors

Thread the meat on skewers.

Place each skewer on a sheet on heavy-duty foil. Lift the foil up around the skewers and pour on the marinade. Double-wrap with foil, being careful not to puncture it with the skewers.

Arrange the packets on a covered barbecue grill over hot coals. Cook for 1 hour or more, turning, until tender.

Unwrap. When the meat is tender, remove the foil, reserving the marinade, and grill the skewers over hot coals until crisp. Turn frequently and baste with the marinade from packets.

To Cook Indoors

Preheat the oven to moderately slow, 325 degrees.

Arrange the meat-threaded skewers in a shallow nonstick roasting pan and pour on the marinade.

Cover the dish with foil and bake for about 1½ hours, until tender.

Remove the skewers from the baking dish to a broiler pan to brown. Turn and baste occasionally with reserved marinade.

Makes 4 servings, about 200 calories each.

MARINATED FLANK STEAK

1 can (10¾ oz.) tomato soup	1 small clove garlic, minced
⅓ cup dry red wine	1 Tbs. finely chopped onion
2 Tbs. finely chopped ripe olives	1½ lb. flank steak, scored

In shallow baking dish combine all the ingredients except the steak. Add the steak and let it marinate at room temperature, turning it once, for 1 hour. Remove the steak.

In a stainless steel saucepan cook the marinade, covered, over low heat, stirring occasionally, for 10 minutes.

Broil the steak 4 inches from heat, brushing it with the marinade, about 4 minutes on each side to the desired degree of doneness. Heat the remaining marinade and serve it with steak.

Makes 6 servings, 205 calories each.

VARIATION

To barbecue, cook the steak 4 inches above glowing coals, brushing it with the marinade, 5 minutes on each side. Serve with the remaining marinade.

MARINATED ROUND STEAK

3 or 4 bay leaves, broken up
1 lb. lean fat-trimmed top round steak, cut into 4 pieces
½ cup dry red wine

¼ cup red wine vinegar
1 clove garlic, minced (optional)
Few drops liquid smoke seasoning (optional)

Spread the broken-up bay leaves in a glass dish and arrange the steak on top of them. In a glass bowl combine the remaining ingredients and pour the mixture over steak. Cover and refrigerate it, turning occasionally, for several hours.

Remove the steak from the marinade and broil or barbecue it to the desired degree of doneness, turning once.

Makes 4 servings, 160 calories each.

SPICED CHUCK STEAK

3 lb. lean fat-trimmed boneless chuck steak, about 2 inches thick
2 tsp. meat tenderizer, plain or garlic-seasoned

⅓ cup minced onion
1 tsp. thyme
1 bay leaf
1 cup red wine vinegar
2 Tbs. mixed pickling spice

Sprinkle the meat with tenderizer and prick it in several places with a fork.

In a shallow dish just large enough to hold steak combine all the remaining ingredients and add the steak. Let it marinate, turning frequently, for 2 to 3 hours at room temperature.

Broil or barbecue the steak about 6 inches from the heat source about 15 minutes on each side. Slice the meat on the diagonal.

Makes 8 servings, 285 calories each.

JAPANESE TERIYAKI MARINADE

¼ cup dry sherry
¼ cup imported soy sauce
½ cup water

¼ tsp. ginger
¼ tsp. MSG (optional)

Combine in a glass bowl.

Makes 1 cup, 4 calories per Tbs.

LEMON MARINADE

¼ cup lemon juice
1½ tsp. garlic salt

1 tsp. basil or oregano
¼ cup water or more if needed

Combine in a bowl.

Makes ½ cup, 2 calories per Tbs.

CUMIN LAMB BURGERS

2 slices stale toasted high-fiber
    bread, diced
¼ cup warm water
1 lb. lean ground lamb shoulder
1 egg, beaten

2 onions, minced
1 tsp. cumin seeds
Salt, or garlic salt, and pepper
Lemon wedges (optional)

In a bowl mash the bread in the water with a fork. Add the remaining ingredients, except the lemon, and toss lightly.

Shape the mixture into 4 patties and broil or barbecue the patties, turning them once, about 3 to 4 minutes per side. (Serve with lemon wedges, if desired.)

Makes 4 servings, 230 calories each.

CURRIED LAMB MEATBALLS

1½ lb. lean ground lamb shoulder
2 onions, minced
2 eggs, lightly beaten, or ½ cup liquid no-cholesterol substitute
2 to 3 tsp. curry powder (or to taste)
½ cup chopped fresh parsley
1 tsp. dried dillweed (optional)
1 cup Raisin Bran cereal, crushed
½ cup skim milk or plain low-fat yogurt
2 Tbs. lemon juice

In a bowl combine the ingredients, except the lemon juice, and toss them lightly to mix well. Shape the mixture into 16 small meatballs.

Broil or barbecue the meatballs, turning them once and basting them with lemon juice, for about 6 to 8 minutes.

Makes 8 servings, 180 calories each, or 170 calories each with egg substitute.

BARBECUED LAMB STEAKS

4 thick lamb steaks, cut from the leg, (about 2¼ lb. in all), halved
½ cup catsup or sugar-free catsup
1 Tbs. wine vinegar
1 tsp. Worcestershire sauce
¼ tsp. garlic salt
Pinch of cayenne

Trim any fat from the lamb and arrange the meat in a broiling pan.

In a bowl combine the remaining ingredients and brush the mixture on the lamb: Broil or barbecue the meat, turning it and brushing it with the liquid, 6 to 7 minutes per side close to heat source.

Makes 8 servings, 185 calories each.

SHISH KEBABS

2 lb. lean fat-trimmed lamb, cut
    into 1½-inch cubes
½ cup wine vinegar
½ cup low-calorie Italian salad
    dressing

4 onions, peeled and quartered
16 mushroom caps

In a glass bowl combine the lamb, vinegar, and diet dressing. Let the lamb marinate, covered, at room temperature for 2 hours, or all day or overnight in the refrigerator.

Thread skewers, alternating lamb and vegetables. Broil or barbecue the skewers close to the heat source, turning and basting them frequently, for about 15 minutes.

Makes 8 servings, 165 calories each.

BARBECUED SMOKED PORK CHOPS WITH PINEAPPLE RINGS

4 lean fat-trimmed ready-to-eat
    center-cut smoked pork chops
    (about 6 oz. each)
1 can (8 oz.) juice-packed
    pineapple rings, including
    juice

¼ tsp. dry mustard or 1 tsp.
    prepared mustard
¼ tsp. pumpkin pie spice

Drain the juice from the pineapple rings and combine it in a glass bowl with the remaining ingredients. Let the chops marinate for 30 minutes. Preheat the broiler or barbecue.

When the heat source is hot, arrange the chops and pineapple rings in a single layer on the rack, about 2 to 3 inches from the heat. When the undersides are brown, turn the chops and cook them briefly, only until heated through.

Makes 4 servings, 250 calories each.

FRUITED HAM ON SKEWERS

¾ lb. ready-to-eat smoked ham
steak, cut into 1-inch cubes
2 seedless oranges, in sections
1 can (8 oz.) juice-packed
pineapple chunks, including
juice

1 unpeeled red apple, cut into
chunks
1 Tbs. lemon juice
1 Tbs. sugar (optional)
2 tsp. prepared mustard

Thread skewers, alternating ham and fruits. In a glass bowl combine the pineapple juice with the remaining ingredients and rotate the skewers in the mixture.

Broil or barbecue the skewers, turning them twice, for about 5 to 6 minutes, until the apple chunks are tender but not soft. Baste with the liquid.

Makes 4 servings, 240 calories each, or 250 with sugar.

POLYNESIAN SKEWERED HAM AND CHICKEN

½ lb. ready-to-eat cured ham
steak, cut into 1-inch cubes
2 skinless, boneless chicken
breasts, cut into 1-inch cubes
1 red bell pepper and 1 green
bell pepper, cut into 1-inch
squares

1 can (16 oz.) unsweetened
pineapple chunks, drained
⅓ cup pineapple juice (from
canned pineapple)
4 Tbs. soy sauce
2 Tbs. salad oil

Thread skewers, alternating ham, chicken, pepper, and pineapple pieces. Transfer the skewers to a shallow pan.

In a bowl combine the remaining ingredients and pour the mixture over the skewers, rotating them.

Broil or barbecue the skewers for 5 minutes on each side, basting them often with the marinade.

Makes 6 servings, 320 calories each.

ROTISSERIE INDIAN CHICKEN

½ cup plain low-fat yogurt
2 Tbs. lemon juice
1 clove garlic, crushed
1 tsp. salt
½ tsp. ground ginger

¼ tsp. ground cumin
¼ tsp. ground turmeric
1 tsp. curry powder
1 whole broiler-fryer chicken
(about 1½ lb.)

In a glass bowl combine the yogurt with the seasonings and add the chicken, coating it well.

Preheat a covered barbecue with a rotisserie attachment to medium setting or 350 degrees.

Secure the chicken to the spit and cook it for about 1 hour or until it is done.

Makes 4 servings, 165 calories each.

POLYNESIAN CHICKEN ON A SPIT

¼ cup soy sauce
1 can (6 oz.) undiluted
pineapple juice concentrate,
defrosted

2 whole broiler-fryer chickens
(about 1½ lb. each)

Combine the soy sauce and pineapple concentrate in a shallow glass bowl, add the chickens, and roll them in the marinade to coat them evenly. Let the chickens marinate, turning them occasionally, for about 1 hour in the refrigerator.

Preheat a covered barbecue or oven equipped with a rotisserie attachment to 350 degrees or medium setting.

Secure the chickens to the spit and cook them about 1 hour, or until they are done.

Makes 8 servings, 195 calories each.

ROTISSERIE LEMON CHICKEN

2 whole broiler-fryer chickens
  (about 1½ lb. each)
⅔ cup lemon juice

⅓ cup soy sauce
1 tsp. crushed tarragon

Preheat a covered barbecue with a rotisserie attachment to 350 degrees.

Secure the chickens to the spit. In a bowl combine the remaining ingredients and brush the mixture over the chickens.

Roast the chickens at medium setting or 350 degrees, basting them occasionally, until they are done, about 1 hour.

Makes 8 servings, 155 calories each.

MARINATED CHICKEN

2 lb. frying chicken, cut into
  pieces
1 clove garlic, minced
3 Tbs. lemon juice
¼ cup olive juice from a jar of
  olives

¼ cup dry white wine or water
3 or 4 bay leaves, broken up
Dash of Tabasco sauce
Salt and pepper
Paprika

Combine all the ingredients in a plastic bag and refrigerate it for 2 to 4 hours, shaking it occasionally.

Remove the chicken from the bag. Broil or barbecue it for about 20 to 25 minutes on each side, until it is cooked through.

Makes 4 servings, 195 calories each.

VEAL BURGERS PARMESAN

1 lb. lean fat-trimmed boneless
  veal shoulder, ground
3 Tbs. grated Parmesan cheese
1 beaten egg or ¼ cup liquid
  no-cholesterol substitute
1 Tbs. lemon juice

2 Tbs. finely minced onion
Salt, or garlic salt, and pepper
½ tsp. basil
1 Tbs. minced fresh parsley
  (optional)

In a bowl combine all the ingredients, toss them lightly, and shape the mixture into 8 patties.

Broil or barbecue the patties 2 inches from the heat source for about 4 or 5 minutes on each side.

Makes 4 servings, 205 calories each, or 195 calories with egg substitute.

CHARCOAL-BROILED SEA STEAKS

1½ lb. cod steaks, fresh or
   defrosted, cut into 6 pieces
¾ cup dry white wine
3 Tbs. lemon juice
Pinch of cayenne or dash of hot
   pepper sauce

⅛ tsp. garlic powder
¼ tsp. oregano
¼ tsp. poultry seasoning
1 Tbs. finely minced scallion
   (optional)
Salt, pepper, and paprika

Arrange the fish in a single layer in a shallow glass dish. In a glass bowl combine the remaining ingredients and pour the mixture over the fish. Let the fish marinate, covered, turning it occasionally, for 4 to 6 hours in the refrigerator, or for 1 hour at room temperature.

Put the fish in a hinged wire grill and sprinkle it with paprika. Barbecue the fish over glowing coals, basting it with remaining marinade, about 8 minutes on each side.

Makes 6 servings, 95 calories each.

SWORDFISH A LA TURK

1 small onion, thinly sliced
8 to 10 bay leaves
1 lb. swordfish steaks

2 Tbs. lemon juice
Salt, or garlic salt, and pepper
1 tsp. olive oil

Arrange the onion and bay leaves in a shallow nonstick pan, add the fish in a single layer, and sprinkle it with lemon juice. Cover and refrigerate the mixture, turning it occasionally, for several hours.

Brush the fish with ½ teaspoon oil and broil it 5 to 6 inches from heat source for 5 minutes. Turn the fish, brush it with the remaining oil, and broil it 5 minutes more, or until it flakes easily.

Makes 4 servings, 155 calories each.

GARLIC-BROILED FISH FILLETS

2 sole or flounder fillets, fresh
   or defrosted
2 tsp. olive oil
2 Tbs. lemon juice

2 small cloves garlic, finely
   chopped
Pinch of oregano (optional)
Paprika (optional)

Arrange the fish in a single layer in a nonstick pan. In a glass bowl combine the oil, lemon juice, garlic, and oregano if desired, and spread the mixture over the fish. (Sprinkle with paprika, if desired.)

Broil or barbecue the fish, without turning it, about 4 inches from the heat source, spooning pan juices over it every 2 minutes for about 6 to 8 minutes.

Makes 2 servings, 140 calories each.

MEDITERRANEAN MARINATED SEA STEAKS

1 lb. fish steaks—cod, halibut,
   or swordfish, fresh or
   defrosted
1 Tbs. mixed pickling spice
2 or 3 bay leaves, broken up
¼ cup cider or white vinegar

½ cup dry white wine
1 clove garlic, minced
Dash of Tabasco sauce
2 tsp. oil
Salt and pepper

Arrange the fish in a single layer on top of the pickling spices and bay leaves in a glass dish. Combine the vinegar, wine, garlic, and Tabasco and pour the mixture over the fish. Let the fish marinate, covered, in the refrigerator, turning it occasionally, for 1 to 2 hours.

Drain the fish and spread it lightly with oil. Broil or barbecue it, turning it once, about 4 minutes on each side, until fish flakes easily. Add salt and pepper to taste.

Makes 4 servings, 115 calories each with cod, 140 each with halibut, or 160 each with swordfish.

More Marinades and Sauces

MANDARIN BASTING SAUCE

½ cup orange juice   ¼ cup soy sauce
¼ cup sugar-reduced orange
  marmalade

In a bowl mix ingredients well. Use as a basting sauce for broiled or barbecued turkey parts.

Makes 1 cup, 190 calories.

BEEFY BARBECUE SAUCE

3 cups tomato juice   ½ tsp. onion salt
¼ cup red wine vinegar   ¼ tsp. coarse pepper
1 clove garlic, crushed   1 beef bouillon cube
2 tsp. dry mustard   ½ tsp. Worcestershire sauce
½ tsp. savory   1 tsp. sugar

Combine the ingredients in a saucepan and simmer until the mixture is reduced by half. Use on lean beefsteaks or hamburgers.

Makes about 1½ cups, 8 calories per Tbs.

CHILI BARBECUE SAUCE

¼ cup chopped celery   ½ cup catsup
1 tsp. chili powder   ¼ cup water
1 can (10½ oz.) condensed   1 Tbs. vinegar
  onion soup   1 tsp. prepared mustard
1 Tbs. cornstarch

Combine the ingredients in a saucepan and cook the mixture over low heat, stirring occasionally, for 10 minutes. Use as a basting sauce when barbecuing chicken pieces.

Makes about 2 cups, 4 calories per Tbs.

SLIM-N-SPICY SAUCE

1 can (8 oz.) plain tomato sauce
2 Tbs. chopped onion
3 Tbs. dill pickle relish

1 tsp. prepared horseradish
Dash of Worcestershire sauce

Combine the ingredients in a saucepan and cook the mixture, stirring, until it bubbles. Serve hot or chilled with fish or poultry, or lean steak or hamburger.

Makes 1¼ cups, 4 calories per Tbs.

BARBECUE STEAK SAUCE

¼ cup chopped celery
¼ cup chopped onion
1 can (10¾ oz.) condensed
   tomato soup
¼ cup water

2 tsp. prepared mustard
1 tsp. prepared horseradish
1 tsp. honey
1 tsp. lemon juice

Combine the ingredients in a saucepan and cook the mixture, stirring occasionally, until the celery and onions are tender. Use as a basting sauce on steak or hamburgers.

Makes about 2 cups, 9 calories per Tbs.

KEBAB SEASONING

½ cup tomato juice
¼ cup chopped onion
½ tsp. garlic salt
⅛ tsp. pepper

2 Tbs. lemon juice
1 tsp. dry mustard
½ tsp. salt

In a glass bowl combine the ingredients. Use the marinade on cubes of lean boneless beef, lamb, or veal, which should be covered and left in the refrigerator overnight. Makes enough to season 2 lb. of boneless meat (8 servings).

Adds 56 calories (about 7 calories to each serving).

HOT-N-SPICY BARBECUE SAUCE

1 cup tomato juice

2 Tbs. lemon juice or vinegar

⅛ tsp. ground allspice

1 Tbs. diced onion

1 Tbs. diced green bell pepper

1 Tbs. prepared mustard

2 Tbs. honey

⅛ tsp. cayenne

1 bay leaf

1 Tbs. diced celery

1 tsp. chili powder

¼ tsp. ground cloves

In a bowl combine the ingredients and mix them thoroughly.

Makes 1½ cups, enough for 12 servings; 8 calories per Tbs.

LIGHT-AND-EASY HORSERADISH SAUCE

¼ cup low-fat mayonnaise

¼ cup plain low-fat yogurt

3 Tbs. prepared horseradish

1 Tbs. minced fresh parsley

1½ tsp. Worcestershire sauce

½ tsp. salt

Pinch of pepper

In a bowl combine the ingredients. Cover the mixture and refrigerate it. Use as a sauce for beef.

Makes ¾ cup, 12 calories per Tbs.

GREEK MARINADE

½ cup plain low-fat yogurt

½ cup lemon juice

1 Tbs. dried mint leaves

1 tsp. oregano

½ tsp. nutmeg

¼ tsp. cinnamon

Salt and pepper to taste

In a bowl combine the ingredients well and spread the marinade over meat, poultry, or fish. Refrigerate the mixture, covered, for several hours.

Makes enough for 4 servings, adds 45 calories, or about 11 calories to each serving.

LIGHT-AND-EASY ORIENTAL DUCK SAUCE

1 can (16 oz.) juice-packed
  pitted apricot halves
⅓ cup soy sauce

2 Tbs. cider vinegar
2 Tbs. honey
¾ cup (6-oz. can) tomato juice

Combine the ingredients in a blender and purée them. Use as a baking or broiling baste for chicken thighs or dark meat turkey roast.

Makes 3 cups, 10 calories per Tbs.

FRENCH WINE MARINADE OR BARBECUE SAUCE

½ cup low-calorie creamy
  French dressing

½ cup dry white wine

In a bowl combine the ingredients and use on lean top round steaks or on lean beef cubes; also good with hamburger, veal, chicken, and seafood.

Makes 1 cup, adds about 12 calories per Tbs.

GINGER MARINADE OR BARBECUE SAUCE

½ cup low-calorie creamy
  French dressing
⅓ cup dry sherry
¼ cup soy sauce

1 Tbs. minced fresh gingerroot
  or dried gingerroot or 2 tsp.
  ground ginger

In a bowl combine the ingredients and use on flank steak, lean meat, poultry, or fish.

Makes about 1 cup, enough for 8 servings; adds 40 calories to each serving.

SOUTH SEAS MARINADE
OR BARBECUE SAUCE

½ cup low-calorie Thousand
Island dressing
¼ cup soy sauce

¼ cup unsweetened pineapple
juice

In a bowl combine the ingredients and use on chicken, lean pork, lamb, beef, or fish.

Makes 1 cup, enough for 8 servings; adds 35 calories to each serving.

MEXICAN MARINADE OR BARBECUE SAUCE

⅓ cup low-calorie Italian salad
dressing
⅔ cup Bloody Mary–seasoned
tomato juice

¼ tsp. instant garlic
½ tsp. ground cumin

In a bowl combine the ingredients and use on chicken, beef, veal, or seafood.

Makes about 1 cup, enough for 8 servings; adds 10 calories to each serving.

CURRIED YOGURT MARINADE OR
BARBECUE SAUCE

½ cup low-calorie French
dressing
½ cup plain low-fat yogurt

2 Tbs. lime juice
1 Tbs. curry powder
1 clove minced garlic

In a bowl combine the ingredients and use on chicken or turkey.

Makes 1 cup, enough for 8 servings; adds 25 calories to each serving.

ITALIAN MARINADE OR BARBECUE SAUCE

⅓ cup low-calorie Italian salad
  dressing

⅔ cup tomato juice
1 clove garlic, minced (optional)

In a bowl combine the ingredients and use on beef, veal, poultry, or seafood.

Makes 1 cup, enough for 8 servings; adds 9 calories to each serving.

More Cookout Ideas

FOILED VEGETABLES

1 package (10 oz.) frozen green
  beans, broccoli, or other
  vegetable

1 Tbs. diet margarine
1 Tbs. water
Salt and pepper

Place the frozen vegetable on a generous length of foil, dot it with diet margarine, and sprinkle it with water. Season with salt and pepper.
Wrap the package tightly and barbecue it, turning it frequently, for 10 to 15 minutes.

Makes 3 servings, about 40 calories each.

PICNIC COLESLAW

1 large head cabbage, shredded
1 onion, chopped
1 grated carrot
¾ cup vinegar
1 tsp. prepared mustard

2 Tbs. salad oil
1 can (6 oz.) frozen undiluted
  apple or pineapple juice
  concentrate
Salt and pepper

Combine the cabbage, onion, and carrot in a large insulated ice bucket. Stir in the vinegar, mustard, and salad oil.
Add the frozen apple or pineapple juice concentrate and keep the bucket tightly closed until serving time. Stir well and season to taste.

Makes 16 servings, 50 calories each.

BARBECUED ORANGES

Seedless oranges   Cinnamon
   1 tsp. brown sugar for each
   orange

Peel each orange and separate it into sections. Place the sections of each orange on foil and sprinkle the sections with sugar and cinnamon.

Wrap each package tightly and place on side of grill until heated through, about 15 to 20 minutes.

Serve for dessert; 95 calories each.

FRUIT KEBABS

Cubes of apples, pears, apricots,   Wine-thinned honey or low-calorie
   bananas, fresh pineapple;   pancake syrup
   slices of peaches, mango,
   cantaloupe; sections of
   tangerine, orange, or
   grapefruit

Thread skewers, alternating the fruits. Before barbecuing, brush each skewer with a light coating of wine-honey (honey thinned with equal parts of wine) or low-calorie syrup.

Grill the skewers over hot coals just until the fruit begins to brown.

A half cupful of fruit and 1 tablespoon of marinade is about 150 calories each with honey marinade, or 110 calories each with diet syrup.

SHORTCAKE-ON-A-STICK

4 slices packaged angel food   Cinnamon
   cake, cut into 2-inch cubes
2 cups juice-packed pineapple
   chunks, drained

Thread skewers, alternating cake and pineapple. Sprinkle the skewers with cinnamon and toast them lightly over coals.

Makes 8 servings, 85 calories each.

8

Slow-Simmered

Dishes

SAVORY STEWS, hearty ragouts, and other slow-simmered combinations of meat and poultry are delicious. But if the two things you can't afford are time and calories, they're not for you. Right?

Wrong!

In this chapter I'd like to demonstrate that you can save work and calories as well as money with long-cooking techniques and lean ingredients. Wouldn't you like to come home to a one-pot beef stew of carrots, onions, and potatoes? Or turkey, tomatoes, and wine with pasta?

Fat and fatty ingredients unnecessarily added to slow-simmer dishes are what give stews and ragouts their fattening image. When you use lean ingredients and techniques that subtract fat instead of adding it, long-cooking combinations take on a much lighter calorie count without losing any of their hearty, rib-sticking appeal. Admittedly, one of the nicest features of slow-simmered dishes is that they *taste* fattening, even though they aren't.

Here are some points to ponder:

The less expensive stew meats have less fat and calories than high-priced steaks and chops. Beef rib is 36 percent fat and 1,819 calories per (boneless) pound, while separable lean beef shoulder or shank stew meat is under 650 calories per pound. Beef bottom round stew meat (separable lean) is only 615 calories per pound.

You can brown meat for stew or ragout with no fat added. Do it under the broiler or brown it in a nonstick pot with cooking spray instead of oil. Be sure to drain and discard any fat that appears during browning.

Young frying chicken can be substituted for older stewing hens and cocks in any slow-simmered poultry dish, thereby cutting the calories dramatically. Young chicken is 382 calories a pound; stewing chicken is 987 calories. Not only do you save calories, you save time as well; young chicken cooks in one-third to one-half the time!

Cubes of dark meat turkey sliced from fresh or defrosted turkey thighs can replace beef or other red meats usually used in slow-simmer dishes. And at far fewer calories: turkey is only 910 calories a pound!

The make-ahead two-step technique for slow-simmered dishes can edit out unwanted fat and calories and fit into your work schedule more easily. Prepare tomorrow's dinner tonight. Allow it to simmer several hours until nearly tender and refrigerate it. At dinnertime tomorrow remove all the hardened fat from the surface and throw it away *before* you add any final ingredients like vegetables or pasta. The dish will be even more tender and flavorful for its overnight wait.

Because slow-simmer dishes keep well and reheat beautifully, you can double, triple, even quadruple ingredients and prepare several make-ahead meals at once. The planned-over leftovers can be portioned into meal-size or single servings, then wrapped and stored in the freezer for homemade thaw-and-serve dinners on nights when there's no time to cook.

Using Fast and Slow Cookers

Directions for the recipes that follow are for conventional types of cookware, but you can easily adapt them for a fast-cooking pressure cooker or a slow-cooking "crock cooker." Whichever you use, simply follow the manufacturer's directions and adjust the cooking times accordingly. With a pressure cooker, add an additional 1½ to 2 cups water for each 20 minutes of cooking time. If there is too much liquid at the end of the cooking time, simmer the mixture uncovered for 5 to 10 minutes, until the excess moisture boils away. You can do the same with slow cookers: remove the cover and change the heat setting to high until the excess liquid is reduced to a sauce. Or thicken a too-liquid sauce by combining a tablespoon of flour (or a teaspoon or two of corn-starch) with some cold water and then stir it in; cook until the sauce is thick.

Here are some ideas to try:

BEEF AND MUSHROOM RAGOUT

1 lb. lean fat-trimmed top round
  steak, cut into 1½-inch cubes
½ tsp. salt or garlic salt
1 cup chopped onion
1 cup fat-skimmed condensed
  beef broth

1 Tbs. Worcestershire sauce
¼ tsp. thyme
½ lb. fresh mushrooms, sliced

Spray a nonstick skillet or Dutch oven with cooking spray. Brown the meat on all sides over moderate heat. Discard any fat.

Season the meat with garlic salt. Add the onion, broth, Worcestershire sauce, and thyme. Cover the dish and simmer it for 30 minutes or more, until the meat is tender.

Add the mushrooms and cook the dish, uncovered, stirring well, until most of the liquid evaporates.

Makes 4 servings, 195 calories each.

BUDGET BOEUF BOURGUIGNON

1½ lb. lean beef arm, fat-trimmed
  and cut into cubes
1 onion, coarsely chopped
1 garlic clove, minced (optional)
1 cup dry red wine
Salt and pepper
1 Tbs. minced fresh parsley or 2
  tsp. dried parsley

1 small bay leaf
1 cup peeled small white
  onions, fresh or defrosted
1 cup sliced carrots, fresh or
  defrosted
1 can (4 oz.) mushrooms,
  undrained

Spray a nonstick pot or Dutch oven with cooking spray. Brown the meat on all sides over moderate heat. Drain any fat.

Add the onion, garlic, wine, salt and pepper to taste, parsley, and bay leaf. Cover the dish and simmer it for about 2 hours, until the meat is nearly tender.

Add the onions and carrots and cook it 10 minutes more, covered.

Add the mushrooms. Uncover the dish and cook the mixture until the liquid is reduced to sauce consistency. Remove all fat and the bay leaf before serving.

Makes 4 servings, 190 calories each.

BEEF BOURGUIGNON

2 lb. lean fat-trimmed top round, cut into 1½-inch cubes

¼ lb. diced Canadian bacon

2 cups Burgundy or other red wine

Salt, or garlic salt, and pepper

1 bay leaf

¼ tsp. poultry seasoning (or a pinch of sage and thyme)

1¼ lb. fresh carrots, cut in 3-inch lengths

1 cup small onions, fresh, defrosted, or canned

2 cups sliced mushrooms, fresh or canned

2 Tbs. chopped fresh parsley

Spray a nonstick pot or Dutch oven with cooking spray. Brown the beef on all sides over moderate heat. Discard any fat.

Add the bacon, wine, and seasonings. Cover the pot and simmer over very low heat for about 2 hours (or more), until the meat is tender.

Add the carrots and simmer for 15 minutes.

Add the onions, mushrooms, and parsley and simmer for 5 minutes.

Uncover the pot and simmer the mixture until most of the liquid evaporates. Remove the bay leaf.

Makes 8 servings, 235 calories each.

SWISS STEAK

2 lb. lean round steak, 1½
   inches thick, trimmed
3 onions, sliced
2 cups canned tomatoes

2 Tbs. flour
2 tsp. salt or garlic salt
Pinch of pepper

Spray a nonstick skillet or Dutch oven with cooking spray. Brown the meat slowly on both sides. Discard any fat. Add the remaining ingredients.

Cover the dish and simmer for about 2 hours until the meat is tender. Check it for tenderness occasionally with a fork. (Add extra water if needed.) Remove any fat before serving.

Makes 8 servings, 185 calories each.

FRUITED BEEF CURRY

1½ lb. lean fat-trimmed boneless
   chuck steak, cut into 1-inch
   cubes
1 can (10½ oz.) fat-skimmed
   condensed beef broth
2 Tbs. lemon juice
1 Tbs. soy sauce
4 Tbs. raisins or dried currants

Salt and pepper
1 Tbs. curry powder
2 onions, thinly sliced
3 Tbs. flour
2 unpeeled red apples, diced
3 Tbs. defatted peanuts or dry-
   roasted cashews, broken up

Spray a nonstick skillet or Dutch oven with cooking spray. Brown the beef quickly over high heat. Discard any fat.

Stir in 1 cup of the broth. Add the lemon juice, soy sauce, raisins, salt and pepper to taste, and curry powder. Cover the pot and simmer it for about 1½ hours, until meat is very tender.

Skim any fat from the surface. Stir in the onions and simmer the mixture, uncovered, for about 5 minutes.

Stir the flour into the remaining broth and add the mixture to the pot, stirring until the sauce is thick. Stir in the apples and peanuts or cashews at the last minute.

Makes 6 servings, 245 calories each.

ROMAN POT ROAST

1½ lb. flank steak
  6 Tbs. grated Romano cheese
  1 tsp. basil
  1 clove garlic, finely minced
    (optional)
Salt and pepper

1 can (16 oz.) Italian tomatoes,
  broken up
¼ cup dry red wine
¾ cup water
½ cup chopped onions

Sprinkle the steak with cheese, basil, and garlic, if desired. Salt and pepper it lightly.

Roll up the steak lengthwise and tie it in several places with kitchen string.

Spray a heavy nonstick skillet or Dutch oven with cooking spray. Brown the steak on all sides over moderate heat. Discard any fat.

Add the tomatoes, wine, water, and onions. Cover the pot and cook the mixture very slowly over low heat for about 2 hours, until the meat is very tender. Uncover the pot for the last 30 minutes to allow the liquid to reduce to a thick sauce.

Makes 6 servings, 210 calories each.

BELGIAN POT ROAST

1½ lb. flank steak
  1 clove garlic, finely minced
    (optional)
  ½ tsp. salt
Pinch of pepper

½ tsp. sage or poultry seasoning
¾ cup low-calorie light beer
1 onion, thinly sliced
1 tsp. brown sugar

Sprinkle the steak with garlic, salt, pepper, and half the sage. Roll up the steak lengthwise and tie it with kitchen string in several places.

Spray a large nonstick skillet or Dutch oven with cooking spray. Brown the steak on all sides over moderate heat. Discard any fat.

Add the beer, onion, brown sugar, and remaining sage. Cover the pot and simmer for 1½ to 2 hours. Uncover the pot and simmer the mixture 6 to 10 minutes until most of the liquid has evaporated.

Makes 6 servings, 175 calories each.

SHANK RAGOUT

3 lb. beef shin slices, 2 inches thick

2 Tbs. Dijon-style mustard (or any "hot" mustard)

2 Tbs. Worcestershire sauce

1 can onion soup, diluted with an equal part of water

½ cup dry white wine or light beer

2 cups sliced carrots, fresh or defrosted

¾ lb. small, peeled potatoes, fresh or defrosted

Salt, or garlic salt, and pepper

Spread the meat with mustard. Brown the meat slowly in a non-stick heavy skillet or Dutch oven. Discard any fat.

Sprinkle the meat with Worcestershire sauce, add the soup and the wine. Cover the pot and simmer the mixture over very low heat for 1 hour or more, until meat is nearly tender. (Add water, if needed.)

Add the carrots and potatoes. Cook the mixture, covered, for 20 minutes, until the meat is tender.

Uncover the pot and simmer the mixture until most of the liquid evaporates. Add salt and pepper to taste.

Makes 4 servings, 475 calories each.

YANKEE BOILED BEEF WITH HORSERADISH SAUCE

3 lb. fat-trimmed boneless bottom round

1 large onion, sliced

1 Tbs. salt

2 or 3 cloves

1 bay leaf

½ tsp. thyme

2 or 3 sprigs of fresh parsley

5 or 6 peppercorns

4 potatoes, peeled and quartered

8 carrots, sliced

1 cup plain low-fat yogurt

3 to 4 Tbs. drained prepared horseradish (or to taste)

Salt and pepper

In a large Dutch oven cover the meat with water. Add the onion, salt, cloves, bay leaf, thyme, parsley, and peppercorns. Simmer the mixture, covered, for 2½ to 3 hours.

Add the potatoes and carrots and cook for 30 minutes.

Slice the meat very thinly against the grain and surround it on a platter with the drained vegetables. In a bowl combine the yogurt and horseradish, season it to taste, and serve it on the side.

Makes 8 servings, 325 calories each.

PAPRIKA VEAL

1½ lb. lean boneless veal cubes
1 Tbs. lemon juice
1 tsp. oil
1½ cups chopped onions
1 clove garlic, minced
1 cup fat-skimmed chicken broth
1 to 2 Tbs. sweet Hungarian paprika
1 cup plain low-fat yogurt
1 Tbs. flour
1 Tbs. minced fresh parsley

In a nonstick skillet or Dutch oven combine the veal, lemon juice, and oil and cook the mixture over moderate heat until it is lightly browned, turning it to prevent it from sticking.

Add the onions, garlic, broth, and paprika. Simmer the mixture, covered, over low heat for about 1 hour or more, until the meat is tender. Uncover the pot and cook the mixture over moderate heat until nearly all the liquid evaporates.

In a bowl combine the yogurt and flour and stir into the pan. Cook and stir over low heat until the sauce is thick. Stir in the parsley.

Makes 6 servings, 215 calories each.

GYPSY ONE-POT VEAL GOULASH

2 lb. lean trimmed veal
   shoulder, cut into 1½-inch
   cubes
1 Tbs. oil
1½ cups tomato juice
2 onions, chopped
2 ribs celery, minced
Salt, or garlic salt, and pepper

2 Tbs. sweet Hungarian paprika
2 tsp. caraway seeds
1 can (16 oz.) tomatoes, well
   broken up
1 cup water
3 cups uncooked curly egg
   noodles

Brown the meat in the oil in a large nonstick skillet or Dutch oven. Discard any fat.

Add the remaining ingredients, except the noodles, stir well, and simmer the mixture, covered, over very low heat for about 1 hour, until the veal is tender.

Stir in the uncooked noodles, a cup at a time. Cover and cook for 10 to 12 minutes, stirring frequently. (Add more water, if needed.)

Makes 8 servings, 310 calories each.

BEEF TONGUE

1 smoked or pickled beef
   tongue (about 4 lb.)
1 bay leaf

1 Tbs. mixed pickling spices
1 clove garlic

In a large pot cover the tongue with water, add the remaining ingredients, and bring the water to a boil. Skim the foam. Simmer the mixture, covered, for 2½ to 4 hours, until the meat is fork-tender.

Drain tongue, peel off its skin, and discard it. Discard any small bones or membranes. Serve the meat hot or cold.

Each 4-oz. serving, 305 calories.

PORK CHOPS WITH APPLE

4 lean trimmed center-cut pork
  chops
2 Tbs. cracker crumbs
1 cup unsweetened apple juice
1½ cups water

1 Tbs. grated onion
Garlic salt and pepper
2 unpeeled firm cooking apples,
  thickly sliced

Moisten the chops with water and press them into the crumbs.

In a nonstick skillet well sprayed with cooking spray brown the chops in a single layer over moderate heat.

Add the remaining ingredients except the apple slices. Cover tightly and lower the heat. Simmer the mixture, turning it occasionally, for about 1 hour, until the chops are very tender. (Add water, if needed.)

Uncover the skillet and simmer the mixture until nearly all the liquid evaporates into a thick sauce.

Add the apples. Cover and cook for about 5 minutes, until the apples are barely tender

Makes 4 servings, 305 calories each.

RAGÙ ALLA BOLOGNESE (ITALIAN MEAT SAUCE)

¾ lb. fat-trimmed lean ground
  round beef
1 or 2 garlic cloves, minced
1 onion, minced
1 rib celery, minced
1 carrot, coarsely shredded, or
  small jar babyfood carrot
  purée

1 can (6 oz.) tomato paste
1 can (16 oz.) tomatoes
  (preferably Italian plum),
  broken up
2 cups water
Salt and pepper
1 tsp. oregano
1 tsp. basil

In a large nonstick skillet or Dutch oven brown the beef. Discard any fat.

Stir in the remaining ingredients. Simmer the mixture, covered, for 50 to 60 minutes. Uncover the mixture and simmer it until the sauce is very thick. Serve over hot pasta.

Makes 4 servings, 195 calories each, plus 155 calories for each cup tender-cooked spaghetti.

FISH BONNE-FEMME STYLE

1 cup sliced fresh mushrooms
2 tsp. butter or margarine
½ cup dry white wine
1 small onion, minced
1 lb. sole or flounder fillets, or
   other thin fish fillets, fresh or
   defrosted

1 cup skim milk
Pinch of nutmeg
Pinch of cayenne or dash of
   Tabasco sauce
2 Tbs. flour
Paprika
2 Tbs. minced fresh parsley

In a nonstick skillet, cook the mushrooms with the butter and 1 Tbs. wine over high heat, stirring, until the liquid evaporates and the mushrooms begin to brown. Remove the mushrooms.

Combine the onion and the remaining wine in the skillet. Top with the fish in a single layer. Simmer the mixture, uncovered, basting with the wine, for about 5 to 8 minutes, until fish is opaque and most of the wine has evaporated. (Add more wine if needed.)

Combine the milk, nutmeg, cayenne or Tabasco, and flour in a covered jar. Shake to blend and stir into the skillet. Simmer until the sauce thickens. Sprinkle the fish with paprika and top with the mushrooms. Sprinkle the dish with parsley and heat it through.

Makes 4 servings, 160 calories each.

SHERRIED TURKEY

2 boned turkey thighs, cut into
   1-inch cubes
½ cup dry sherry
1 small bay leaf
½ tsp. poultry seasoning
½ tsp. coarse pepper
2 tsp. salt or garlic salt

1 Tbs. minced fresh parsley
2 cups sliced carrots, fresh or
   defrosted
2 cups sliced onions
1 lb. fresh mushrooms, thinly
   sliced

In a heavy nonstick skillet or Dutch oven well sprayed with cooking spray arrange the turkey, skin side down, in a single layer. Brown the cubes over moderate heat, turning them to brown evenly. Discard any fat.

Add the other ingredients, except the carrots, onions, and mushrooms. Simmer the mixture, covered, for 1 hour or more, until the turkey is tender.

Skim off the fat and add the carrots and onions. Cover and simmer for 20 minutes.

Add the mushrooms and cook the mixture, stirring occasionally, until the liquid is reduced to a sauce consistency.

Makes 10 servings, 300 calories each.

TURKEY CHILI

2 lb. raw ground turkey or bulk turkey sausage, defrosted if frozen
1 cup chopped onion
2 cloves garlic, minced
1 cup minced celery
1 can (16 oz.) tomatoes, broken up

2 Tbs. golden raisins
2 Tbs. vinegar
1 can (10 oz.) fat-skimmed beef broth
Salt and pepper
2 tsp. chili powder, or more to taste
1 tsp. cumin seeds (optional)

In a nonstick skillet or Dutch oven brown the turkey slowly over moderate heat, breaking it into chunks. Discard any fat.

Add the remaining ingredients. Simmer the mixture, covered, for 1 hour. Skim off any fat.

Uncover and simmer until most of the liquid is evaporated. (Serve with cooked brown rice, if desired.)

Makes 8 servings, 145 calories each, or 245 calories each with ½ cup serving of rice.

SWEET-AND-SOUR TURKEY CUBES

1 young boned turkey thigh,
  cut into 1½-inch cubes
2 tsp. prepared mustard
2 onions, chopped
1 clove garlic, minced (optional)
1 can (8 oz.) plain tomato sauce
1 can (8 oz.) stewed tomatoes,
  well broken up
½ cup juice-packed crushed
  pineapple, undrained
2 Tbs. red wine vinegar
3 Tbs. raisins
Salt and pepper
1 cup fat-skimmed turkey or
  beef broth

Toss the turkey with the mustard and in a nonstick skillet well sprayed with cooking spray, brown it, uncovered, over moderate heat. Stir to prevent sticking. Discard any fat.

Add the remaining ingredients. Simmer the mixture, covered, over low heat for about 1½ hours, until the turkey is tender. Uncover, raise the heat, and cook until the sauce is thick. (Serve with rice, if desired.)

Makes 5 servings, 340 calories each, or about 100 extra calories per ½ cup of rice.

SAVORY TURKEY CUBES

1 boned turkey thigh, cut into
  1½-inch cubes
1½ cups tomato juice
1 tsp. prepared mustard
2 tsp. Worcestershire sauce
4 onions, quartered
3 ribs celery, thinly sliced
1 clove garlic (optional)
Salt and pepper
¾ cup cold water
1 tsp. cornstarch

In a nonstick skillet or Dutch oven well sprayed with cooking spray cook the turkey skin side down over moderate heat, turning it to prevent sticking, until it browns. Discard any fat.

Add the remaining ingredients, except the water and cornstarch. Simmer the mixture, covered, over very low heat for 1½ hours or more, until the turkey is tender. (Add water if needed.)

Skim off any fat. In a small bowl combine the water and cornstarch and stir until smooth. Stir into the pot, until the sauce thickens and clears

Makes 5 servings, 325 calories each.

9
Sensational
Soups

MOTHER was right: soup *is* good for you! Medical researchers have also turned up some convincing evidence that soup can alleviate the symptoms of the common cold. How? They're not sure. Maybe the steamy vapors help to unclog nasal plumbing. Maybe good-tasting soup makes it easy to follow the drink-lots-of-liquid prescription. Whatever the reason, soup is not only good but it's good for you. And it doesn't have to be bland or boring. It can be hot and spicy, cool and refreshing; a first course, whole meal, or quick lunch. It can be extravagant or inexpensive, elegant or ethnic, time-consuming to make or short-order.

Best of all, it needn't be fattening. Because soup is liquid, lightening its calorie count by skimming off fat is easy. Even "cream" soups can be calorie-light when fats are kept to a minimum.

In this chapter are recipes for a variety of soups that have one thing in common: they're long on satisfaction but light in calories. Despite the light calorie counts, many of these soups are nutritional "heavyweights" that can be complete meals in themselves.

Homemade Broth

Homemade broths are easy to make and have many uses: the fat-skimmed liquid can start a hearty vegetable soup, add flavor to spaghetti sauce, or be the basis for a fat-free gravy. Broth can be used as the cooking liquid for vegetables, then simmered down into a self-making sauce—no butter needed! The meat reserved from the bones used for broth making can appear in salads or sandwich fillings. And because the homemade variety can be made without salt, MSG, or other additives, it can also be low fat, no salt, additive free.

CHICKEN BROTH I

1 lb. chicken backs and necks
1 qt. water
1 onion, halved
1 rib celery, halved

1 tsp. salt (optional)
1 tsp. MSG (optional)
1 small bay leaf (optional)

Combine ingredients in a soup pot and simmer the mixture for 1 hour or longer, covered, until all the meat falls from the bones. (Or cook it in a pressure cooker, according to the manufacturer's directions, for 20 minutes.) Strain the broth and chill it. When cold, skim the fat and spoon the broth by the cupful into small covered jars, being sure to leave a 1-inch headroom.

Remove the meat from the bones and reserve it or freeze it for other uses.

Makes approximately one quart, about 22 calories per cup.

VARIATIONS

Chicken Broth II: Substitute a 2-lb. package of chicken wings.

Turkey Broth I: Substitute a large turkey neck and add 1 tsp. poultry seasoning, if desired.

Turkey Broth II: Reserve the meaty carcass from a leftover turkey. Fit it into a large stockpot or pressure cooker and add as many quarts of water as needed to cover. Increase the other seasonings accordingly.

Meat Broth I: Spread meaty beef, veal, or pork bones in a shallow broiling pan and brown them under the broiler. Put the bones in a large stockpot or pressure cooker, cover with water, add seasonings. Simmer until the meat falls off bones.

Meat Broth II: Reserve meaty bones left over from steaks, chops, or roasts and freeze them in plastic bags. (Have separate freezer bags for beef, pork, and veal.) Put the frozen bones in a large stockpot or pressure cooker, cover with water, and add seasonings. Simmer until the meat falls off bones.

Broth Concentrates: To save room in the freezer, simmer fat-skimmed broth in an uncovered pot until it is reduced by half. The result will be very strong and flavorful. Cool and pour into babyfood jars, leaving headroom. Skim the fat and freeze.

Frozen Broth Cubes: Pour concentrate broth into ice-cube trays and freeze solid. Remove to plastic bags, label, store in the freezer.

Salt-Free Broths: Omit salt from the master recipe and season with lemon juice and additional herbs after defrosting. Don't add salt substitutes before freezing.

CHILLED CONSOMMÉ DELIGHT

1 can (10½ oz.) condensed consommé, chilled

½ cup melon balls (cantaloupe, watermelon)

In bowl combine the consommé and melon. Serve in chilled bowls. (Garnish with yogurt, if desired.)

Makes 2 servings, about 65 calories each.

CHICKEN CURRY SOUP

1 can (10½ oz.) condensed chicken broth
½ cup plain low-fat yogurt
½ cup water

1 tsp. curry powder
½ cup unpeeled chopped apple
2 Tbs. toasted flaked coconut

In saucepan combine all the ingredients, except the apple and coconut. Simmer the mixture a few minutes.

Add the apple and coconut and heat through.

Makes 4 servings, about 55 calories each.

DRUMSTICK SOUP

1 turkey drumstick	½ tsp. MSG
3 cups water	½ tsp. poultry seasoning
Salt	2 cups skim milk
1 onion	4 Tbs. flour
1 rib celery	Minced parsley (optional)
1 bay leaf	

In a saucepan combine all the ingredients, except the milk and flour. Cook the mixture, covered, over moderate heat for 1 to 1½ hours, or until the turkey is tender.

Strain the broth and let the drumstick cool. Set broth aside until any fat rises to surface and skim it off. Heat the broth to boiling. Stir the milk and flour together and stir the mixture into the broth, until it simmers.

Remove the meat from the drumstick and cut into bite-size pieces. Stir the meat into the broth and heat it until it is heated through. (Garnish with parsley, if desired.)

Makes 4 meal-size servings, about 265 calories each.

CREAM OF MUSHROOM SOUP

¾ lb. fresh mushrooms	1 Tbs. arrowroot
1 small onion, chopped	1 can (13 oz.) evaporated skim
2 cups fat-skimmed chicken or	milk
turkey broth	Salt and pepper
1 Tbs. flour	

In a saucepan combine the mushrooms, onion, and broth. Simmer the mixture, covered, over low heat for about 15 minutes.

In a blender blend the mixture on high speed until the mushrooms are minced.

Return the mixture to the saucepan and reheat it to boiling. In a bowl combine the flour, arrowroot, and milk and pour into saucepan. Cook the mixture, stirring, until it thickens. Season to taste, cover, and simmer for 5 minutes.

Makes 8 servings, 65 calories each.

CREAM OF CHICKEN SOUP

1 cup finely diced celery
¼ cup minced onion
1 cup grated carrot
2 Tbs. chopped fresh parsley
2 cups fat-skimmed chicken
(or turkey) broth

Salt and pepper
1 tsp. MSG (optional)
2 cups skim milk
¼ cup flour

In a large saucepan combine all the ingredients, except the milk and flour. Simmer the mixture, covered, for 15 minutes.

Combine the milk and flour in a jar and shake well. Stir into soup.

Simmer the mixture, stirring frequently, over very low heat, for 5 minutes.

Makes 6 servings, about 70 calories each.

CREAM OF PEA SOUP

2 packages (10 oz. each) frozen
peas
¼ cup chopped onion
1 cup boiling water

3 cups skim milk
3 Tbs. flour
1 tsp. salt

In a saucepan cook the peas and onion in the boiling water, until just tender, about 7 minutes.

Sieve the mixture or purée it in a blender.

Combine the milk and flour in a 2-quart saucepan. Over low heat cook and stir the mixture until it is slightly thickened. Stir in the purée and salt, and heat just to boiling.

Makes 6 servings, 95 calories each.

CREAM OF POTATO SOUP

3 potatoes, peeled and sliced
1 onion, chopped
2 cups fat-skimmed chicken or
   turkey broth
1½ cups water

1 can (13 oz.) evaporated skim
   milk
Salt and white pepper
2 Tbs. minced fresh parsley

Combine the potatoes, onion, broth, and water in a saucepan and simmer the mixture, covered, over low heat for 35 minutes.

In a blender blend the mixture on high speed until it is smooth. Return it to the saucepan and heat it to boiling. Add the milk and simmer for 5 minutes. Season to taste. Garnish with parsley.

Makes 8 servings, 80 calories each.

CREAM OF TURKEY AND BROCCOLI SOUP

1½ cups fat-skimmed turkey or
   chicken broth
1 cup diced cooked white meat
   turkey
1 package (10 oz.) cut broccoli

1 onion, minced
Pinch of poultry seasoning
   (optional)
1 cup skim milk
2 tsp. cornstarch

In a saucepan combine all the ingredients, except the milk and cornstarch. Cover the mixture and heat to boiling. Separate the broccoli pieces; add to the broth mixture and simmer, covered, for 10 minutes.

In a bowl stir the milk and cornstarch together until smooth and stir the mixture into the saucepan. Cook the soup, stirring, until it is bubbling.

Makes 2 meal-size servings, 270 calories each.

TURKEY, WINE, AND MUSHROOM SOUP

Meaty turkey frame from leftover
roast turkey
1 onion, chopped
1 cup sherry
3 cups water
Pinch of nutmeg
½ teaspoon MSG (optional)

½ lb. fresh mushrooms, coarsely
chopped
1 tsp. butter or margarine
¼ cup chopped fresh parsley
2 cups skim milk
2 Tbs. cornstarch
Salt and pepper

Combine the turkey frame, onion, sherry, water, nutmeg, and MSG, if desired, in a large pot. Cover it and simmer for 1½ to 2 hours.

Strain the broth and refrigerate it for several hours. (You should have about 3 cups; add water if needed.)

Pick meat from the bones, mince and refrigerate it, covered.

In a large nonstick skillet brown the mushrooms in the butter and add the turkey meat and parsley.

Skim the fat from the broth and add the broth to the skillet. Heat to boiling.

In a bowl combine the milk and cornstarch and stir the mixture into the skillet. Cook the soup over moderate flame, stirring, until it is hot and bubbling. Season to taste.

Makes about 6 servings, about 75 calories each.

ASKO'S FINNISH FISH SOUP

1 lb. perch or other white fish,
cut into chunks
3 large potatoes, peeled and
cubed
1 large onion, sliced

Salt and pepper
2 cups water
1 cup skim milk
¼ cup minced fresh parsley
2 Tbs. snipped chives

In a kettle combine the fish, potatoes, onion, and salt and pepper to taste, pour in the water, and bring the mixture to a boil. Reduce the heat and simmer, covered, for about 20 minutes, until the fish is opaque and the potatoes are tender.

Add the milk and bring the soup to the boiling point. Add the parsley and chives and heat through.

Makes 4 meal-size servings, 240 calories each.

LIGHT FISH CHOWDER

1 large onion, thinly sliced
2 Tbs. diet margarine
2 cups boiling water
2 potatoes, peeled and cubed
2 carrots, scraped and thinly
  sliced
1 rib celery, thinly sliced

1 lb. fish fillets, cubed
2 cups skim milk
2 Tbs. flour
Salt and pepper
2 Tbs. minced fresh parsley
Paprika

Spread the onion in a shallow layer in a large nonstick skillet or electric fry pan, add the margarine, and cook the mixture, covered, for 1 minute. Uncover and cook until the liquid evaporates and the onion is soft.

Add the boiling water, potatoes, carrots, and celery and simmer over low heat, covered, for 10 minutes.

Add the fish and cook the mixture, covered, until the potatoes are just tender and the fish is opaque.

Combine the milk and flour in a large covered jar and shake to blend. Gently stir into the skillet and add salt and pepper to taste. Cook, stirring for 5 minutes, until the mixture simmers and thickens slightly. Sprinkle the chowder with parsley and paprika to taste.

Makes 6 meal-size servings, about 180 calories each.

EASY NEW ENGLAND CLAM CHOWDER

2 cans (7 oz. each) minced
  clams
2 onions, chopped
1 can (10½ oz.) cream of celery
  soup
1 soup can water

2 potatoes, peeled and diced
2 ribs celery, sliced
1 tsp. thyme
Salt and pepper
Minced fresh parsley (optional)

Drain the clams and reserve the juice. In a saucepan combine the juice with the remaining ingredients.

Simmer the mixture for 25 to 30 minutes, add the clams, and heat them through. (Garnish with parsley, if desired.)

Makes 10 servings, about 70 calories each, or 4 meal-size servings, 175 calories each.

EASY MANHATTAN CLAM CHOWDER

1 can (20 oz.) minced clams,
 undrained
1 can (16 oz.) tomatoes, well
 broken up
3½ cups water
¼ tsp. thyme
1 Tbs. cornstarch (optional)

1 cup thinly sliced onions
1 cup minced celery
1 tsp. salt
Pinch of pepper
1 Tbs. minced fresh parsley
3 Tbs. bacon-flavored bits

In a kettle combine all the ingredients, except the bacon bits. Cover and simmer over low heat, stirring occasionally, until the celery is tender, about 25 minutes. Serve the chowder sprinkled with the bacon bits.

Makes 10 servings, about 65 calories each.

HEARTY CHICKEN CHOWDER

1 broiler-fryer chicken with
 giblets (about 2½ lb.)
5 cups water
1 cup sliced carrots
3 medium onions, thinly sliced
1 cup diced celery
1 bay leaf

6 peppercorns
1 Tbs. dried parsley
3 tsp. salt
1½ cups skim milk
⅓ cup flour
¼ tsp. thyme
½ cup frozen peas, thawed

Combine the chicken, water, carrots, onions, celery, bay leaf, peppercorns, parsley, and 2 tsp. salt in a large saucepan. Bring the liquid to a boil, reduce the heat, and simmer, covered, for about 45 minutes, or until the chicken is tender.

Remove the chicken and let it cool. Strain and refrigerate the broth, discarding the bay leaf and peppercorns. Reserve and refrigerate the vegetables.

Remove the chicken meat from the bones and cut it into chunks. Skim the fat from the broth.

Blend the broth with the milk and flour in a saucepan and cook the mixture 2 to 3 minutes, until it is slightly thickened. Add the remaining salt and thyme, stir in the chicken, peas, and reserved vegetables. Simmer the chowder for 10 minutes.

Makes 6 meal-size servings, 265 calories each.

BLENDER GAZPACHO

1 cucumber, peeled and diced
½ small onion, sliced
3 Tbs. red wine vinegar
5 stuffed green olives

½ tsp. basil or oregano (optional)
Pinch of cayenne or dash of hot
   pepper sauce (optional)
4 cups chilled tomato juice

Combine all the ingredients, except tomato juice, in a blender. Add 2 cups tomato juice (or as much as blender will hold) and blend the mixture until smooth.

Combine the soup with the remaining tomato juice. Serve chilled garnished with thin cucumber slices, if desired.

Makes 6 servings, 45 calories each.

TURKEY ZUCCHINI SOUP

2 turkey drumsticks, fresh or
  frozen
4 cups water
2 onions, thinly sliced
2 cups thinly sliced celery
1 bay leaf
½ tsp. poultry seasoning
  (optional)

1 tsp. MSG (optional)
Ice cubes and water
2 cups sliced zucchini, fresh or
  defrosted
Salt, pepper, minced fresh parsley

Put the turkey drumsticks in a pot large enough to let them lie flat. (It's not necessary to defrost the turkey, if frozen.) Add water, onions, celery, and seasonings. Heat the mixture to boiling, cover, and simmer until the meat is tender, about 1 to 1½ hours. Remove from heat.

Fill a 2-cup measure with ice cubes, fill it to the top with cold water, and pour the liquid into the pot. When the turkey is cool enough to handle remove from broth, separate meat, and cut it into bite-size chunks. Skim fat from broth.

Add the zucchini to broth and simmer the mixture, covered, until the zucchini is tender, about 5 minutes. Add the turkey and heat through. Add salt, pepper, and minced parsley to taste.

Makes 8 meal-size servings, about 200 calories each.

MEX-TEX TACO SOUP

2½ cups fat-skimmed chicken, turkey, or beef broth or 1½ cups fat-skimmed canned broth, diluted

2 onions, coarsely chopped

2 green bell peppers, seeded and diced

1 cup tomatoes, canned, undrained, broken up

½ cup loosely packed, fresh chopped parsley

1 tsp. chili powder (or to taste)

1 tsp. oregano

¾ tsp. ground cumin

1 bay leaf

1 clove garlic, minced

Salt and pepper

1 cup diced cooked chicken, turkey, or beef

6 cheese-flavored corn chips, broken up

2 Tbs. shredded extra-sharp cheddar or American cheese

Hot pepper sauce (optional)

Combine all the ingredients, except the meat, corn chips, and cheese, in a soup pot or pressure cooker, cover, and simmer the mixture for 30 minutes (or for 10 minutes in a pressure cooker, following the manufacturer's directions). Uncover, remove the bay leaf, and stir in meat. Cook until heated through. To serve, sprinkle the soup with corn chips and top with cheese, if desired. (Add hot pepper sauce, if desired.)

Two meal-size servings, 290 calories each without cheese, about 315 calories each with cheese.

SOUP JARDINIÈRE

1 Tbs. diet margarine

1 onion, chopped

3 medium potatoes, peeled and diced

2 carrots, scraped and sliced

1 rib celery, sliced

2 Tbs. chopped fresh parsley

5 cups fat-skimmed chicken or turkey broth

Melt the margarine in a kettle, add the onion, and saute for 5 minutes. Add the potatoes, carrots, and celery and cook 2 minutes more, stirring, to prevent sticking.

Add the remaining ingredients, cover the kettle, and simmer for 1 hour. Serve as is or purée in a blender and reheat.

Makes 8 servings, about 80 calories each.

VEGETABLE BEEF SOUP

2 cups cooked fat-trimmed
  cubed lean beef
2 cans (10½ oz. each)
  condensed beef broth
2 soup cans water (2½ cups)
1 onion, minced

1 package (10 oz.) frozen mixed
  vegetables
2 Tbs. chopped fresh parsley
2 tsp. prepared horseradish
  (optional)

In a saucepan, combine the ingredients and heat, stirring occasionally.

Makes about 7 servings, 120 calories each, or 4 meal-size servings at 215 calories each.

HAM AND CHICKEN NOODLE SOUP

1 cup diced cooked ham
1 cup shredded carrot
1 cup chopped onion
1 cup minced celery
2 cans (10½ oz. each),
  fat-skimmed condensed
  chicken broth

2 soup cans water (2½ cups)
1 cup diced cooked chicken or
  turkey
⅛ tsp. thyme
¼ cup chopped fresh parsley
1 cup uncooked medium
  noodles

Combine all the ingredients in a large saucepan, bring the liquid to a boil, and reduce the heat. Cook for 10 minutes, stirring occasionally, or until the noodles are done.

Makes 8 servings, 135 calories each, or 4 meal-size servings at 270 calories each.

10

Vegetable

Variety

LUCKILY for the "light and easy"-minded cook, vegetables are now "in." Mother Nature's new chicness had done more to improve the image of vegetables than all the lectures of grandmothers and nutritionists put together. Today it's gauche to confess a prejudice against parsnips.

Fashion notwithstanding, there are still grown-ups with secret "greenophobia," an unreasonable fear that anything that's "good for you" is probably inedible. Sometimes this feeling is simply held over from childhood. Other times it's based on a bad experience. In past decades, the vegetables served in many homes and restaurants (and most school cafeterias) really were close to inedible! Fortuitously, the popularity of salads and oriental food has brought about a revolution in the way vegetables are cooked. Today, crispness and crunch, fresh flavor, and color are the sought-after qualities; vegetables are now quick-cooked with the least amount of liquid. Remember, there's really no such thing as an undercooked vegetable, if it suits your palate.

Here are some tips to help you make light of vegetables:

- Try to introduce yourself and your family to new vegetables when they're in season and their flavor and quality are at their peak.

- Buy yourself a vegetable steamer and steam the produce in the least possible amount of liquid.
- Cook vegetables in broth and serve the sauce with the vegetable. The vitamins won't disappear, as they do when vegetables are cooked in water that's drained away. Or try tomato juice or fruit juice (keep cooking time short; acid liquids can affect the color of green vegetables).
- Add spices and herbs for flavor and variety. No butter needed!
- Instead of butter, margarine, or high-fat sauces, use low-calorie mayonnaise or salad dressings as toppings.
- Fresh vegetables in season are best, but frozen vegetables are better than poor quality out-of-season ones. Cheaper, too!
- For the most flavor and texture and the best nutrition at the least cost choose plain frozen vegetables instead of those packed in sauces. Commercially sauced vegetables are often double or triple in calories.

Vegetables are Mother Nature's "Vitamin Pills"!

Vitamin A—found in dark green, yellow, and orange vegetables: squash, carrots, tomatoes, asparagus, spinach, and broccoli.

Vitamin C—found in tomatoes, potatoes, cabbage, brussels sprouts, broccoli, and mustard greens.

For the most nutrition and flavor, it's important to choose quality vegetables and store them to retain their freshness until used.

Shopping for Vegetables

A good shopping strategy is to buy fresh vegetables for the first part of the week and frozen vegetables for the rest of the week, or until your next marketing trip.

Look for fresh, wrinkle-free, bruise-free ones.

Purchase carrots and other root vegetables without their tops. Otherwise, the foliage continues to "grow," drawing moisture and nutrition away from the edible portion of the vegetable during storage.

Avoid over- or undersized vegetables. Immature produce lacks flavor; overgrown vegetables may be tough or seedy. Misshapen vegetables are often inferior in taste and nutrition.

STEAMED FRESH ASPARAGUS

Wash asparagus in cold running water. Snap off the tough woody ends. Steam to the desired crunchiness or tenderness using one of these methods:

Covered Skillet

Put a round cake rack or trivet in the skillet and add water, up to the level of the rack. Lay the asparagus on top of the rack. Cover the skillet and steam them to desired tenderness.

In a Coffeepot

Stand the spears in a coffee percolator. Pour in two inches of water, cover the coffeepot, and steam asparagus to desired tenderness.

In a Microwave Oven

For crunchy asparagus, lay the spears in a single layer on a paper plate. Cover with another paper plate. Cook on full power for 30 seconds. Open the door, check the texture, then rotate the plate. Continue to cook at 30-second intervals until crisp and hot. The time depends on the thickness of the stalks, and how many you're cooking at once.

4 medium-size fresh spears, cooked, are 12 calories; 1 lb. fresh, cooked, is 91 calories.

Top hot asparagus with a dollop of low-calorie mayonnaise, fresh lemon juice, or a shake of bottled low-calorie Italian salad dressing . . . no butter needed.

ARTICHOKE HEARTS IN TOMATO SAUCE

1 package (9 oz.) frozen artichoke hearts	½ tsp. dried oregano
1 cup tomato juice	1 Tbs. grated onion or 1 tsp. instant onion

In a nonstick saucepan combine the ingredients and simmer 6 to 7 minutes. Uncover and continue to cook an additional minute or two, until artichoke hearts are tender and the sauce is thick. Serve with the cooking sauce.

Makes 3 servings, 40 calories each.

ARTICHOKE HEARTS WITH LEMON

1 package (9 oz.) frozen
  artichoke hearts
¾ cup fat-skimmed undiluted
  chicken broth, canned,
  homemade, or reconstituted

¼ tsp. dried basil
Salt, or onion salt, and pepper
Juice of 1 lemon

In a saucepan, combine the ingredients, except lemon juice, and simmer them 6 to 7 minutes, until the artichoke hearts are tender and the cooking liquid is reduced. Remove from the heat and stir in the lemon juice. Serve hot, with the cooking liquid poured over the artichoke hearts.

Makes 3 servings, 45 calories each.

DILLED BRUSSELS SPROUTS

10 oz. fresh brussels sprouts
½ cup fat-skimmed condensed
  chicken broth

Pinch of dried dillweed

Combine the ingredients in a saucepan. Simmer the mixture, covered, for 5 minutes.

Uncover and simmer, stirring frequently, until nearly all the liquid has evaporated. If sprouts require more cooking, add a little water.

Makes 2 servings, 60 calories each.

FIVE-MINUTE SAUCY BROCCOLI

1 package (10 oz.) chopped
  frozen broccoli, defrosted
2 Tbs. low-calorie mayonnaise
¼ cup boiling water

1 Tbs. minced fresh onion or 1
  tsp. dried onion flakes
  (optional)
Salt and pepper

In a saucepan combine all ingredients except broccoli; mix well. Stir in defrosted broccoli. Cover and simmer 3 minutes. Uncover and continue to simmer until nearly all the liquid has evaporated.

Makes 3 servings, 45 calories each.

BROCCOLI AU GRATIN

1 package (10 oz.) frozen broccoli cuts, defrosted	Salt and pepper
	Pinch of cayenne pepper
1 cup skim milk	4 Tbs. extra-sharp shredded
2 Tbs. instant-blending flour	cheddar cheese

Preheat the oven to moderate, 350 degrees.

Arrange defrosted broccoli in an ovenproof casserole. In a nonstick saucepan combine milk and flour and stir over low heat until sauce simmers and thickens. Season to taste. Pour sauce over broccoli and sprinkle with cheese. Bake for 15 minutes.

Makes 4 servings, 85 calories each.

EGGPLANT HALVES ALLA PARMIGIANA

4 small eggplants, unpeeled and halved lengthwise	1 clove garlic, minced (optional)
	1 tsp. oregano
1 can (16 oz.) plain tomato sauce	8 Tbs. grated Parmesan cheese
	Salt and pepper
1 small onion, minced	

Preheat the oven to moderately low, 325 degrees.

Arrange the eggplant, cut side up, in a casserole. In a bowl combine the tomato sauce, onion, and garlic and pour the mixture over the eggplant. Sprinkle with oregano.

Cover the casserole tightly with foil and bake it for about 50 to 60 minutes, or until the eggplant is tender.

Sprinkle the top with Parmesan cheese, season to taste, and bake 10 minutes more.

Makes 8 servings, 90 calories each.

VARIATION

Substitute 8 tsp. grated extra-sharp Romano for the Parmesan. Only 70 calories per serving.

ORANGE GINGER BEETS I

1 jar (16 oz.) sliced beets
2 Tbs. defrosted undiluted
  orange juice concentrate
2 Tbs. water

1 tsp. cornstarch
¼ tsp. ground ginger
Salt and pepper

Heat beets in their own juice. Combine the remaining ingredients, stir them smooth, then blend the mixture into the simmering beet juice over low heat, until the sauce is thick.

Makes 4 servings, 65 calories each.

VARIATION

Orange Ginger Beets II: Substitute 3 Tbs. fresh orange juice for the water and 1 Tbs. low-sugar orange marmalade for the orange juice concentrate; 55 calories per serving.

CABBAGE WEDGES IN TOMATO-PINEAPPLE SAUCE

1 small or ½ large head of
  cabbage
2 cups tomato juice

1 cup unsweetened pineapple
  juice

Cut cabbage into 4 even wedges, with leaves attached to the base. In a saucepan combine the juices, add the cabbage wedges, and simmer, covered tightly, just until cabbage wedges are tender-firm, about 8 minutes. Pour the sauce from the pan over the wedges.

Makes 4 servings, 80 calories each.

SPICED SHREDDED CARROTS

1 lb. fresh carrots, unpared and
  thoroughly scrubbed
3 Tbs. frozen apple juice
  concentrate, undiluted
¼ cup water

3 Tbs. raisins
Pinch of cinnamon, apple pie
  spice, or cardamom
Salt and pepper to taste

Shred the carrots in a food processor or an electric food grinder or shred by hand.

Combine them with the remaining ingredients in a saucepan. Cover and simmer for 2 minutes.

Uncover and simmer until most of the liquid has evaporated.

Makes 4 servings, 85 calories each.

CARROTS AND CELERY CASSEROLE

1 envelope or cube of chicken
  bouillon
½ cup boiling water
½ lb. sliced carrots, fresh or
  defrosted

1 rib celery, sliced
1 onion, sliced
Small bay leaf (optional)
2 Tbs. dry sherry

Preheat the oven to moderate, 350 degrees.

Dissolve the bouillon in boiling water in a heatproof cup.

Combine the ingredients in a casserole and bake it, covered for 30 minutes. Remove bay leaf before serving.

Makes 4 servings, 40 calories each.

GLAZED CARROTS AND ONIONS

3 chicken bouillon cubes
1 lb. (6 medium) carrots,
  scraped, cut in quarters
Boiling water

12 small white onions, peeled
1 Tbs. butter or margarine
2 Tbs. sherry

Place 2 bouillon cubes and carrots in a large saucepan. Add boiling water to cover carrots, stir to dissolve the bouillon cubes, then simmer, covered, for 10 minutes. Add onions, cook about 5 minutes longer, or until vegetables are tender. Drain.

Melt butter in pan. Add sherry. Stir in remaining bouillon cube until dissolved. Add vegetables and stir about 3 minutes over medium heat until golden-brown and glazed.

Makes 6 servings, 85 calories each.

PICKLED CARROTS

20 oz. frozen sliced carrots
¾ cup apple juice concentrate or cider concentrate, defrosted
¾ cup water
¾ cup cider vinegar
1 Tbs. mixed pickling spices
Salt and pepper

Combine ingredients and simmer 5 minutes. Cool, then chill several hours in refrigerator.

Remove carrots with a slotted spoon. Strain liquid to remove whole spices; pour strained liquid over carrots. Serve chilled.

Makes 6 servings, 100 calories each.

CELERY RATATOUILLE

4 ribs celery
2 tsp. olive oil
1 small onion, chopped
1 clove garlic, minced (optional)
4 cups (½ lb.) unpeeled cubed eggplant
1 green bell pepper, seeded, diced
1 medium zucchini, sliced
Salt and pepper
Pinch basil or thyme

Cut trimmed celery into 1-inch lengths; set aside. In a large saucepan or skillet, heat oil, add onion and garlic, and saute them for 5 minutes. Add remaining ingredients; cover and cook 15 minutes. Remove cover and cook 30 minutes longer, stirring occasionally. Serve hot or cold.

Makes 8 servings, 60 calories each.

CELERY AND MUSHROOM SAUTE

4 tsp. butter or margarine
3 cups sliced fresh mushrooms
4 cups thinly sliced celery
¼ cup water or chicken broth
Salt, or onion salt, and pepper
Soy sauce (optional)

Melt 2 tsp. butter in a large skillet. Add mushrooms; saute 5 minutes or until golden. Remove from the skillet. Melt the remaining butter in the skillet. Add the celery; saute 5 minutes. Add the water (or broth) and seasonings to taste. Cover and simmer for 5 minutes. Stir in the mushrooms; heat through.

Makes 6 servings, 45 calories each.

CORN BAKED IN HUSKS

Fresh corn in husks   Salt and pepper
Butter, margarine, or diet
    margarine

Preheat the oven to moderately high, 375 degrees.
Peel back the cornhusks but don't remove them. Remove and discard the cornsilk. Spread each ear of corn lightly with ½ tsp. butter, margarine, or diet margarine. Sprinkle lightly with salt and pepper. Fold cornhusks back over corn. Wrap each ear in foil. Bake 30 to 35 minutes or grill over medium coals about 20 minutes, turning occasionally.

Each ear about 90 calories with butter or margarine or 80 calories with diet margarine.

CAULIFLOWER AU GRATIN

1 package (10 oz.) frozen   Salt, or seasoned salt, and pepper
    cauliflower, defrosted   2 Tbs. shredded extra-sharp
½ cup skim milk   cheddar cheese
¼ cup water   2 tsp. seasoned bread crumbs
1 tsp. cornstarch

Preheat the oven to moderate, 350 degrees.
Allow cauliflower to defrost at room temperature. Arrange defrosted uncooked cauliflower in a shallow ovenproof casserole. In a small non-stick saucepan combine milk, water, and cornstarch and stir over low heat until simmering. Pour sauce over cauliflower, sprinkle with cheese and bread crumbs, and add salt and pepper to taste. Bake uncovered for 15 to 30 minutes.

Makes 4 servings, 55 calories each.

CURRIED CAULIFLOWER

1 medium head fresh
  cauliflower or 2 packages (10
  oz. each) frozen cauliflower
½ cup water
1 tsp. butter or margarine

1 cup skim milk
2 Tbs. instant-blending flour
½ tsp. curry powder
Salt, or butter-flavored salt, and
  pepper

If using fresh cauliflower, wash and break up into florets. In a saucepan combine them with water, butter, and ½ cup milk. Cover and cook over low heat until just tender, about 10 minutes. Remove the cauliflower with a slotted spoon to a serving dish.

Combine the remaining milk with the flour and curry powder; stir smooth. Heat the cooking liquid over low heats, stir in the flour mixture, and continue to stir over low heat until the sauce is thick. Season to taste, and pour sauce over the cauliflower.

Makes 6 servings, 50 calories each.

GREEN BEANS AND TOMATOES WITH BASIL

1 can (8 oz.) stewed tomatoes,
  well broken up
¼ cup finely chopped onion

¼ cup water
¼ tsp. basil or oregano
10 oz. green beans, defrosted

Combine all the ingredients except the beans in a saucepan and simmer the mixture, covered, for 8 minutes.

Add the beans and simmer, uncovered, stirring often, until they are tender and most of the liquid is reduced to a thick sauce.

Makes 6 servings, 25 calories each.

CREAMED GREEN BEANS

1 bag (20 oz.) French-style
  green beans, fresh or partially
  defrosted
1 onion, minced
1 red bell pepper, seeded and
  diced

1 cup fat-skimmed condensed
  chicken broth
1 cup skim milk
2 Tbs. flour
8 tsp. American-style grated
  cheese

Combine the vegetables and broth in a nonstick saucepan and simmer the mixture, covered, for 5 minutes.

In a bowl combine the milk and flour well. Stir it into the saucepan and cook, stirring, until the sauce is thick. Sprinkle with cheese.

Makes 8 servings, 65 calories each.

MIDDLE EASTERN GREEN BEANS

½ lb. fresh green beans, tipped and sliced, or 1 package (10 oz.), defrosted

1 cup crushed peeled tomatoes or 1 can (8 oz.) stewed tomatoes

1 onion, chopped
1 clove garlic, minced
½ cup chopped fresh parsley
4 Tbs. water
1 lemon

In a saucepan combine all the ingredients except lemon and simmer them 20 minutes. Garnish with lemon wedges or season with lemon juice to taste.

Makes 4 servings, 55 calories each.

CINNAMON RUTABAGA

3 cups peeled diced rutabaga (yellow turnip), fresh or frozen
¾ cup (6-oz. can) apple juice

Salt, or butter-flavored salt, and pepper
Cinnamon

In a covered saucepan cook rutabaga with apple juice until very tender, about 15 minutes. Remove rutabaga and mash in a bowl with a potato masher or process smooth in a food processor, blender, or electric mixer. Season to taste with salt, pepper, and cinnamon.

Makes 6 servings, 35 calories each.

SAUTEED MUSHROOMS

½ lb. fresh mushrooms, whole
   or sliced
2 tsp. butter

¼ cup dry white wine or sherry
Salt and pepper

If mushrooms are small, leave them whole. Combine the ingredients in a nonstick skillet which has been sprayed with cooking spray. Cook and stir over high heat until all of the liquid evaporates.

Makes 4 servings, 45 calories each.

NUTMEG SQUASH

1 acorn squash
4 Tbs. water
4 Tbs. orange, apple, or
   pineapple juice concentrate,
   defrosted, undiluted

2 tsp. butter, margarine, or diet
   margarine
Salt and pepper
Nutmeg

Preheat the oven to moderately hot, 400 degrees.

Halve the squash, scrape out seeds, and arrange the halves cut side up in a shallow baking dish. Fill each cavity with 2 Tbs. water, 2 Tbs. juice concentrate, 1 tsp. butter or margarine and sprinkle with salt, pepper, and nutmeg. Cover the pan with foil and bake 30 minutes. Uncover; continue baking until squash is tender, basting occasionally with the sauce in the cavity of the squash. Split each squash half in two to serve.

Each serving (¼ squash): 80 calories with orange juice, 75 calories with apple or pineapple juice (subtract 5 calories if using diet margarine).

SQUASH KEBABS

1 medium yellow squash,
   quartered and cut into 1-inch
   pieces
4 small onions

1 Tbs. low-calorie Italian salad
   dressing
1 Tbs. grated Parmesan cheese
Garlic salt and pepper

Thread skewers, alternating squash and whole onions.

Brush the skewers with salad dressing and sprinkle them lightly with cheese. Broil or barbecue the skewers 2 inches from heat source, turning frequently, for about 8 minutes.

Makes 4 servings, 45 calories each.

ITALIAN SQUASH AND PEPPERS

1 green bell pepper, seeded, cut into 1-inch squares
½ onion, sliced
¾ cup tomato juice

Pinch of oregano or basil
1 medium zucchini or yellow summer squash, thinly sliced

In a saucepan combine all of the ingredients, except the zucchini or squash, and simmer them, covered, 5 minutes. Add the zucchini or squash and simmer, covered, 3 minutes more.

Makes 4 servings, 30 calories each.

APPLE SAUERKRAUT I

1 lb. fresh or canned sauerkraut
½ cup unsweetened applesauce
½ cup water

1 small onion, chopped (optional)
2 tsp. caraway seeds (optional)

Combine ingredients in a saucepan and simmer covered, for 30 to 40 minutes.

Makes 4 servings, 45 calories each, or 60 calories each with optional ingredients.

VARIATION

Apple Sauerkraut II: Omit applesauce; increase water to ¾ cup. Core and quarter 1 large unpeeled McIntosh apple. Lay the unpeeled apple quarters on top of the sauerkraut. Cover and simmer 30 to 40 minutes. Before serving, lift the peel from the apple quarters. Stir apple pulp into the sauerkraut.

Makes 4 servings, 50 calories each.

ITALIAN TOMATO PEPPER SKILLET

1 can (8 oz.) stewed tomatoes
1 green bell pepper, or 2 Italian frying peppers, seeded and diced
½ small onion, chopped
Pinch of oregano or basil
¼ cup water

In a nonstick saucepan combine all ingredients and simmer the mixture over low heat for 12 to 15 minutes. Uncover and simmer for 3 minutes more, until thick.

Makes 3 servings, 40 calories each.

ZUCCHINI AND CARROTS IN ORANGE SAUCE

1½ cups orange juice
1 package (10 oz.) frozen sliced carrots
1 package (10 oz.) frozen sliced zucchini
2 Tbs. minced onion or 2 tsp. onion flakes (optional)
Salt and pepper
1 tsp. cornstarch
¼ cup cold water
1 Tbs. minced parsley (optional)

In a saucepan heat the orange juice to boiling, add the carrots, and simmer, covered, for 10 minutes. Add the zucchini and onion, if desired, and salt and pepper to taste. Cover and simmer until the vegetables are just tender, about 4 to 5 minutes. Combine cornstarch and cold water, add to the sauce, and stir over low heat until the mixture thickens. Sprinkle with parsley, if desired.

Makes 6 servings, 60 calories each.

EGGPLANT AND ZUCCHINI ITALIANO

1 small eggplant (¾ lb.), unpeeled, cubed
2 zucchini, sliced
2 onions, halved and sliced
1 can (6 oz.) tomato paste
1 can (10½ oz.) chicken or beef broth, undiluted but fat-skimmed
1 tsp. dried oregano or basil
Salt, or garlic salt, and pepper

Combine the vegetables in a pot. In a bowl stir the tomato paste and the broth together until smooth. Stir in remaining ingredients, then add mixture to pot and simmer, covered, for 30 to 40 minutes. (Refrigerate or freeze the leftovers; reheat gently.)

Makes 8 servings, 50 calories each.

ORIENTAL STIR-FRIED ZUCCHINI *good*

2 tsp. salad oil
2 Tbs. water
1 lb. zucchini, quartered lengthwise and cut into 2-inch strips

1 onion, halved and thinly sliced
2 Tbs. soy sauce

Spray a large nonstick skillet with cooking spray. Add oil, water, zucchini, and onion in a shallow layer. Cook the mixture over high heat for 5 minutes, stirring occasionally, until water evaporates. Sprinkle with soy sauce.

Makes 4 servings, 55 calories each.

OVEN-EASY ORIENTAL VEGETABLE MEDLEY

1 bag (20 oz.) mixed Japanese or Chinese vegetables (without sauce), defrosted
1 Tbs. salad oil

½ cup fat-skimmed beef or chicken broth or water
2 Tbs. soy sauce
1 tsp. sesame seeds (optional)

Preheat the oven to hot, 450 degrees.
Stir ingredients together. Spread in a shallow layer in a nonstick 11- by 17-inch pan which has been liberally sprayed with cooking spray. Bake uncovered 6 to 8 minutes, stirring once or twice.

Makes 6 servings, 85 calories each, or 90 calories each with sesame seeds).

MINESTRONE VEGETABLE CASSEROLE

2 tomatoes, peeled and diced
1 cup shredded cabbage
1 onion, halved, thinly sliced
1 rib celery, thinly sliced
1 Tbs. chopped fresh parsley
Pinch of basil or oregano

Salt, or garlic salt, and pepper
½ cup condensed beef broth,
   fat-skimmed
2 tsp. grated Pamesan or
   Romano cheese

Preheat the oven to moderate, 350 degrees.

Combine vegetables in a covered casserole. Season to taste. Pour on broth and sprinkle with cheese and bake, covered, for 30 to 40 minutes.

Makes 6 servings, 35 calories each.

FREEZER SALAD

1 package (10 oz.) frozen mixed
   vegetables
¼ cup boiling water

¼ cup low-calorie Italian salad
   dressing
½ small red onion, in rings

Break up frozen vegetables in a bowl. Pour on boiling water, stir in salad dressing, and add onion. Cover and leave at room temperature until defrosted. Store in refrigerator at least 5 hours, stirring once or twice to blend flavors.

Makes 4 servings, 60 calories each.

CHEESE SAUCE

¾ cup instant nonfat dry milk
2 Tbs. cornstarch
½ tsp. salt
¼ tsp dry mustard

Pinch of pepper
2 cups water
10 slices low-calorie process
   cheese

Combine dry milk, cornstarch, salt, mustard, and pepper in a non-stick saucepan, add water, and stir thoroughly. Cook over low heat, stirring, until the mixture simmers and thickens.

Add cheese and stir until melted. Use on vegetables.

Makes 2½ cups, 20 calories per Tbs.

Salads and Salad Dressings

for All Seasons

SALADS are the light cook's ace in the hole for enjoyable eating with a minimum of fat and calories. A salad before or with a meal can cut down the serving size of more fattening foods. Or a salad can be the whole meal.

Meal-size salads are also the light cook's fast-food. Lean leftovers tossed with greens and imaginatively seasoned can be assembled into tasty dinners in less time than it takes to heat a frozen dinner or wait in line for takeout burgers and fries.

But despite their light image, salads *can* be calorie-costly if they're drowned in heavy dressings. What you put on those greens can multiply their calorie count a hundredfold. I've seen salad makers top 10 calories' worth of lettuce with 400 calories in blue cheese.

One thing light cooks can be grateful for is the wide range of bottled commercial low-calorie salad dressings in nearly every variety—French, Italian, Russian, Thousand Island, Roquefort and blue cheese, garlic, creamy Italian, coleslaw, green goddess, Caesar, cucumber, sweet and sour—whatever you like, there's a version to choose.

If you prefer to make your own dressing, this chapter offers recipes that duplicate the taste and texture of some of the fattening favorites . . . without the fats and calories.

APPLE SLAW

2 Tbs. raisins
1 Tbs. vinegar
1 tsp. prepared mustard
Salt or garlic salt to taste
1 cup plain low-fat yogurt

1½ cups chopped unpeeled apple
Lemon juice
4 cups shredded green or red cabbage
½ cup chopped celery

Combine the raisins, vinegar, mustard, salt, and yogurt in a small bowl. Cover and chill.

Mix the apple with the lemon juice and toss with the other ingredients.

Makes 8 servings, about 45 calories each.

CAULIFLOWER BOWL

3 cups raw cauliflower buds
1 Tbs. lemon juice
1 small head lettuce, torn
1 cup thinly sliced radishes
1 small onion, thinly sliced

Salt and pepper
Dried dillweed
1 cup low-calorie creamy Italian salad dressing

In a bowl toss the cauliflower with the lemon juice. Add the remaining vegetables, seasonings, and salad dressing and toss.

Makes 8 servings, 35 calories each.

WALDORF CELERY SLAW

2 unpeeled red apples, diced
4 ribs celery, sliced
2 Tbs. raisins
3 Tbs. low-fat mayonnaise

2 Tbs. low-fat vanilla yogurt
1 Tbs. chopped walnuts
Salt and pepper

In a bowl combine all the ingredients and mix well.

Makes 6 servings, 65 calories each.

MINTED CUCUMBER SLICES

2 Tbs. chopped fresh mint or 2
  tsp. dried mint
1 Tbs. fresh snipped dillweed or
  1 tsp. dried dillweed
⅛ tsp. garlic salt
1 cup plain low-fat yogurt

2 unpeeled cucumbers, scored
  and thinly sliced (about 6
  cups)
Salt
Chopped fresh parsley

Combine the mint, dillweed, garlic salt, and yogurt in a small bowl. Cover and chill it.

Sprinkle the cucumbers with salt and chill them for 30 to 45 minutes, tossing occasionally.

To serve, drain the cucumbers well and in a bowl toss with the yogurt mixture. Garnish with parsley.

Makes 6 servings, 35 calories each.

GOLDEN FRUIT SALAD

1 unpeeled golden Delicious
  apple, diced
¼ cup seedless grapes, halved
2 ribs celery, thinly sliced

2 Tbs. low-fat mayonnaise
2 Tbs. plain low-fat yogurt
Pinch of ground cinnamon
  (optional)

In a bowl combine the ingredients and chill. Arrange on beds of lettuce and sprinkle with cinnamon, if desired.

Makes 4 servings, 45 calories each.

SQUASH SALAD BOWL

1 small head Romaine lettuce,
  torn
1 medium zucchini, thinly
  sliced

1 small red onion, thinly sliced
2 Tbs. minced Italian parsley
1 cup low-calorie Italian-
  seasoned salad dressing

In a salad bowl combine the ingredients.

Makes 8 servings, 30 calories each.

SALADE NIÇOISE

¼ cup dry red wine
¼ cup red wine vinegar
1 Tbs. olive oil
Dash of Worcestershire sauce
   1 clove garlic, minced (optional)
   1 Tbs. chopped fresh parsley
     (optional)
¼ tsp. oregano
1½ cups cooked sliced green
     beans or 10-oz. package,
     defrosted

1 cooked white potato, peeled
     and thinly sliced
4 medium stuffed green olives,
     sliced
2 ripe tomatoes, diced
1 can (6½ or 7 oz.) water-
     packed solid white tuna,
     drained and flaked
4 hard-cooked eggs, sliced

In a large bowl combine the first 7 ingredients. Add to the dressing the beans, potatoes, and olives. Cover the mixture and refrigerate for several hours to allow the flavors to blend.

Just before serving, toss the salad with the remaining ingredients.

Makes 4 servings, 255 calories each.

TOMATO STUFFED WITH CHICKEN-PINEAPPLE SALAD

  1 cup plain low-fat yogurt
¼ tsp. leaf tarragon or pinch of
    dried tarragon
Salt to taste
   1 can (8 oz.) juice-packed
     crushed pineapple, drained

1½ cups diced cooked chicken or
    turkey
½ cup chopped celery
6 tomatoes
6 Tbs. toasted slivered almonds
    (optional)

Combine the yogurt, tarragon, and salt in a small bowl. Cover and chill it.

In another bowl, combine the pineapple, chicken, and celery and chill it.

Toss the yogurt mixture with the chicken mixture.

Cut tomatoes not quite through the skin into wedges. Open and fill with the chicken mixture. Top with almonds, if desired.

Makes 6 servings, about 140 calories each, or 200 calories each with almonds.

ITALIAN SUPPER SALAD

2 cups diced or shredded turkey
  salami
4 cups torn lettuce
2 cups thinly sliced fresh
  mushrooms
½ zucchini or cucumber, thinly
  sliced

8 cherry tomatoes, halved
¼ cup sliced scallions (optional)
8 Tbs. low-calorie Italian salad
  dressing
Salt and pepper to taste

In a bowl combine the ingredients and toss them gently.

Makes 4 servings, 280 calories each.

TACO SALAD

4 cups shredded iceberg lettuce
¼ cup onion, minced
1 green bell pepper, seeded and
  chopped
⅔ cup low-calorie Italian salad
  dressing

1 clove garlic, minced
¼ tsp. ground cumin
6 Tbs. coarsely shredded extra-
  sharp cheddar cheese
12 cheese-flavored tortilla chips,
  broken up

In a bowl combine all the ingredients, except the cheese and chips, and toss. Top with the cheese and chips.

Makes 6 servings, 80 calories each.

COTTAGE CHEESE POTATO SALAD

2 cups peeled diced cooked
  potatoes
2 hard-cooked eggs, chopped
½ cup sliced celery
⅓ cup sliced radishes
⅓ cup chopped scallions
8 thinly sliced green olives

1 Tbs. olive liquid (from the jar)
2 Tbs. low-calorie Italian
  dressing
¼ cup plain low-fat yogurt
2 cups low-fat cottage cheese
Salt and pepper to taste
Paprika (optional)

In a bowl combine the ingredients in the order in which they are listed. Chill the salad for several hours. Mound on lettuce.

Makes 8 servings, 100 calories each.

WALDORF SALAD

½ cup plain low-fat yogurt
1 Tbs. low-fat mayonnaise
Salt and pepper
⅛ tsp. cinnamon
¼ tsp. grated lemon rind
  (optional)

2 cups unpeeled chopped red
  apples
Lemon juice
1½ cups chopped celery
4 Tbs. raisins
2 Tbs. chopped walnuts

In a bowl combine the yogurt, mayonnaise, salt and pepper to taste, cinnamon, and lemon rind, if desired.

Mix the apples with the lemon juice and add to the other ingredients. Add celery, raisins, and walnuts. Toss.

Makes 8 servings, about 55 calories each.

FRENCH HERB DRESSING

2 Tbs. liquid pectin
2 Tbs. olive oil
4 Tbs. olive liquid (from jar of
  green olives)
4 Tbs. cider vinegar
4 Tbs. unsweetened cider or
  apple juice

1 tsp. prepared yellow mustard
1 tsp. dried marjoram or other
  herbs
Salt, or garlic salt, and pepper

Combine in a covered jar. Season to taste. Shake well before serving.

Makes 1 cup, 18 calories per Tbs.

WHITE FRENCH DRESSING

1 cup low-fat cottage cheese
2 tsp. vinegar or lemon juice
½ tsp. tarragon
1 small garlic clove, crushed

Onion salt and pepper
1 cup plain low-fat yogurt
Few sprigs of parsley

In a blender blend the first 5 ingredients until smooth.

In a bowl combine the mixture with the yogurt. Cover and chill. Use on tossed salads. (Keeps for several days, covered, in the refrigerator.)

Makes about 2 cups, 10 calories per Tbs.

ITALIAN CHEESE DRESSING

5 Tbs. low-fat mayonnaise
4 Tbs. white or cider vinegar
⅓ cup water
2 Tbs. grated Parmesan or
Romano cheese

1 tsp. dried oregano
Salt, or garlic salt, and pepper

Beat or fork-blend ingredients together. Season to taste. Refrigerate in a covered jar. Shake well before serving.

Makes 1 cup, 17 calories per Tbs.

ITALIAN TOMATO DRESSING

¾ cup (6-oz. can) plain tomato
juice
2 Tbs. salad oil
2 Tbs. red wine vinegar
1 clove garlic, chopped, or
pinch of instant garlic

2 Tbs. chopped parsley
1 tsp. dried basil or oregano
Salt (if needed) and pepper

Combine all the ingredients in a covered jar and shake up. Season to taste. Shake well before serving.

Makes 1 cup, 19 calories per Tbs.

CREAMY ITALIAN DRESSING

1 cup part-skim ricotta cheese
1 hard-cooked egg, quartered
2 Tbs. lemon juice
1 tsp. prepared mustard

1 tsp. onion salt
Pinch of sugar (optional)
1 tsp. oregano or basil (optional)

In a blender blend all the ingredients until smooth.

Makes 1¼ cups, 16 calories per Tbs.

CREAMY GREEK SALAD DRESSING

3 Tbs. lemon juice
3 Tbs. low-fat mayonnaise
3 Tbs. part-skim ricotta cheese
3 Tbs. water
1 clove garlic, peeled

4 Tbs. fresh parsley
3 Tbs. fresh mint or 2 tsp. dried
   mint
Salt and pepper

Combine in a blender or food processor and blend smooth. Season to taste. Refrigerate.

Makes 1 cup, 14 calories per Tbs.

CITRUS SALAD DRESSING

1 large juice orange, peeled
¼ cup lemon juice
3 Tbs. salad oil
2 or 3 sprigs of parsley

1 tsp. dried mint or marjoram or
   other herbs to taste
Salt and pepper to taste

Purée the orange in a blender or in a food processor with the steel blade.

Add the remaining ingredients and process until the parsley is minced. Store in refrigerator and shake well before serving.

Makes 1½ cups, 20 calories per Tbs.

FETA CHEESE DRESSING

1 oz. feta cheese
½ cup low-calorie Italian salad
  dressing

2 Tbs. low-fat mayonnaise
5 Tbs. plain low-fat yogurt
1 tsp. dried mint or marjoram

Crumble cheese. Stir remaining ingredients smooth. Add the crumbled cheese. Refrigerate.

Makes 1 cup, 16 calories per Tbs.

FRUIT SALAD DRESSING

4 Tbs. low-fat mayonnaise
4 Tbs. low-fat cottage cheese
3 Tbs. lemon juice
⅓ cup unsweetened pineapple
  juice

1 tsp. curry powder
Salt and pepper

Blend smooth in a blender or food processor. Season to taste. Refrigerate.

Makes 1 cup, 16 calories per Tbs.

CITRUS FRENCH DRESSING

3 Tbs. salad oil
4 Tbs. lemon juice
½ cup unsweetened orange
  juice

¼ tsp. dry mustard or ½ tsp.
  prepared mustard
Salt, or garlic salt, and pepper

Combine in a covered jar. Season to taste. Shake well before serving.

Makes about 1 cup, 30 calories per Tbs.

TOMATO FRENCH DRESSING

2 Tbs. salad oil   2 Tbs. vinegar
¾ cup (6-oz. can) tomato juice   Salt, or seasoned salt, and pepper

Combine the ingredients in a jar. Season to taste. Cover. Shake well before using.

Makes 1 cup, 18 calories per Tbs.

ORANGE FRUIT DRESSING

2 tsp. grated orange rind   1 cup orange yogurt
Salt and pepper to taste   ⅛ tsp. cinnamon

In a bowl combine the ingredients and chill. Use on fruit salads.

Makes about 1 cup, 15 calories per Tbs.

JAPANESE GINGER DRESSING

½ cup low-calorie French   1 Tbs. soy sauce
  dressing   3 Tbs. dry sherry
2 tsp. ground ginger   ¼ cup white grape juice

Combine the ingredients in a covered jar. Shake before serving.

Makes 1 cup, 15 calories per Tbs.

HAWAIIAN FRUIT SALAD DRESSING

½ cup low-calorie French   1 tsp. curry powder
  dressing   ⅓ cup unsweetened pineapple
1 Tbs. soy sauce   juice
1 tsp. ground ginger   2 Tbs. lime juice

Combine the ingredients in a covered jar. Shake well before serving.

Makes 1 cup, 12 calories per Tbs.

CARIBBEAN DRESSING

1 Tbs. salad oil
3 Tbs. lime juice
½ cup low-calorie French dressing
¼ cup canned peach or mango nectar or unsweetened pineapple juice

1 tsp. ground allspice
Salt and pepper

Combine the ingredients in a covered jar. Season to taste. Shake well before serving.

Makes 1 cup, 20 calories per Tbs.

OLIVE OIL AND VINEGAR DRESSING

2 Tbs. olive oil
4 Tbs. olive liquid (from a jar of green olives)
4 Tbs. cider vinegar

2 Tbs. liquid pectin
¼ cup water
Salt, or garlic salt, and pepper
Dried herbs to taste

Combine the ingredients in a covered jar. Season to taste. Cover and refrigerate. Shake well before serving.

Makes 1 cup, 16 calories per Tbs.

SPICY MEXICAN DRESSING

¾ cup (6-oz. can) Bloody Mary–seasoned tomato juice
¼ cup low-calorie Italian-seasoned salad dressing

1 clove garlic, chopped
¼ tsp. ground cumin
2 Tbs. grated cheddar or American cheese

Combine ingredients in a covered jar. Refrigerate. Shake well before serving.

Makes 1 cup, 8 calories per Tbs.

CHEESE FRENCH DRESSING

1½ cups low-fat cottage cheese
½ cup bottled French dressing
¼ cup crumbled Roquefort
    cheese

1 Tbs. prepared horseradish

In a blender blend all the ingredients until smooth. Refrigerate the mixture until serving time.

Makes 2¼ cups, 25 calories per Tbs.

BLENDER GREEN MAYONNAISE

1 avocado, peeled and cut into
    chunks
1 raw egg
2 Tbs. lime juice

½ tsp. yellow prepared mustard
Salt, or celery salt, and pepper to
    taste

In a blender blend all the ingredients until smooth. Store in the refrigerator.

Makes about ½ cup, about 20 calories per Tbs.

YOGURT LOUIS DRESSING

½ cup chili sauce
1 Tbs. chopped scallion
1 Tbs. lemon juice

Salt to taste
1½ cups plain low-fat yogurt

In a bowl combine the ingredients. Cover and chill. Serve with cold shellfish.

Makes 2 cups, 11 calories per Tbs.

LIGHT MAYONNAISE

1 cup plain low-fat yogurt
2 hard-cooked eggs
1 tsp. celery salt

2 Tbs. lemon juice
½ tsp. dry mustard
½ tsp. sugar

In a blender blend the ingredients until smooth.

Makes about 1¼ cups, about 13 calories per Tbs.

BLUE CHEESE DRESSING

¼ cup crumbled blue cheese
1 tsp. vinegar
½ tsp. sugar (optional)

Salt and pepper to taste
1 cup plain low-fat yogurt
2 Tbs. water

In a bowl combine the ingredients. Cover and chill.

Makes about 1 cup, about 15 calories per Tbs.

LIGHT THOUSAND ISLAND DRESSING

3 Tbs. chili sauce
3 Tbs. pickle relish
1 Tbs. finely chopped onion
1 tsp. vinegar

1 tsp. prepared mustard
½ tsp. salt
1 cup plain low-fat yogurt
2 Tbs. low-fat mayonnaise

In a blender blend the ingredients until smooth. Cover and chill.

Makes 1½ cups, 11 calories per Tbs.

12

Potatoes, Pasta,

and Rice

A GENERATION AGO economy-minded cooks were urged to stretch their menus by using such filling foods as potatoes, pasta, and rice. Then some best-selling diet fads told us that starchy foods were fattening and that the route to slimness called for lots of meat and protein. Today you still see people turn thumbs down to baked potato (90 calories), but ask instead for a second helping of prime ribs (500 calories). The fact is these so-called starchy foods are both filling and nonfattening as well as nutritious and inexpensive. Potatoes, pasta, and rice are calorie-light because their fat content is virtually zero. What can make these delicious foods fattening are sauces and garnishes high in fat: creamy toppings, melted butter, and cheese.

This chapter shows you how to lighten the calories of these favorite foods.

LIGHT-AND-EASY OVEN FRENCH FRIES

2 unpeeled medium potatoes, cut in thick strips	1 Tbs. salad oil Salt, pepper, paprika

Preheat the oven to hot, 450 degrees.

Slice the potatoes into a bowl of ice water to crisp them, drain, and toss them with oil to coat them lightly.

Spread potato strips in a single layer on a nonstick cookie sheet, and bake, turning them frequently, until golden brown and tender, about 30 to 40 minutes. Sprinkle generously with salt, pepper, and paprika.

Makes 4 servings, 75 calories each.

LIGHT-AND-EASY SCALLOPED POTATOES

2 cups pared raw potatoes, thinly sliced
1½ cups skim milk
1 Tbs. instant-blending flour

Salt and pepper to taste
1 Tbs. grated Parmesan cheese
Paprika

Preheat the oven to moderate, 350 degrees.

Combine the potatoes and the milk in a nonstick saucepan and simmer over low heat for 15 minutes. Spoon a layer of potatoes into a nonstick baking dish and sprinkle them with some of the flour, salt, and pepper. Repeat until all the potatoes are used. Pour the milk which is left in the saucepan over the potatoes, and sprinkle with the Parmesan and paprika.

Cover and bake the potato mixture 10 minutes, or until potatoes are tender. Remove the cover and bake 10 minutes longer.

Makes 4 servings, 105 calories each.

MILKMAID'S POTATO CASSEROLE

2 cups cooked diced potatoes
½ cup plain low-fat yogurt
½ cup low-fat cottage cheese

2 Tbs. chopped onion
1 Tbs. chopped parsley
Salt, or garlic salt, and pepper

Preheat the oven to moderate, 350 degrees.

Combine all the ingredients in a nonstick 9-inch cake pan. Bake, uncovered, for 25 to 30 minutes.

Makes 6 servings, 60 calories each.

ITALIAN POTATO CASSEROLE

4 medium potatoes, peeled and
  sliced
2 tomatoes, sliced, or 1 can (8
  oz.) tomatoes, broken up

1 onion, chopped
½ tsp. oregano or basil
Salt, or garlic salt, and pepper

Preheat the oven to moderately hot, 400 degrees.

Combine the ingredients in a nonstick baking dish, and bake, covered, for 30 minutes. Uncover and bake 15 to 20 minutes until potatoes are tender.

Makes 8 servings, 65 calories each.

FRENCH POTATOES AND MUSHROOMS

2 cups pared potatoes, thinly
  sliced
½ cup mushrooms, thinly sliced
1 can (10½ oz.) onion soup,
  undiluted

¼ tsp. dried thyme
Dash of pepper

Preheat the oven to moderate, 350 degrees.

Combine the ingredients in a nonstick 9-inch square baking pan and bake, covered, for 30 minutes. Uncover and bake 15 minutes more, or until vegetables are tender.

Makes 6 servings, 65 calories each.

PARSLEY POTATOES

6 medium potatoes, peeled and
  thinly sliced
½ cup minced onion

1 cup fat-skimmed chicken
  broth
½ cup chopped parsley

Combine all of the ingredients except parsley in a large saucepan, and simmer, covered, for 10 minutes. Add the parsley and continue simmering, uncovered, until the potatoes are tender, about 5 minutes.

Makes 8 servings, 75 calories each.

POTATOES AND GREEN BEANS

3 medium potatoes, peeled and
cubed
Pinch of basil or oregano
1 cup fat-skimmed chicken
broth

1 package (10 oz.) French-style
green beans, defrosted
2 tsp. cornstarch
1 Tbs. cold water

In a saucepan combine potatoes, basil, and broth and simmer, covered, for 15 minutes. Add the green beans and cook 5 to 8 minutes, or until the vegetables are tender. Drain, reserving ¾ cup cooking liquid.

Combine cornstarch with the cold water and stir into the vegetable cooking liquid. Cook and stir until thickened, about 2 minutes. Add the vegetables; reheat.

Makes 8 servings, 50 calories each.

LINGUINE WITH CHICKEN SAUCE

1 skinless boneless chicken
breast, cut into 1-inch cubes
¼ lb. Canadian bacon, cut into
1-inch cubes
1 tsp. butter or margarine
1 cup fat-skimmed undiluted
chicken broth
1 cup dry white wine

5 cups tender-cooked protein-
enriched linguine, drained
½ cup low-fat cottage cheese
3 oz. Swiss cheese, shredded
½ cup minced fresh parsley
Pinch of nutmeg
Salt and pepper

In a large nonstick skillet or electric fry pan sprayed with cooking spray, brown the chicken and bacon in the butter in a single layer over moderate heat, turning to prevent them from sticking. Remove from the skillet. Drain any fat.

Combine the remaining ingredients in the skillet and cook, stirring constantly, over moderate heat until most of the liquid evaporates and the pasta is well coated with the cheese. Stir in the bacon and chicken and heat through. Serve immediately.

Makes 6 meal-size servings, 290 calories each.

LINGUINE AND LITTLENECKS

2 doz. littleneck clams, rinsed
and picked over
1 can (16 oz.) plain tomato
sauce
½ cup dry sherry
1 small onion, minced
½ to 1 tsp. oregano, basil, or pizza
seasoning

1 clove garlic, minced (optional)
4 oz. tender-cooked (without
salt) protein-enriched linguine
or spaghetti, drained.
1 Tbs. grated extra-sharp
Romano cheese

Combine all the ingredients, except the pasta and cheese, in a pot and heat the mixture to boiling. Cover, lower the heat, and simmer until the clams open, about 8 to 10 minutes. Discard any clams that don't open.

Serve the spaghetti sauce on the hot pasta and sprinkle it with cheese.

Makes 2 servings, 450 calories each.

GREEK SPAGETTI AND MEATBALLS
WITH EGGPLANT SAUCE

1 lb. lean ground round or
ground lamb
1 egg, beaten or ¼ cup no-
cholesterol substitute
2 Tbs. chopped fresh mint or
parsley or 2 tsp. dried
Salt and pepper
3 cups peeled and diced
eggplant
1 can (10½ oz.) fat-skimmed
beef broth

1 cup water
1 can (6 oz.) tomato paste
1 onion, chopped
1 clove garlic, minced
⅛ tsp. nutmeg
½ tsp. oregano
8 cups tender-cooked protein-
enriched spaghetti or linguine
or macaroni, drained
8 tsp. grated extra-sharp
Romano cheese

In a bowl combine the meat, egg, mint or parsley, salt and pepper to taste. Shape the mixture into 16 tiny meatballs and brown them under the broiler, turning once.

In a large pot combine the eggplant, broth, water, tomato paste, onion, garlic, nutmeg, and oregano, heat to boiling, and add the meatballs. Cover the pot and simmer for 30 minutes.

Uncover and simmer the mixture until the sauce is thick. Serve over hot pasta and sprinkle with cheese.

Makes 8 servings, under 300 calories each.

SPEEDY SPAGHETTI AND TUNA

2 tomatoes, peeled and diced, or 8-oz. can tomatoes, broken up
1 can (6 oz.) tomato paste
½ tsp. poultry seasoning
1 tsp. basil or oregano
½ tsp. fennel seed
Garlic salt and pepper
1½ cups cold water
1 can (6½ or 7 oz.) water-packed tuna, drained and flaked.
8 oz. tender-cooked protein-enriched spaghetti, drained.

Combine the ingredients, except the pasta, in a pot. Simmer the mixture, covered, for 15 minutes. Serve over the hot spaghetti.

Makes 4 servings, 320 calories each.

BARLEY ROMANO

1 can (16 oz.) Italian tomatoes, undrained
2 cups tomato juice
½ cup pearl barley
1 onion, chopped
1 green bell pepper, seeded and chopped
¼ tsp. oregano
4 Tbs. grated extra-sharp Romano cheese

In a saucepan combine all the ingredients, except the cheese, cover, and simmer over low heat, stirring occasionally, for 1 hour or more, until all the liquid is evaporated and the barley is tender.

Serve sprinkled with cheese.

Makes 6 servings, 120 calories each.

HAM, MACARONI, AND CHEESE

4 oz. uncooked protein-
  enriched elbow macaroni
  (about 1¼ cups)
¼ cup plain low-fat yogurt
1 egg, lightly beaten
1 small onion, finely minced
1 tsp. prepared mustard
Dash of Tabasco or
  Worcestershire sauce
  (optional)

1 cup diced cooked ham
1 cup coarsely shredded extra-
  sharp cheddar or American
  cheese
Salt and pepper
2 Tbs. minced fresh parsley

In a pan boil macaroni in salted water about 16 minutes, until it is very tender. Drain and return to the pan.

Over very low flame stir in each ingredient in the order given and cook the mixture until heated through.

Makes 4 servings, 325 calories each.

DAIRY NOODLE CASSEROLE

1¼ cups skim milk
1½ Tbs. cornstarch
1 Tbs. lemon juice
Dash of Worcestershire sauce
1 tsp. prepared mustard
Pinch of cayenne (optional)
  2 Tbs. minced fresh parsley or 2
    tsp. dried parsley
  2 cups (5 oz.) tender-cooked
    medium egg noodles, drained

1 can (4 oz.) mushroom pieces,
  drained
1 small onion, peeled and
  minced
16 oz. low-fat cottage cheese
Salt and pepper
  5 Tbs. grated sharp American
    cheese
  2 Tbs. seasoned bread crumbs

Preheat the oven to moderate, 350 degrees.

Combine the milk and cornstarch in a saucepan and cook the mixture, stirring, over low heat until it simmers and thickens. Stir in lemon juice, Worcestershire sauce, mustard, cayenne, if desired, and parsley.

Combine the sauce with the noodles, mushrooms, onion, and cottage cheese in a casserole and sprinkle it with the grated cheese and bread crumbs.

Bake the dish, uncovered, for 25 to 30 minutes.

Makes 6 main-course servings, 215 calories each, or 12 side-dish servings, 105 calories each.

CHICKEN AND MACARONI IN RED PEPPER SAUCE

½ lb. skinless boneless chicken breast, cut into 1-inch cubes
1 can (16 oz.) stewed tomatoes
2 red bell peppers, seeded and diced
2 small onions, chopped
2 cups water

2 Tbs. chopped fresh mint or 2 tsp. dried mint
¼ tsp. nutmeg
½ tsp. oregano
¼ tsp. cinnamon
4 oz. dry elbow macaroni

In a large nonstick skillet sprayed with cooking spray brown the chicken quickly, turning to prevent sticking. Remove the chicken.

Combine all the remaining ingredients, except the macaroni, in the skillet and heat the mixture to boiling. Stir in the macaroni, a little at a time, cover tightly, and simmer over low heat, stirring occasionally, for about 15 minutes, until the macaroni is very tender.

Uncover and simmer until nearly all the liquid evaporates.

Stir in the chicken and cook, stirring frequently, until it is heated through.

Makes 3 servings, 370 calories each.

SEASONED RICE

¼ cup finely minced celery
1 Tbs. finely minced onion
¾ cup fat-skimmed condensed
   chicken or beef broth

½ cup water
¼ cup raw brown rice
1 Tbs. minced fresh parsley
Salt (if needed) and pepper

In a saucepan combine the ingredients, cover, and simmer for 45 minutes or more, until all the liquid is absorbed and the rice is tender.

Makes 2 servings, 110 calories each.

BROWN RICE

1 cup raw brown rice
3 cups fat-skimmed turkey
   broth

Salt and pepper

In a saucepan, stir the rice into boiling broth. Reduce the heat to a simmer, cover tightly, and simmer for 45 minutes, until all the liquid is absorbed. Season to taste

Makes 4 cups, 90 calories per ½ cupful.

MEXICAN BEEF AND RICE

4 onions, minced
2 ribs celery, minced
2 green bell peppers, seeded
   and diced
½ tsp. oregano
½ tsp. ground cumin (optional)
1 tsp. chili powder (or to taste)

2 cups tomato juice, plain or
   spicy
1½ cups instant rice
2 cups cooked fat-trimmed
   diced roast beef
4 Tbs. shredded sharp cheddar
   cheese (optional)

Combine the onions, celery, peppers, seasonings, and tomato juice in a nonstick skillet or saucepan, cover, and simmer for 5 minutes.

Stir in the rice and beef, reheat to boiling, and remove the pan from heat. Cover tightly and let it stand for 5 minutes, until the liquid is absorbed.

Stir well and serve sprinkled with cheese, if desired.

Makes 4 whole-meal servings, 385 calories each, or 415 calories each with cheese.

INDIAN CURRIED RICE

1 cup chopped onion
1 cup minced celery
1 cup thinly sliced mushrooms
2 cups fat-skimmed chicken
   broth
1 cup raw rice
3 Tbs. golden raisins
Salt, or garlic salt, and pepper

½ tsp. poultry seasoning
1 tsp. curry powder (or to taste)
¼ tsp. allspice, or mixed apple
   pie spices
1 red unpeeled apple, cored and
   diced
8 tsp. toasted sunflower seeds,
   or sliced almonds

Spray a large nonstick skillet with cooking spray. Spread the onions, celery, and mushrooms in a shallow layer. Add ¼ cup chicken broth. Cook, uncovered, over high heat, until the broth evaporates and the vegetables begin to brown. Stir them to prevent sticking.

Add the remaining broth and heat to boiling. Stir in the remaining ingredients except the apple and sunflower seeds or almonds. Lower the heat; cover and simmer 15 to 20 minutes, until the rice is tender and the liquid has evaporated. Stir in the apple and heat through. Fluff with a fork. Sprinkle with the sunflower seeds or sliced almonds just before serving.

Makes 8 servings, 145 calories each.

LIGHT-AND-EASY ORIENTAL UNFRIED RICE

1 egg, lightly beaten, or ¼ cup
  no-cholesterol egg substitute
½ cup sliced onion
½ cup slant-sliced celery
½ cup mixed red and green
  chopped bell peppers, fresh or
  defrosted, or ½ cup sliced
  mushrooms
1 cup fat-skimmed chicken
  broth
1 cup instant rice
1 cup fresh or canned bean
  sprouts, rinsed and drained
Soy sauce

Spray a nonstick skillet with cooking spray. Pour the egg or substitute into the cold skillet. Cook uncovered, undisturbed, over low heat until the egg is nearly set. Break the egg into shreds with the tines of a fork.

Add the onion, celery, pepper or mushrooms, and broth. Heat to boiling. Reduce the heat, cover, and simmer 5 minutes. Add the rice and bean sprouts. Heat to boiling. Cover tightly, turn off the heat, and leave undisturbed for 5 minutes. Uncover. Cook and stir over moderate heat until the rice is dry and heated through. Add soy sauce to taste.

Makes 6 servings, 100 calories each with egg, or 7 calories less per serving with egg substitute.

CREOLE RICE

1 slice lean smoked pork
  breakfast strip
½ cup chopped onion
1 clove garlic, minced
1 cup water
2 cups peeled, chopped
  tomatoes, fresh or canned and
  undrained
½ cup chopped green bell
  pepper
¼ cup chopped parsley
1 tsp. prepared mustard
1 bay leaf
⅛ tsp. red pepper flakes (or to
  taste)
Salt and pepper
1 cup raw rice

Dice the breakfast strip. Spray a nonstick skillet with cooking spray. Fry the diced strip—with no fat added—until it is very crisp and well rendered of fat. Drain and discard the fat. Set the browned pork pieces aside.

Combine the onion and garlic with 2 Tbs. of water in the skillet. Cover and cook over moderate heat 2 minutes. Uncover and continue to cook, stirring occasionally, until the liquid evaporates and the onions begin to brown. Stir in the remaining ingredients, except the rice. Mix well; heat to boiling. Stir in the rice. Cook until boiling resumes, then lower the heat and cover the pan and simmer for 15 to 20 minutes, until the rice is tender and the liquid is absorbed. Remove the bay leaf. Stir in the reserved pork pieces.

Makes 8 servings, 115 calories each.

VARIATION

Jambalaya Dinner:
Follow the preceding recipe. Add 1 lb. peeled, deveined raw shrimp or 1 lb. diced raw chicken cutlets to the skillet during the last 10 minutes of cooking; 170 calories per serving with shrimp; 175 calories per serving with chicken.

LIGHT-AND-EASY FRUITED RICE FOR POULTRY

½ cup minced celery
1 cup any unsweetened fruit juice (orange, pineapple, apple, etc.)
1 cup instant rice
1 tsp., envelope, or cube chicken bouillon

2 Tbs. golden raisins, or minced apricots, or other dried fruits (optional)
Dash of cinnamon or pumpkin pie spice (optional)

Cook the celery in the fruit juice, covered, for 5 minutes. Stir in the remaining ingredients, mixing well. Heat to boiling. Remove from the heat; cover tightly and wait 5 minutes. Uncover and heat through over low heat.

Makes 6 servings, 80 calories each with orange or apple juice, 85 calories each with pineapple juice; raisins add about 10 calories per serving.

BAKED RICE MILANESE

1 cup chopped onions
1 Tbs. water
1 tsp. butter or margarine
1½ cups chopped green bell
 pepper
3 cups cooked rice

Salt and pepper
½ tsp. basil
1 can (8 oz.) tomato sauce
6 Tbs. shredded extra-sharp
 cheddar cheese

Preheat the oven to moderate, 350 degrees.

Spray a nonstick skillet with cooking spray. Combine the onions, water, and butter or margarine. Cook and stir over moderate heat until the water evaporates.

Add the bell pepper, rice, seasonings, and tomato sauce. Turn the mixture into a greased 1½-qt. casserole. Top with the cheese. Bake for 20 minutes.

Makes 8 servings, 130 calories each.

POLYNESIAN PINEAPPLE RICE AND PEPPERS

1 cup minced celery or ½ cup
 minced celery and ½ cup
 chopped onion
1 green bell pepper, seeded,
 thinly sliced into strips
1 cup fat-skimmed chicken
 broth

1 can (8 oz.) unsweetened
 crushed pineapple, undrained
1 cup instant rice
Soy sauce

Cook the celery, (onion), and bell pepper in the chicken broth for 5 minutes. Stir in the pineapple and rice. Heat to boiling. Remove from the heat and cover tightly. Wait 5 minutes. Uncover and cook over low heat until the moisture evaporates and the rice is fluffy and tender. Season to taste with the soy sauce.

Makes 6 servings, 95 calories each.

ITALIAN RICE AND TOMATOES

1 can (8 oz.) stewed tomatoes, broken up

2 Tbs. minced onion or 2 tsp. instant onion

½ tsp. chopped garlic or pinch of instant garlic (optional)

½ tsp. dried basil or oregano

½ cup instant rice

2 Tbs. water or dry white wine

Salt (if needed) and pepper

1 Tbs. grated sharp Romano cheese (optional)

Combine all of the ingredients, except the grated cheese, in a saucepan. Heat to boiling. Remove from the heat and cover tightly for 5 minutes. Uncover and stir over a moderate flame until the rice is dry. Sprinkle with the cheese before serving, if desired.

Makes 6 servings, 40 calories each (wine and cheese add 5 calories per serving).

INDIAN TOMATO-SPICED RICE

2 tsp. butter

2 Tbs. water

1 cup finely chopped onions

2 cups tomato juice plus dash of Tabasco, or Bloody Mary mix

1 cup long-grain rice

2 cloves garlic, minced

¼ tsp. ground ginger

Pinch of ground clove

Salt or butter-flavored salt

Pinch of pepper

3 Tbs. fresh chopped parsley

Combine the butter, water, and onion in a nonstick saucepan. Cook uncovered, until the water evaporates and the onions are browned. Stir to prevent sticking.

Add the remaining ingredients, except the parsley. Heat to boiling. Cover tightly and cook over low heat until the rice is tender. Stir in the parsley.

Makes 8 servings, 160 calories each.

LEMON-PARSLEY RICE
FOR SEAFOOD AND POULTRY

1 cup instant rice
¼ cup loosely packed fresh
  parsley, chopped
1 Tbs. lemon juice

Salt, or butter salt, and pepper
Pinch of dried tarragon (optional)
1 cup water or fat-skimmed
  chicken broth

Combine all of the ingredients and heat to boiling. Remove from the heat and cover tightly. Wait 5 minutes. Fluff with a fork before serving.

Makes 6 servings, 60 calories each with water, or 65 calories each with broth.

MOCK SAFFRON RICE

2 tsp. butter
2 Tbs. water
1 cup thinly sliced onions
4 cups boiling water
2 cups raw long-grain rice

2 Tbs. chopped parsley or 2 tsp.
  parsley flakes
1 tsp. tumeric
⅛ tsp. ground cumin
1½ tsp. salt or butter-flavored salt

Combine the butter, water, and onions in a nonstick saucepan. Cook uncovered, until the water evaporates and the onions are golden. Stir to prevent sticking. Add the remaining ingredients and heat to boiling. Cover and simmer over low heat until the rice is tender.

Makes 10 servings, 150 calories each.

SEAFOOD SAUCE

1 cup thinly sliced mushrooms,
  fresh or canned
2 tsp. butter or margarine
½ cup dry sherry or dry white
  wine
1 lb. sea scallops or fillets of
  sole or flounder, cut in 1½-
  inch cubes

Salt and pepper
Pinch of nutmeg
2 Tbs. flour
1 cup skim milk
2 Tbs. grated Parmesan cheese
2 slices low-fat cheese, chopped
  or cut into julienne strips
1 Tbs. minced fresh parsley

In a nonstick skillet or electric fry pan, cook the mushrooms with the butter and 1 tablespoon wine over high heat until the liquid evaporates and the mushrooms brown. Remove mushrooms.

Combine the scallops or fish and remaining wine in the skillet, sprinkle with salt, pepper, and nutmeg and simmer the mixture, uncovered, for about 5 to 8 minutes, until the seafood is opaque and most of the wine has evaporated. (Spoon the wine over the seafood occasionally while it cooks.)

In a jar combine the flour and milk and shake until blended. Add it to the skillet and stir gently until the sauce thickens. Season to taste.

Add the cheese, mushrooms, and parsley and heat the mixture through.

Makes 4 servings, 190 calories each.

SPINACH PESTO SAUCE FOR SPAGHETTI

1 cup fresh parsley
2 or 3 cloves garlic
  2 Tbs. dried basil or ⅓ cup fresh
  basil
  2 Tbs. olive oil
  2 Tbs. low-calorie Italian salad
  dressing

Salt and pepper
  4 cups fresh spinach, rinsed
  and trimmed
  ½ lb. spaghetti or linguine
  7 Tbs. grated Parmesan cheese

Combine all the ingredients except the spinach and cheese in a blender or in a food processor with the steel blade. Process until the parsley is minced, add the spinach, a little at a time, and process until it is finely minced.

Cook ½ lb. spaghetti or linguine, drain it, and return it to the pot.

Add the cheese and toss the pasta lightly until the cheese is melted. Add the sauce and over very low heat mix the pasta until it is well coated.

Makes 4 servings, about 345 calories each.

VARIATION

For fewer calories omit the olive oil and increase the salad dressing to 4 tablespoons; about 285 calories each serving.

LIGHT TOMATO SAUCE

2 tsp. olive oil	½ cup water or fat-skimmed
3 Tbs. olive liquid (from a jar)	undiluted chicken or beef
1 onion, finely minced	broth
1 clove garlic, minced (optional)	½ cup dry white wine or water
1 can (28 oz.) crushed tomatoes	1 or 2 tsp. oregano or basil
1 can (6 oz.) tomato paste	Salt and pepper

In a nonstick saucepan or skillet sprayed with cooking spray cook first 4 ingredients, uncovered, over moderate heat until the olive liquid evaporates and the onion begins to turn soft. Stir to prevent sticking. Do not allow onions to brown.

Stir in the remaining ingredients, mix well, simmer the mixture, covered, stirring occasionally, for 30 minutes.

Uncover and simmer the sauce a few more minutes until it is reduced to the desired thickness.

Makes 4 cups, about 70 calories per ½ cupful.

VARIATIONS

Omit the olive oil and combine all the ingredients according to the preceding directions. Only about 60 calories per ½ cup.

To make in a pressure cooker, add an additional ½ cup water. Cover and cook under pressure for 10 minutes according to the manufacturer's directions. Reduce pressure and remove cover; simmer to the desired thickness.

EASY MEAT SAUCE

¾ lb. lean ground round	¼ cup dry red or white wine or
1 onion, minced	water
1 can (16 oz.) plain tomato	1 tsp. oregano or Italian herbs
sauce	1 clove garlic, minced (optional)

In a large nonstick skillet or electric fry pan sprayed with cooking spray brown the meat in one layer over moderate heat. Discard any fat.

Add the remaining ingredients and simmer the mixture, uncovered, stirring occasionally, until the sauce is thick, about 10 to 15 minutes.

Makes 4 servings, 160 calories each.

BROCCOLI PRIMAVERA SAUCE
FOR SPAGHETTI

1 cup fat-skimmed chicken
    broth, fresh or canned
1 package (10 oz.) frozen cut
    broccoli, defrosted
1 onion
½ tsp. oregano (optional)

⅛ tsp. nutmeg
⅔ cup skim milk
1 Tbs. flour
Salt and pepper
2 Tbs. grated Parmesan cheese

In a nonstick skillet or electric fry pan heat the broth to boiling over high heat.

Add the broccoli, onion, oregano, and nutmeg and simmer the mixture, uncovered, stirring frequently, until nearly all the liquid evaporates.

Stir the milk and flour into the skillet and simmer the sauce for 3 to 4 minutes over low heat, stirring, until it is thick. Add salt and pepper to taste. Sprinkle with Parmesan.

Makes 2 servings, 150 calories each. (Recipe may be doubled or tripled.)

ITALIAN VEAL SAUCE

1 lb. lean ground veal shoulder
1 can (6 oz.) tomato paste
1 can (10 oz.) fat-skimmed beef
    or chicken broth

1 onion, finely minced
Salt, or garlic salt, and pepper
½ tsp. basil or mixed pizza herbs

In a large nonstick skillet or electric fry pan sprayed with cooking spray brown the veal over moderate heat, breaking the meat into chunks. Discard any fat.

Stir in the remaining ingredients and simmer, covered, for 10 minutes. Simmer, uncovered, stirring often, for 5 minutes, until the sauce is very thick.

Makes 4 servings, 221 calories each; add 155 calories per cupful of pasta.

SPAGHETTI SAUCE RUSTICA

2 lbs. ripe tomatoes
2 onions, finely chopped
2 ribs celery, finely minced
¾ cup minced fresh parsley
1 can (12 oz.) tomato paste
1 cup dry white wine or water

2 Tbs. fresh minced basil or
  oregano or 2 tsp. dried
Salt and pepper
1 or 2 cloves garlic, minced
  (optional)

Combine all the ingredients in a heavy nonstick pot, cover, and heat to boiling. Lower the heat and simmer the mixture for 45 minutes. Uncover and simmer until the sauce is very thick.

Makes 4 servings, about 155 calories each; with cupful of pasta, 340 calories.

PESTO SAUCE FOR PASTA OR POTATOES

1 cup part-skim ricotta cheese
1 clove garlic, peeled
1 egg or ¼ cup liquid no-cholesterol
  egg substitute
½ cup fresh parsley, fresh basil,
  or fresh spinach leaves

Salt and pepper
2 Tbs. grated low-fat Swiss-type
  cheese or Parmesan cheese
  (optional)

Have the ingredients at room temperature. Combine them in a blender or food processor. Using the steel blade, blend with on-off motions until the vegetables are chopped and the sauce is smooth. Stir into hot drained spaghetti or linguine, hot cooked sliced potatoes, or spoon onto baked potatoes.

Makes 4 servings, 110 calories each with egg; 100 calories each with egg substitute; cheese adds 15 calories per serving.

SOUR CREAM SAUCE FOR POTATOES

1 cup uncreamed low-fat
   cottage cheese
⅓ cup plain low-fat yogurt or
   buttermilk

1 to 2 Tbs. lemon juice (optional)
   ¼ cup sliced chives or scallions
Salt, or seasoned salt, and pepper
Paprika (optional)

Have the ingredients at room temperature. Combine all of the ingredients, except paprika, in a blender or food processor. Using the steel blade, blend with on-off motion until the sauce is smooth and the chives are chopped.

Stir the sauce into hot cooked sliced potatoes, or spoon onto baked potatoes (or into hot drained noodles). Sprinkle with paprika, if desired.

Makes 4 servings, 55 calories each with yogurt; 50 calories each with buttermilk.

SUGGESTED TOPPINGS FOR POTATOES

Chopped fresh herbs: parsley,
   chives, basil, dill, mint
Hot skim milk or chicken broth
   seasoned with herbs
Grated Parmesan cheese
Mock Sour Cream: low-fat cottage
   cheese and lemon juice
   whipped in the blender

Chopped onion with coarsely
   grated black pepper
Chive-spiked low-fat cottage
   cheese or plain low-fat yogurt
Equal parts sour cream and skim
   milk, blended
Mashed avocado

13

Making Light of Breakfast

and Brunch

THE ADVICE—eat a better breakfast—isn't just for kids. Studies show that breakfast skipping impairs performance at any age and for any occupation. If your brain turns fuzzy during a midmorning sales conference, the likely culprit is no breakfast, or the wrong breakfast.

A light breakfast isn't a "right" breakfast if it consists solely of coffee and sweet rolls. Caffeine and sugar may get you going, but that quick blast of energy will probably flicker out once you've dealt with the commuter crush. If you arrive at your desk tired and shaky, you need to set off on a proper breakfast.

The right light breakfast should include some protein. While we Americans usually get all the protein we need (and more) during the course of the day, we tend to overdose on protein at the wrong end of the clock, winding up the workday with big servings of protein foods just when we need them least. It would cost us less in both cash and calories to consume less meat with lunch and dinner and add more lean protein to our wake-up meal.

Unfortunately, many of the big breakfast foods are heavy in fat, sugar, calories, and cholesterol. Most traditional breakfast and brunch menus read like a diet doctor's forbidden list: eggs, bacon, sausage, French toast, pancakes, butter, jam, jelly, and syrup.

You can lighten the calories of these traditional foods without sacrificing flavor. Here are some suggestions:

Eggs—You can fry eggs, scramble them, or make an omelet in a nonstick skillet with no fat added. Simply spray the skillet well with cooking spray before the eggs are added. Set the flame a bit lower than you ordinarily would and watch the eggs carefully to prevent them from sticking. (Each tablespoon of oil you don't use saves 115 to 125 calories.) You can save even more calories and eliminate cholesterol completely by making an omelet or scrambled eggs with frozen no-cholesterol substitute. Defrost before using according to carton directions. You can save about 80 calories by using equivalent substitute instead of two eggs.

Pancakes and waffles—Among the mixes buckwheat is your best buy in terms of calories and protein. Or look for a high-protein soy-added pancake mix in the health food store. Don't add any fat or oil to the mix, regardless of the directions, and use skim milk and egg substitute if you're watching your cholesterol. Use a nonstick griddle or waffle iron, well sprayed with cooking spray, to make pancakes or waffles and stretch them by folding in berries, diced apples, or other unsweetened fruit.

French toast—This delight can also be made in a nonstick skillet sprayed with cooking spray. You can use high-fiber diet bread in place of ordinary bread and low-calorie no-cholesterol egg substitute in place of eggs. The milk should be skim, of course.

Healthful toppings—Pancakes, waffles, and French toast really don't need butter or margarine, so simply omit it and save 100 calories a tablespoon. Instead of syrup (pure sugar, pure calories) top such breakfast foods with cinnamon-spiced applesauce or crushed unsweetened pineapple, gently warmed in a saucepan. Or make your own fruit syrups.

Breakfast meats—Ordinary bacon is 69 percent fat and breakfast sausage is 50 percent fat. Use instead Canadian bacon, 980 calories per pound; lean-frying fat-reduced pork strips, 1,508 calories per pound; turkey sausage, 880 calories per pound. Or pan-fry lean smoked meats in a nonstick skillet with no fat added. For example: (per pound) cooked ham is 1,061 calories, turkey ham is 640 calories, turkey pastrami is 566 calories, and turkey bologna is 880 calories.

Muffins and breads—Using conventional recipes, these breakfast foods may be fillers with little nutritive value. Try using less shortening and sugar to make them low-cal wholesome treats.

Breakfast cereals—For a speedy start that's light on fuss and calories, consider cereal. A cupful of low-calorie high-protein Special K with a half cupful of skim milk and a half cupful of sliced strawberries, fresh blueberries, or peaches is high in health, low in calories.

Today most cereal boxes are nutritionally labeled. But comparisons are difficult to make because quantities differ, according to weight. For example, an ounce of Wheaties and an ounce of Alpen may have the same calorie counts—110—but you can consume only a quarter cupful of Alpen for those 110 calories. It takes five times as much—1¼ cups— to make up an ounce of Wheaties. Many of the new "health food" cereals contain significant amounts of added fat. Consequently, their calorie counts are relatively high. Some of the granola-type cereals are actually more fattening than the sugar-coated kidstuff types.

To help you choose, below is a checklist of how some of today's best-known cereals compare.

Note: Calculations are approximate, rounded off, based on information supplied on manufacturer's labels at the time of writing. Formulations may change, however. For the most current information on the calorie count of your favorite cereal, check the box.

"Light" Cereal Guide

ONE OUNCE OF CEREAL EQUALS:	PROTEIN GRAMS PER OZ.	FAT GRAMS PER OZ.	CARBO-HYDRATE GRAMS PER OZ.	CALORIES PER OZ.	CUPS PER OZ.	CALORIES PER CUP
Puffed Wheat, Quaker	3.80	0.40	22.4	102	2	51
Puffed Rice, Quaker	1.80	0.20	25.0	112	2	56
Kix	2.50	0.60	23.8	112	1½	75
Corn Flakes, Kellogg	2.10	0.40	24.4	105	1⅓	79
Honeycomb	1.60	0.10	25.0	108	1⅓	81
Total	2.50	0.50	23.0	101	1¼	81
Special K	5.70	0.34	20.8	109	1¼	87
Shredded Wheat, Nabisco	2.30	0.64	18.6	87	1*	(87)
Wheaties	3.00	1.00	23.0	110	1¼	88
Corn Flakes, General Mills	2.40	0.30	24.3	111	1¼	89
Cheerios	3.80	2.00	20.2	112	1¼	90
Wheat Stax	2.30	2.00	21.9	114	1¼	91
Rice Chex	1.33	0.85	24.7	112	1⅛	100
Shredded Wheat, Spoon-size	2.70	0.74	21.8	102	25*	(102)
Sugar-Frosted Mini-Wheats	2.60	0.26	23.1	105	25*	(105)
Cinnamon Mini-Wheats	2.60	0.26	23.1	105	25*	(105)
Quisp	1.30	2.70	23.1	122	1⅙	105
Product 19	2.41	0.30	23.0	106	1	106
Rice Krispies	1.84	0.09	24.8	106	1	106

*Biscuits

ONE OUNCE OF CEREAL EQUALS:	PROTEIN GRAMS PER OZ.	FAT GRAMS PER OZ.	CARBO-HYDRATE GRAMS PER OZ.	CALORIES PER OZ.	CUPS PER OZ.	CALORIES PER CUP
Pep	2.40	0.37	23.0	106	1	106
Cocoa Puffs	1.70	0.30	25.0	107	1	107
Team	1.67	0.42	24.3	107	1	107
Post Toasties	2.00	0.10	24.0	108	1	108
Clackers	1.90	2.30	22.1	108	1	108
Org-Honey Wheat Puffs	1.60	0.30	25.0	109	1	109
Buc Wheats	3.00	1.00	23.0	110	1	110
Boo Berry	1.00	1.00	23.0	110	1	110
Frankenberry	2.00	1.00	24.0	110	1	110
Count Chocula	2.00	1.00	24.0	110	1	110
Sugar Pops	1.60	0.16	25.7	110	1	110
Sugar Smacks	1.87	0.43	25.0	110	1	110
Trix	1.50	0.30	25.2	110	1	110
Lucky Charms	2.20	1.00	23.6	110	1	110
Corn Bursts	1.60	0.20	25.4	110	1	110
Sugar Jets	2.10	1.10	23.7	111	1	111
Kaboom	1.60	0.70	24.6	111	1	111
Frosty O's	2.10	1.00	23.9	111	1	111
Sugar-Sparkled Twinkles	1.90	0.80	24.2	112	1	112
Apple Jacks	1.25	0.20	25.9	112	1	112
Fruit Loops	1.70	1.10	24.7	113	1	113
Cocoa Krispies	1.30	0.62	21.5	113	1	113
Crispy Critters	2.20	1.10	23.0	113	1	113
Alpha-Bits	2.20	1.10	23.0	113	1	113
Cinnamon Crunch	1.30	2.60	22.2	117	1	117
Puffa Puffa Rice	0.85	2.60	23.9	120	1	120
All-Bran, Kellogg	3.00	1.00	19.0	60	½	120
Sugar Crisp Wheat Puffs	1.70	0.70	25.0	107	⅞	122
Fruity Pebbles	0.90	0.10	25.0	111	⅞	127
Cocoa Pebbles	0.90	0.10	25.0	111	⅞	127
Frosted Rice Krinkles	0.90	0.10	25.0	111	⅞	127
40% Bran Flakes, Kellogg	2.80	0.40	22.1	104	¾	139
Krumbles	2.80	0.21	23.0	105	¾	140
Sugar-Frosted Flakes	1.36	0.04	25.4	107	¾	143
40% Bran Flakes, Post	2.50	0.30	21.0	97	⅔	146
Grape-Nut Flakes	2.50	0.30	22.0	101	⅔	152
Vanilla Crunch	1.30	1.70	23.8	116	¾	155
Crunchberry	1.30	2.10	23.8	119	¾	159
Oat Flakes	5.10	1.30	19.0	107	⅔	161
Life	5.10	0.60	20.0	107	⅔	161
Captain Crunch	1.30	3.00	22.8	123	¾	164
Wheat Chex	3.00	1.00	23.0	110	⅔	165
Pink Panther	1.00	0.10	25.0	112	⅔	168
Peanut Butter Crunch	2.10	3.80	21.3	128	¾	171
Raisin Bran, Post	2.00	0.30	21.0	92	½	184
Cinnamon Raisin Bran, Post	2.00	0.30	21.0	92	½	184
All Bran, Kellogg	3.43	0.62	19.2	96	½	192
Bran Buds, Kellogg	3.15	0.54	19.9	98	½	196
Raisin Bran, Kellogg	2.30	0.31	22.5	100	½	200
Kellogg Concentrate	11.30	0.06	15.3	106	⅓	318
Heartland	2.07	2.55	22.0	120	⅜	320
Granola, Raisin-Nut	3.00	5.00	19.0	130	⅓	390

ONE OUNCE OF CEREAL EQUALS:	PROTEIN GRAMS PER OZ.	FAT GRAMS PER OZ.	CARBO-HYDRATE GRAMS PER OZ.	CALORIES PER OZ.	CUPS PER OZ.	CALORIES PER CUP
Nature Valley Granola	3.00	5.00	19.0	130	⅓	390
Grape-Nuts	2.50	0.10	23.0	104	¼	416
Alpen	3.50	2.00	19.0	110	¼	440
Quaker with Raisin-Nuts	2.00	5.00	17.0	120	¼	480
Granola, Honey-Almond	4.50	4.50	17.0	125	¼	500
Granola, Kretschmer	4.50	4.50	17.0	125	¼	500
Quaker 100% Natural	3.00	6.00	15.0	130	¼	520

YOGURT SCRAMBLED EGGS

3 eggs
¼ cup plain low-fat yogurt

Salt and pepper

In a bowl beat the ingredients together. In a nonstick skillet sprayed with cooking spray cook the eggs gently over low heat, lifting the edges and letting the liquid portion run beneath to set.

Makes 2 servings, 140 calories each.

HAM AND MUSHROOM FRITTATA

1 onion, minced
½ lb. fresh mushrooms, sliced thin
2 tsp. butter or margarine
1 tsp. dry white wine or water
8 eggs, lightly beaten

½ tsp. salt
Pinch of dry mustard
Pinch of pepper
1 cup diced, cooked ham
Paprika

In a nonstick skillet or large omelet pan sprayed with cooking spray combine the onion, mushrooms, butter or margarine, and wine and cook the mixture, stirring, over medium heat until the wine evaporates.

Pour the eggs over the mushroom mixture, season to taste, and spread the ham over the eggs.

Cover tightly and cook over low heat for about 10 minutes, until the eggs are set. Sprinkle with paprika, cut into wedges, and serve.

Makes 4 servings, 275 calories each.

HIGH-FIBER BREAD "PANCAKES"

2 large eggs
½ cup skim milk
1½ tsp. baking powder

4 slices high-fiber bread, wheat or white

Combine all the ingredients in a blender and blend until smooth.

Heat a nonstick griddle sprayed with cooking spray over moderate heat, pour on the batter by one-third cupfuls, and tip and turn the griddle slightly to spread it. Lower the heat.

Cook pancakes until the tops are lightly bubbled and slightly dry. Turn and cook the other sides until golden.

Makes 8 pancakes, 50 calories each.

FRUIT-FLAVORED PANCAKES

1 cup pancake mix
½ tsp. baking soda
1 egg or ¼ cup liquid no-
cholesterol substitute
¾ cup apple or other
unsweetened fruit juice

½ cup water
1 tsp. vanilla
Cinnamon or apple pie spice

In a bowl stir the pancake mix and baking soda together, add the egg, juice, ¼ cup water, and vanilla, and stir until well blended. (Add more water, if needed.)

Heat a nonstick griddle well sprayed with cooking spray over moderate heat until hot. Pour in the batter by scant quarter cupfuls and cook pancakes, turning them once. Sprinkle with spice and serve with unsweetened applesauce (50 calories per half cup).

Makes 4 brunch servings, 165 calories each, or 155 calories each with no-cholesterol egg substitute.

LIGHT WAFFLES

1 whole egg
½ cup pancake mix, regular,
　buttermilk, or whole wheat

1 tsp. salad oil
½ cup skim milk
Vanilla

In a bowl stir the ingredients together.

Preheat a nonstick waffle maker well sprayed on both sides with cooking spray. When a drop of water bounces and sizzles, pour on the batter and close.

Open the maker when waffles stop steaming.

Makes 2 servings, about 205 calories each.

VARIATIONS

Spice Waffles: Add ½ tsp. cinnamon, pinch of nutmeg and clove or allspice. (Top with hot applesauce, if desired.)

Waffle "Shortcakes": Prepare waffles as directed. Divide into 4 sections. Top each hot waffle section with ½ cup chilled sliced fresh berries or peaches (sweetened to taste, if necessary).

HIGH-FIBER FRENCH TOAST

1 egg or ¼ cup liquid no-
　cholesterol substitute
Few drops of vanilla (optional)

Salt or butter-flavored salt
2 slices high-fiber bread

Fork-blend the egg and flavorings in a small shallow bowl. Allow the bread to soak in it for 3 to 5 minutes, turning the slices, until all the egg is absorbed.

Heat a nonstick skillet sprayed with cooking spray over moderate heat. Add the bread and cook it, turning once, until both sides are golden. (This toast is so moist and flavorful, it needs no butter.) Top with 1 Tbs. Light Honey Pancake Syrup, page 166.

Each slice (plain), 90 calories, or 70 calories each with no-cholesterol substitute.

FAST APPLESAUCE

3 to 4 large cooking apples,
    peeled and thinly sliced
    ½ cup water or unsweetened

apple, white grape, or
orange juice (optional)

In a heavy saucepan combine the apples and water or juice, cover tightly, and simmer for 4 to 5 minutes. Fork-stir until chunky or whip smooth.

Makes 4 half-cup servings, 75 calories each with water, or about 90 calories each with juice.

LIGHT BUTTER

½ lb. butter, at room
  temperature
1 container (8 oz.) diet
  margarine, chilled

1 cup ice water
Dash of salt

Combine the ingredients in a mixer bowl and whip them with an electric mixer until thick and creamy. Chill, covered, in the refrigerator.

Makes 3 cups, 50 calories per Tbs.

HONEY-MAPLE SYRUP

¼ cup honey
¼ cup pure maple syrup
1 Tbs. cornstarch

Dash of salt
1 cup cold water

Blend the ingredients in a saucepan and heat, stirring, until the mixture simmers and thickens.

Makes 1½ cups, 21 calories per Tbs.

LIGHT HONEY PANCAKE SYRUP

1 Tbs. cornstarch
⅔ cup honey

Pinch of salt
1 cup cold water

Combine all the ingredients in a nonstick saucepan and cook the mixture over low heat, stirring, until it simmers.

Lower heat and simmer for 1 minute.

Makes 1⅔ cups, 25 calories per Tbs.

VARIATIONS

Maple Syrup: Add 2 tsp. maple flavoring.

"Extra-light" Syrup: Reduce the honey to ½ cup, which makes 1⅓ cups, 16 calories per Tbs.

Pineapple Syrup: Prepare Extra-Light Syrup, remove from heat, and stir in 1 can (6 oz.) defrosted undiluted pineapple juice concentrate. Makes 2 cups, 22 calories per Tbs.

Apple Juice Syrup: Follow the preceding directions, but substitute undiluted apple juice concentrate. Makes 2 cups, 21 calories per Tbs.

SAUSAGE AND MUSHROOMS

1 lb. low-fat turkey or veal bulk
  breakfast sausage, fresh or
  defrosted
1 clove garlic, minced
1 cup tomato juice

½ lb. fresh mushrooms, thinly
  sliced
2 medium onions, thinly sliced
1 green bell pepper, seeded and
  sliced into strips

In a large nonstick skillet or electric fry pan sprayed with cooking spray cook the sausage over moderate heat until the underside is brown. Break it into chunks. Turn and brown evenly. Drain any fat.

Stir in the remaining ingredients and simmer, covered, for 5 minutes. Uncover and cook, stirring frequently, until nearly all the liquid reduces to a thick sauce. (For a luncheon or supper dish, serve with soy sauce, if desired.)

Makes 4 servings, 270 calories each.

LIGHT PORK SAUSAGE

2 lb. lean ground pork
1 lb. ground raw turkey
1 level Tbs. poultry seasoning
1½ Tbs. salt
1½ tsp. pepper

Pinch of red pepper flakes
3 Tbs. red wine
1 Tbs. liquid smoke seasoning
(optional)

In a bowl combine all the ingredients and toss them lightly. Using a heaping teaspoonful, shape small flat patties.

Line a baking sheet with foil or freezer wrap and place the patties on it 1 inch apart. Freeze.

To cook, remove the desired number of patties and broil them under high heat, turning once, until they are done. Pork must be well cooked before eating.

Makes 3 pounds of sausage meat, 855 calories per pound. Makes 24 patties, 105 calories each.

COUNTRY-STYLE LIGHT VEAL SAUSAGE

2 lb. lean ground veal
1 tsp. thyme or sage or poultry
    seasoning
2 tsp. salt

1 tsp. pepper
2 Tbs. lemon juice
Dash of liquid smoke seasoning
(optional)

In a bowl combine the ingredients and toss them lightly. Shape 16 flat patties.

To pan-fry, place the patties in a cold nonstick skillet and warm slowly. Cook them over moderate heat, turning frequently. Do not press down on them with a spatula. Discard the fat.

Makes sixteen 2-oz. patties, 80 calories each.

LIGHT-AND-EASY BISQUIX MIX

6 cups sifted flour   3 Tbs. baking powder
1 Tbs. salt

Mix the ingredients and store in a covered container. No refrigeration needed!

BISQUIX

Preheat the oven to moderately hot, 425 degrees.

To 1 cup bisquix mix stir in 2 Tbs. soft butter or margarine, plus ¼ cup skim milk (enough to make a soft dough). The dough should leave the sides of the bowl and form a soft ball.

Put dough on floured board or pastry cloth and knead lightly several times. Roll dough about ½ inch thick and with a floured biscuit cutter cut rounds 1½ inches in diameter. Bake the biscuits on an ungreased baking sheet for 15 minutes, until they are golden.

Makes 8 biscuits, 80 calories each.

VARIATIONS

Substitute diet margarine and reduce the milk to 3 Tbs.; 70 calories each biscuit.

For cheese biscuits, add ¼ cup grated cheese to 1 cup of bisquix mix before adding milk; 95 calories per biscuit.

For orange biscuits, combine 1 tsp. grated orange rind with 5 Tbs. undiluted orange juice concentrate. Spoon a little of the mixture on each biscuit before baking; 100 calories per biscuit.

For drop biscuits, increase milk to ½ cup and drop dough by spoonfuls onto the ungreased baking sheet. Bake at 425 degrees for 10 to 15 minutes; 85 calories per biscuit.

BLUEBERRY CHEESE MUFFINS

¼ cup creamed cottage cheese   1¼ tsp. baking powder
1 egg   ⅓ cup skim milk
¾ cup sifted flour   2 Tbs. sugar
½ tsp. salt   1 cup fresh blueberries

Preheat the oven to moderately hot, 425 degrees.

In a bowl beat the cottage cheese and egg together.

Stir flour, salt, and baking powder together and add to cheese-egg mixture. Add the milk and the sugar and stir lightly.

Gently stir in the blueberries. Spoon the mixture into muffin paper cups or nonstick muffin tins sprayed with cooking spray and bake for 16 to 18 minutes.

Makes 10 muffins, 70 calories each.

VARIATION

Use low-fat cottage cheese and omit the sugar; 55 calories per muffin.

LIGHT-AND-EASY JOHNNYCAKES

½ cup sifted flour   1 tsp. salt
½ cup yellow cornmeal   1 egg
1 tsp. baking powder   ½ cup creamed cottage cheese
½ tsp. baking soda   ⅓ to ¾ cup water

Preheat fry pan or griddle.

In a bowl mix all the ingredients together, adding more water if needed.

Pour the batter on fry pan or griddle sprayed with cooking spray to make 4-inch-diameter pancakes. When they bubble, turn to brown.

Makes 8 pancakes, 80 calories each.

VARIATION

Use 99 percent fat-free cottage cheese and use 2 egg whites or ¼ cup liquid no-cholesterol substitute; 65 calories each.

RAISIN BRAN LOAF

3 cups sifted flour	1 cup whole bran cereal
1 tsp. salt	6 Tbs. raisins
4 tsp. baking powder	2 eggs
3 Tbs. sugar	1 cup skim milk

Preheat the oven to moderate, 375 degrees.

In a bowl sift the flour, salt, and baking powder together. Stir in the sugar, cereal, and raisins. Beat the eggs and milk together and stir into the batter, only until mixed.

Pour the batter into a nonstick bread pan and bake it for 50 minutes.

Makes 20 slices, ⅜-inch thick, 100 calories each.

APPLE-RAISIN MUFFINS

3 slices slightly stale low-calorie high-fiber bread, wheat or white, diced	½ tsp. baking soda
	1 tsp. apple pie spice
	1 cup applesauce
1 cup instant non-fat dry milk	2 eggs
½ tsp. baking powder	4 Tbs. raisins

Preheat the oven to moderate, 375 degrees.

Combine the bread and the dry ingredients in a blender and blend until the bread is crumbed.

Add the remaining ingredients, except raisins, and blend thoroughly. Stir in the raisins.

Spoon into nonstick muffin cups sprayed with cooking spray. Bake for 25 minutes, or until they are golden brown.

Makes 12 muffins, 75 calories each.

VARIATION

Use unsweetened applesauce and omit the raisins; 60 calories each.

LIGHT HOT CHOCOLATE

1½ Tbs. unsweetened cocoa	½ cup instant nonfat dry milk
Pinch of salt	2 cups cold water
Pinch of cornstarch	½ tsp. vanilla

Combine the dry ingredients in a saucepan. Stir in the water and cook over moderate heat, stirring, until the mixture simmers and is smooth.

Remove from heat and stir in the vanilla.

Makes 3 servings, 75 calories each.

VARIATION

To make in a blender, omit the cornstarch. Combine the dry ingredients and add boiling water. Blend until smooth.

14

Sandwiches and Other Bread-Based Meals

EVER SINCE the Earl of Sandwich put his main course between two slices of bread so that he could make a quick getaway from the table, sandwiches have been the quintessential light meal. Unfortunately, many are heavy in calories and uninspired in flavor.

It's generally the filling, not the bread, that makes sandwiches a "heavy" choice for the figure-conscious. (The carbohydrate-counting craze of a decade ago still has people believing that bread is the culprit. Luncheonette menus continue to feature the trite "diet plate" with bread removed: usually a greasy fried hamburger, creamed cottage cheese, and canned peaches in sugar syrup . . . 500 calories or more!) Ironically, many of the choices on the regular sandwich menu are more slimming: roast beef, ham, or sliced turkey, for example. Even egg or tuna salad made with regular mayonnaise can weigh in at a lower calorie count than the ubiquitous hamburger–cottage cheese diet plate.

There's no need to avoid the convenience of sandwich meals just because you want to lighten your calorie intake. Trimming calories from America's favorite meal is easy. Consider:

Breads

Regular white bread is about 70 calories a slice; dark breads are about the same, but the slices are often larger.

High-fiber bread is only about 50 calories a slice. It's more satisfying because the fiber is more filling.

Sandwich-thin slices or melba-thin bread is about 55 calories a slice. You can make slim slices by buying bread unsliced.

Diet or protein bread is usually lower in calories, but not always. Look for the calorie counts on the label. Some brands are as low as 40 to 50 calories a slice.

Gluten bread is made from a special low-starch flour and is available in small thin sandwich slices at about 35 calories each.

True French and Italian breads are made without shortening, sugar, or eggs, so the calories are lower than an equivalent slice of regular bread. Unfortunately, most labels don't give calorie information, but they do list ingredients. Avoid French breads that list anything other than flour, salt, yeast, and water.

Pita bread, or pocket bread, is another low-calorie alternative. The dough is essentially the same as French and Italian bread, with no added shortening, sugar, or eggs.

Hard rolls and hamburger and hot dog rolls can be made light by removing some of the doughy center.

Fillings

Many sandwich fillings, including most cold cuts and deli meats, most hard cheese, and all salad fillings made with mayonnaise, add unnecessary calories. Here are some lighter alternatives.

Use lean roast meat and poultry, such as roast beef, turkey breast, and boiled ham.

Use turkey alternatives to deli meats: turkey bologna, turkey pastrami, turkey salami, turkey ham—all cured and seasoned the same way as the more fattening beef and pork products.

Use homemade salad fillings made with low-calorie mayonnaise.

Use diet or part-skim cheese instead of hard cheese and lighten cheese calories by as much as half.

This section makes light of sandwiches and other bread-based meals.

EGG SALAD SANDWICH FILLING

4 hard-cooked eggs, chopped
1½ cups low-fat small-curd
  cottage cheese
½ cup finely chopped celery

2 tsp. Worcestershire sauce
2 tsp. prepared mustard
Salt and pepper to taste
Paprika (optional)

In a bowl combine the ingredients. Chill before using.

Makes eight ⅜-cup servings, 75 calories each.

COTTAGE TUNA SANDWICH SPREAD

½ cup low-fat uncreamed
  cottage cheese
1 can (3½ oz.) water-packed
  tuna, drained

2 Tbs. low-fat mayonnaise
3 Tbs. minced celery
2 Tbs. chopped scallions

Mash all of the ingredients together with a fork or combine them in a food processor with the plastic blade and mix with quick on-off motions, just until blended. Chill until serving time.

Fills 3 sandwiches, 100 calories each (spread only).

CHEESE AND OLIVE SPREAD

1 cup plain low-fat pot cheese
  (uncreamed cottage cheese)
2 Tbs. olive liquid (from the jar)

Dash of Tabasco sauce (optional)
¼ cup Spanish stuffed green
  olives, finely minced

Combine all of the ingredients, except the olives, in a food blender or a food processor, using the metal blade. Cover and blend until smooth. Fold in the minced olives. Chill.

Makes about 1¼ cups, 9 calories per Tbs.

SALAMI SALAD SANDWICH FILLING

1 cup low-fat cottage cheese
3 slices (3 oz.) turkey salami or
turkey bologna, minced

2 Tbs. dill pickle relish
Salt, or onion salt, and pepper

Combine all of the ingredients and refrigerate several hours, if possible, for the flavors to blend.

Makes enough for 4 sandwiches, 95 calories each (filling only).

HAM AND EGG SALAD SANDWICH FILLING

½ cup minced cooked ham
(boiled ham)
3 hard-cooked eggs, peeled and
chopped

5 Tbs. minced celery
2 Tbs. dill pickle relish
1 Tbs. low-fat mayonnaise
Salt and pepper

Combine all of the ingredients and refrigerate for several hours, if possible, for the flavors to blend.

Makes enough for 4 sandwiches, 115 calories each (filling only).

PRIMAVERA SANDWICH SPREAD

1 cup low-fat large-curd cottage
cheese
½ tsp. caraway seed
½ small carrot, raw, shredded

2 radishes, shredded
Onion salt and pepper
1 sprig parsley, minced
(optional)

Combine all of the ingredients and refrigerate for a few hours, if possible, for the flavors to blend. Serve on melba-thin slices of rye or pumpernickel bread.

Makes enough for 4 sandwiches, 55 calories each (spread only).

LIGHT-AND-EASY GRILLED HAM AND CHEESE SANDWICH

2 slices high-fiber bread
2 tsp. prepared sharp mustard
  (optional)
2 thin slices (1½ oz.) low-
  calorie cheese

2 slices (2 oz.) lean cooked ham
  (boiled ham)

Lightly spread the bread with the mustard, if desired. Place a slice of cheese on each bread slice. Top with the sliced ham and close the sandwich.

Spray a nonstick skillet well with cooking spray or spray both sides of a two-sided nonstick electric sandwich grill. Place the sandwich on a cold grill or skillet.(If using a skillet, weight the sandwich by placing a small pot on top of it.) Cook it slowly over low heat (or on the low setting of the electric grill). Turn the sandwich with a spatula to brown the other side.

Each sandwich, 300 calories (mustard adds about 10 calories).

VARIATIONS

Low-fat turkey bologna, turkey salami, or turkey pastrami may be substituted for the ham; 20 calories less with turkey bologna or turkey salami, 60 calories less with turkey pastrami.

Or try a grilled chicken-cheese sandwich, substituting chicken roll for the ham; 40 calories less.

HAMBURGERS ORIENTALE

1 lb. lean ground round
1 can (2 oz.) mushroom pieces,
  drained and chopped

Pinch of cayenne
½ tsp. ground ginger
2 Tbs. soy sauce

In a bowl combine all the ingredients, except the soy sauce. Shape the mixture into 4 patties, broil over coals or under a broiler, turning them once, and basting liberally with the soy sauce.

Makes 4 servings, 160 calories each.

LIGHT REUBEN SANDWICH

2 slices melba-thin seeded rye
    bread
2 Tbs. low-calorie Thousand
    Island salad dressing
2 oz. lean corned beef round,
    thinly sliced

2 Tbs. well-drained sauerkraut
    or thinly sliced dill pickles
2 thin slices (1 oz.) low-fat
    Swiss-style cheese or part-
    skim mozzarella

Spread the bread lightly with the salad dressing. Top each slice of bread with corned beef, a tablespoon of sauerkraut or wafer-thin pickle slices, and a slice of cheese. Slip the open sandwich halves under the broiler until they are heated through and the cheese is melted. Serve with a knife and fork or put the sandwich halves together and slice into quarters.

Each sandwich, 265 calories.

GREEK BURGERS

1 lb. lean ground lamb
1 small onion, finely chopped
1 tsp. garlic salt
¼ tsp. cinnamon

¼ tsp. nutmeg
1 tsp. dried mint or oregano
1 cup plain tomato juice

In a bowl combine the meat with the seasonings and add just enough tomato juice to moisten the mixture. Shape into 4 patties.
    Broil over coals or under a broiler, turning them once and basting with the remaining tomato juice.

Makes 4 servings, about 170 calories each.

ROQUEFORT BURGERS

1 lb. lean ground round
1 small onion, minced

1 cup low-calorie Roquefort
    salad dressing

In a bowl combine the ingredients. Shape into 4 patties. Broil over coals or under a broiler, turning them once.

Makes 4 servings, 190 calories each.

TEXAS BURGERS

1 lb. lean ground beef round
1 tsp. onion salt
1 tsp. chili powder
4 Tbs. chopped green bell
pepper

¾ cup (6-oz. can) plain or spicy
tomato juice
2 slices (2 oz.) regular or diet
American-style cheese, halved

In a bowl combine the meat, seasonings, and pepper. Shape into 4 patties. Broil over coals or under a broiler, turning them once and basting frequently with tomato juice. Top each burger with a piece of cheese at the last minute and return to the broiler until it melts.

Makes 4 servings, 215 calories each with regular cheese, or 190 calories each with diet cheese.

BEEFBURGERS IN PITA POCKETS

1 lb. lean ground beef round
Garlic salt and pepper
¼ tsp. cinnamon
¼ tsp. nutmeg
1 tsp. marjoram
½ tsp. basil or oregano
2 Tbs. lemon juice

2 medium pita breads, halved
and split open
1 small onion, thinly sliced
1 small tomato, thinly sliced
½ small cucumber, thinly sliced
4 tsp. minced fresh parsley

Season the beef with salt, pepper, spices, and herbs. Shape into 4 patties.

Broil over coals or under a broiler, basting with the lemon juice.

Fill each pita pocket with a burger and top it with sliced onions, tomato, cucumber, and parsley.

Makes 4 servings, 250 calories each.

VARIATION

Substitute lean ground lamb. Makes 4 servings, 250 calories each.

BEEFBURGER AND SPROUTS IN PITA POCKETS

6 oz. lean ground beef round, shaped into 2 patties
2 Tbs. soy sauce
Garlic salt and pepper to taste
1 5-inch pita bread, halved and split open
2 Tbs. chopped scallions or raw onion
½ cup chopped fresh bean sprouts
2 Tbs. catsup

Season the hamburgers with the soy sauce, garlic salt, and pepper as they broil.

Fill each pita pocket with a burger and top it with onion and sprouts. Garnish with catsup and additional soy sauce, if desired.

Makes 2 servings, 235 calories each.

PITA TACOS

4 small (1 oz. each) or 2 medium (2 oz. each) pita breads
½ lb. lean ground beef bottom round
1 can (8 oz.) stewed tomatoes, broken up
4 Tbs. chopped onion
4 Tbs. chopped bell pepper
Garlic salt and pepper
1 tsp. chili powder (or to taste)
1 cup shredded iceberg lettuce
4 Tbs. shredded sharp cheese

Split the pita breads into half-moons.

Break up the beef in a nonstick skillet which has been sprayed with cooking spray. Cook and stir over high heat until the meat is browned. Drain and discard any fat.

Add the tomatoes, onion, bell pepper, and seasonings. Cook and stir over high heat until most of the liquid has evaporated.

Stuff the mixture into pita bread pockets, dividing it evenly. Add the lettuce and cheese.

Makes 4 servings, 285 calories each.

MUSHROOM BURGERS IN PITA POCKETS

6 oz. lean ground beef round,
  shaped into 2 patties
Pinch of poultry seasoning
Salt and pepper
1 5-inch pita bread, halved and
  split open

¼ cup chopped onion
½ cup sliced fresh mushrooms
¼ cup dry white wine

Brown the hamburgers quickly in a small nonstick skillet over high heat, seasoning them with the seasonings. Discard any fat.

Fill each pita pocket with a burger. Combine the remaining ingredients in the skillet and cook over high heat, stirring, for 1 minute. Spoon the mixture over the hamburgers.

Makes 2 servings, 215 calories each.

FRENCH BREAD PIZZA WITH EVERYTHING ON IT

1 long skinny loaf French or
  Italian bread
1 onion, sliced
1 green bell pepper, seeded and
  sliced crosswise
1 cup sliced fresh mushrooms
1 clove garlic, minced (optional)

1½ cups plain tomato sauce
½ cup shredded part-skim
  mozzarella cheese
2 Tbs. grated sharp Romano
  cheese (optional)
Salt, pepper, oregano, basil, red
  pepper flakes to taste

Preheat the oven to moderately hot, 425 degrees.

Halve the bread lengthwise, and pull out the doughy center, leaving only the crust.

Layer the vegetables on the hollowed-out loaves, sprinkle with garlic, if desired, and spoon on the tomato sauce. Sprinkle with the mozzarella and Romano, if desired, and seasonings.

Bake the crusts, uncovered, on a shallow nonstick baking pan or sheet sprayed with cooking spray for 20 minutes.

To serve, slice each in half.

Makes 4 servings, about 195 calories each; optional ingredients add about 15 calories each serving.

VARIATIONS

Mexican Chicken Pizza: Dice ½ lb. raw chicken cutlets (or turkey steaks) into 1-inch cubes and use in place of the mushrooms. Substitute 1 tsp. cumin seeds or ½ tsp. ground cumin for the basil (or omit cumin and red pepper flakes and season with chili powder to taste). 250 calories per serving.

French Bread Sausage Pizza: Shape ¼ lb. low-fat turkey or veal breakfast sausage into tiny meatballs and use in place of the mushrooms. Sprinkle with 1 tsp. fennel seeds, if desired. 240 calories per serving.

French Bread Salami Pizza: Cube ¼ lb. low-fat turkey salami (if using presliced turkey salami, cut it into julienne strips) and use in place of the mushrooms. 240 calories per serving.

French Bread Pizza Marinara: Drain and flake a 6½- or 7-oz. can of water-packed solid white meat tuna and use in place of the mushrooms. Sprinkle lightly with lemon juice; 245 calories per serving. (Tiny shrimp or crab meat can also be used. With shrimp, 225 calories per serving; with crab meat, 240 calories per serving.)

Raider's Pizza: Raid the refrigerator and use thinly sliced zucchini, thinly sliced green stuffed olives, crumbled cooked leftover hamburger, lean thinly sliced roast beef, diced vine-ripe tomatoes, diced cooked white meat poultry, lean deli meats, other shredded low-fat cheese.

Italian Bread Pizza Pie: Use a round loaf of Italian bread or a round doughnut-shaped bread with a hole in the center. Halve it and pull out the doughy center, leaving only the thin crust. Fill with thinly sliced fresh vegetables, top with plain tomato sauce, shredded part-skim mozzarella, and Italian herbs, as desired. Bake for 20 minutes in a preheated moderately hot 425-degree oven.

MINUTE STEAK SANDWICHES

For each serving:
   3 oz. thinly sliced lean beef
     round ("minute steaks" or
     "sandwich steaks")
Meat tenderizer, plain or seasoned
   2 slices high-fiber bread,
     toasted, or 1 small (1-oz.) pita
     bread

Thin slice raw onion (optional)
   1 slice tomato (optional)
   4 thin pickle slices (optional)

Moisten the minute steak with warm water. Sprinkle with the meat tenderizer and pound with a studded meat mallet. Turn steak and repeat. Wait 15 to 20 minutes. Spray a nonstick skillet with cooking spray until slick. Heat the skillet over a high flame. Add the steaks and sear quickly on both sides (steaks should be medium-rare; total cooking time about 1 minute).

Serve each steak between the toasted fiber bread slices or in split pita bread circles. Top as desired with sliced onion, tomato, pickle.

Each 3-oz. steak, 115 calories. Bread adds 50 calories per slice of high-fiber bread, or 80 calories per 1-oz. pita bread.

15

Entertaining

TODAY, every host and hostess can be sure that at least some of the people on the guest list will be looking for slimmer alternatives to the usual calorie-laden party fare . . . for lighter, less alcoholic ways to socialize. It's hospitable to be able to offer both: the expected, and the unexpectedly light. At the very least it's self-defense! You'll be less tempted by the calorie-rich cheese spreads you've set out for your guests if you've also got a tray of crisp vegetable chips and spicy low-fat dips. And don't be surprised if the healthy stuff is more popular.

In this chapter I've collected some ideas for light entertaining: buffet dishes for a crowd and dips for more casual get-togethers.

Calorie-Light Dip Bases

Instead of sour cream at nearly 1,000 calories a pint or cream cheese at 850 an 8-ounce package, whip up your own low-fat dip base at only one-half or one-third the calories. Try these out in your blender:

- Combine 2 cups small-curd cottage cheese and ½ cup buttermilk and blend until smooth.
- Combine 2 cups small-curd cottage cheese, 2 Tbs. lemon juice, and ½ cup skim milk and blend until smooth.

- Combine 2 cups dry-curd cottage cheese and 1 cup plain low-fat yogurt and blend until smooth.
- Put plain low-fat yogurt in a paper coffee filter cone and allow it to drain in the refrigerator for several hours until it reaches the right thickness.
- Combine 1 cup sour half-and-half and 1 cup plain low-fat yogurt and blend until smooth.
- Combine a softened 3-oz. package cream cheese with 1 cup part-skim ricotta cheese and blend until smooth.
- Combine an 8-oz. package low-fat "imitation" cream cheese with 1 cup skim milk and blend until smooth.
- Combine an 8-oz. package Neufchatel cheese with 1 cup skim milk and blend until smooth.
- Combine a 3-oz. package cream cheese with 1 cup large-curd creamed cottage cheese and ½ cup skim milk and blend until smooth.

To one cup of base, add any of the following:

- Garlic Dip: 1 garlic clove, minced, or ⅛ tsp. instant garlic, plus 1 tsp. salt and 2 Tbs. chopped fresh parsley.
- Onion Dip: 1 Tbs. dry onion flakes and 1 envlope (or teaspoon) instant beef broth.
- Mexican Dip: 1 Tbs. each of minced green bell pepper, minced red bell pepper, and chili sauce and ½ tsp. onion salt.
- Blue Cheese Dip: Freeze a chunk of blue cheese, then grate it. Stir in 2 Tbs. of cheese, 1 tsp. Worcestershire sauce, 1 tsp. garlic salt.
- Monterey Dip: Freeze a chunk of extra-sharp Monterey Jack or American cheese, then grate it. Add 5 Tbs. grated cheese, 2 Tbs. minced red or green bell pepper, 1 Tbs. minced onion, and ½ tsp. salt.
- Seafood Dip: 5 Tbs. chili sauce, 2 Tbs. lemon juice, 1 Tbs. grated onion, 1 or more tsp. prepared horseradish, and ½ tsp. garlic salt.
- Curry Dip: 5 Tbs. low-fat light mayonnaise, 1 Tbs. granulated sugar substitute or 2 tsp. honey, ½ tsp. salt, and 1 tsp. curry powder.

Or try this:

- Combine your favorite dip base with a half packet of dry salad dressing mix—green goddess, garlic French, cheese-Italian, blue cheese, smoky bacon, and so on.

Guide to Party Calories

Say nuts to nuts! They're half fat. Macadamia nuts are the worst, 18 calories each! If you must, choose dry-roasted peanuts or soy nuts (neither are really nuts . . . they're beans!)

Cheese and crackers: Ordinary saltines, at 12 calories each, are less fattening than crackers with more oil or fat. Most "natural" cheeses range between 105 and 110 calories an ounce. Processed cheese, 100 and 105 an ounce. Spreads (they contain some moisture), 65 and 80 per ounce.

Part-skim, low-fat, and "diet" cheeses can vary widely; some have only half the calories of regular cheese, while others are nearly as fattening. Check the lablels.

Chips and dips: Potato chips are about 8 calories apiece. Skinny salted pretzel sticks are 1 calorie each. A whole cupful of unbuttered popcorn, flavored with butter salt, is only 25 calories.

Dips depend on the base. Onion dip made with sour cream is about 35 calories per level tablespoon, but only 12 calories when made with plain yogurt. With cream cheese, a whopping 58! Commercial ready-to-use dips are 25 to 30.

Nibbles and noshes: For small shrimp, 10 each; large shrimp, 20; cocktail franks, 50 each; herring, 50 calories an ounce; caviar, 42 per tablespoon; liver paste, 45 per tablespoon; medium olives, about 6 each.

Here's the news on booze; remember, the higher the proof, the higher the calories; 100-proof liquor is 125 calories per 1½-ounce shot; 94-proof, 115; 90-proof, 110; 86-proof, 105.

Nix on sweet mixers: Regular ginger ale and tonic are 85 calories per 8 ounces; cola, 7-Up, and Sprite, between 95 and 100. Sugar-free mixers (Fresca, 7-Up, ginger ale, etc.) have only a trace. Bitter Lemon is one of the most fattening, 128 calories. Fruit juices can be even higher.

What about water? Calorically speaking, it's free, although today it's considered trendy to pay for it. (In blindfold taste tests, many people prefer club soda from the supermarket to fancy-priced imports.) If you resent paying for—and hauling home—high-priced water in snobby bottles, why not make your own! If you want fizz, check the housewares department for a gadget that allows you to charge water (and other beverages) with bubbles.

Go light on beer: Regular beer and ale average around 150 calories per 12-ounce can or bottle; "light" beers can vary from a low of 70 calories (Olympia Gold) to a high of 134 (Michelob Light). Most average around 100, but check the label.

The word on wine: Wine calories depend on the sugar content and the concentration of alcohol. The lighter (lower proof) and dryer (less sweet) the wine is, the fewer calories. A sweet dessert wine like sherry or port can be as high as 150 calories for a 3-ounce glass. Light dry table wines can be half that. Wine labels will probably never have calorie counts but take a clue from the alcohol content listed on the label and choose a relatively low-alcohol wine. Also, try "spritzers"—light, tall drinks of dry wine served over ice, diluted with sparkling water. Beware commercially bottled sangria (wine and fruit juice). It generally has added sugar and averages around 100 calories per 3 ounces.

Nonalcoholic Party Drinks

BITTER ORANGE SPRITZ

1 juice orange, squeezed
6 to 8 oz. sparkling water

Dash of bitters (optional)

Combine with ice cubes in a tall glass; about 75 calories.

GRAPE SPRITZ

¼ cup bottled undiluted grape juice

¼ lemon, squeezed (optional)
6 to 8 oz. sparkling water

Combine with ice cubes in a tall glass; about 40 calories.

POLYNESIAN SPRITZ

⅓ cup unsweetened canned pineapple, apricot, peach, or mango juice

6 to 8 oz. sparkling water

Combine with ice cubes in a tall glass. Pineapple or peach, 40 calories; mango, 45 calories; apricot, 25 calories.

CIDER SPRITZ

2 Tbs. undiluted cider   6 to 8 oz. sparkling water
  concentrate, defrosted

Combine with ice cubes in a tall glass; 60 calories

Other fruit spritzes to make with juice concentrate: pineapple, 65 calories; orange or tangerine, 55 calories; grapefruit, 50 calories.

HAWAIIAN SPRITZ

2 Tbs. undiluted orange juice   ½ cup sparkling water
  concentrate, defrosted
¼ cup unsweetened pineapple
  juice

Combine with ice cubes in a tall glass; 95 calories.

Dips and Hors d'Oeuvres

COTTAGE CHEESE CHILI DIP

½ cup low-fat cottage cheese or   1 tsp. oregano
  part-skim ricotta   1 tsp. ground cumin
¼ cup chili sauce   Salt to taste
1 tsp. Tabasco   ½ cup plain low-fat yogurt

In a small mixing bowl beat the cottage cheese and chili sauce together until fairly smooth. Beat in the seasonings.
  Fold in the yogurt. Cover and chill.

Makes about 1¼ cups, 11 calories per Tbs. with cottage cheese, or 15 calories per Tbs. with ricotta.

LIGHT CALIFORNIA DIP

1 cup 99% fat-free small-curd cottage cheese or part-skim ricotta

¼ cup skim milk
½ of a 1½-oz. package dehydrated onion soup

In a blender, blend the ingredients until smooth. Refrigerate for 30 minutes before serving. (May be thinned more with milk if desired.)

Makes 1¼ cups, 13 calories per Tbs. with cottage cheese, or 22 calories per Tbs. with ricotta.

CURRIED COTTAGE CHEESE DIP

1 cup low-fat cottage cheese or part-skim ricotta
½ tsp. salt
¾ tsp. curry powder

2 Tbs. water
1 tsp. lemon juice
¼ cup sweet pickle relish

In a blender blend all the ingredients, except the relish, until smooth.

Stir in the relish. Serve with raw vegetables or salad greens.

Makes 1¼ cups, 12 calories per Tbs. with cottage cheese, or 21 calories per Tbs. with ricotta.

CREAMY CURRY DIP

½ cup plain or pineapple low-fat yogurt
4 Tbs. low-fat mayonnaise
5 Tbs. low-calorie French dressing

3 Tbs. unsweetened orange juice concentrate, defrosted
¼ tsp. pumpkin pie spice
1 to 2 tsp. curry powder (or to taste)

In a bowl combine the ingredients. Serve with cubes of ham or turkey, pear cubes dipped in lemon juice, green grapes, pineapple chunks, melon balls, tangerine sections, or orange chunks.

Makes 2 cups dip, 11 calories per Tbs., with pineapple yogurt, 12 calories per Tbs.

COTTAGE CHEESE GARLIC DIP

1 cup low-fat cottage cheese or
  part-skim ricotta
2 Tbs. chopped fresh parsley

1 small clove garlic
1 Tbs. grated onion
Salt and pepper to taste

In a blender or in a food processor with the steel blade blend the ingredients until smooth. Cover and chill.

Serve with raw vegetables, crackers, or chips.

Makes 1 cup, 11 calories per Tbs. with cottage cheese, or 22 calories per Tbs. with ricotta.

SEAFOOD DIP

1 cup chili sauce
¼ cup lemon or lime juice
¼ cup prepared horseradish

1 Tbs. Worcestershire sauce
2 Tbs. minced onion or 2 tsp.
  instant onion

Combine all of the ingredients and chill. Serve with cold cooked shrimp, crab fingers, or small scallops speared on toothpicks.

Makes about 1½ cups, 14 calories per Tbs.

TUNA COTTAGE CHEESE DIP

2 cups low-fat creamed cottage
  cheese or part-skim ricotta
1 clove garlic
1 can (6½ or 7 oz.) water-
  packed solid white tuna,
  drained
1 Tbs. minced onion

1 Tbs. lemon juice
1 Tbs. prepared horseradish
¼ tsp. Worcestershire sauce
¼ tsp. hot pepper sauce
2 Tbs. low-fat mayonnaise
Salt, or celery salt, and pepper to
  taste

In a blender or in a food processor with the steel blade blend all the ingredients until smooth.

Makes 2½ cups, 15 calories per Tbs. with cottage cheese, or 24 calories per Tbs. with ricotta.

ROQUEFORT DIP

8 oz. low-calorie cream cheese,
 softened
¼ cup crumbled Roquefort
 cheese

½ cup plain low-fat yogurt
2 tsp. lemon juice
Salt to taste

In a small mixing bowl beat the cheese together until fairly smooth.
Beat in the yogurt, lemon juice, and salt. Cover and chill.

Makes about 1¾ cups, 21 calories per Tbs.

PRIMAVERA DIP

1 cup part-skim ricotta cheese
1 cup plain low-fat yogurt
2 Tbs. finely grated carrot
1 Tbs. finely grated onion
2 tsp. finely grated green bell
 pepper

1 tsp. salt
⅛ tsp. garlic powder
Dash of pepper or Tabasco

Beat the ricotta and yogurt together in a small mixing bowl. Blend
in the carrot, onion, bell pepper, salt, garlic, and pepper or Tabasco.
Cover and chill. Use as a dip for raw vegetables.

Makes about 2 cups, 15 calories per Tbs.

BRAUNSCHWEIGER SPREAD

¼ lb. Braunschweiger or
 liverwurst
1 cup 99% fat-free pot cheese
 or dry cottage cheese
1 packet (1½ oz.) dry onion
 soup mix

Generous dash of Worcestershire
 sauce
3 Tbs. dill pickle relish (or to
 taste)

Combine all of the ingredients in a blender or food processor. Using the steel blade, blend smooth. Refrigerate until serving time. Serve with saltine crackers.

Makes 2 cups, 23 calories per Tbs.

CHICKEN OR TURKEY CURRY SPREAD

1 cup finely minced cooked
white meat chicken or turkey
3 Tbs. low-fat mayonnaise
2 Tbs. low-fat yogurt, plain or
lemon

1 Tbs. dill pickle relish
½ tsp. curry powder (or to taste)

Combine all of the ingredients and chill.

Makes 1 cup, 25 calories per Tbs.

BLUE CHEESE WINE SPREAD

¼ cup (2 oz.) blue cheese
1 package (8 oz.) low-calorie
cream cheese, softened
1 clove garlic, minced
3 Tbs. plain low-fat yogurt
1 tsp. Worcestershire sauce

2 tsp. lemon juice
2 Tbs. Chablis or other dry
white wine
Salt and pepper
Paprika (optional)

Combine all of the ingredients, except the paprika, in a food processor. Blend smooth, using the steel blade. Cover and chill. Spread on crackers. Sprinkle with paprika, if desired.

Makes 1¾ cups, 24 calories per Tbs.

CHEESE BALL

3 cups (12 oz.) shredded extra-
sharp cheddar cheese
½ cup low-fat cottage cheese
½ cup plain low-fat yogurt

½ tsp. Worcestershire sauce
¼ cup minced ripe olives
½ cup chopped fresh parsley

In a small mixing bowl beat all the cheese together until smooth. Add the yogurt and Worcestershire sauce and beat until creamy. Stir in the olives. Cover and chill.

Shape into a ball and roll in parsley. Refrigerate.

Let the ball come to room temperature before serving.

Makes 3 cups, 35 calories per Tbs.

MARINATED MUSHROOMS

1 lb. fresh mushrooms
4 cups water
2 Tbs. white vinegar
¼ cup chopped onion
2 Tbs. chopped fresh parsley

3 Tbs. lemon juice
2 tsp. sugar (optional)
¼ tsp. thyme
Salt and pepper to taste
¾ cup plain low-fat yogurt

In a saucepan simmer the mushrooms in the water and vinegar for 10 minutes, covered. Drain and cool.

In a bowl, combine the remaining ingredients. Stir in the mushrooms. Chill, covered, for several hours or overnight.

Makes 8 servings, 35 calories each.

HOLIDAY RAW MUSHROOMS

1 lb. small white fresh
mushrooms
½ cup part-skim ricotta cheese
1 Tbs. chopped green bell
pepper
1 Tbs. chopped red sweet
pepper or canned pimiento

2 Tbs. chopped scallion or
onion
Pinch of oregano
Salt and pepper

Wash mushrooms and remove the stems. Chop the stems finely and stir with remaining ingredients. Season to taste, then spoon the filling into the mushroom caps. Chill.

Makes 8 servings, 40 calories each.

CHEESE-STUFFED MUSHROOMS

1 lb. fresh mushrooms
1 small onion, minced
2 tsp. butter or margarine
1 Tbs. minced parsley

4 Tbs. low-fat cottage cheese
3 Tbs. seasoned bread crumbs
Salt, or garlic salt, and pepper

Wash mushrooms, remove and chop stems. In a nonstick skillet combine the chopped stems with onion and butter and stir over medium heat until the liquid evaporates and the mixture is tender. Add the mushroom-onion mixture to the parsley, cheese, and bread crumbs; mix well. Season to taste.

Stuff the filling into the mushroom caps and arrange them on a broiling pan. Broil until the filling is lightly browned.

Makes 8 servings, 45 calories each.

TUNA-STUFFED MUSHROOMS

1 lb. fresh mushrooms
1 can (7 oz.) water-packed
   tuna, flaked
3 Tbs. diet mayonnaise

1 Tbs. minced celery
1 Tbs. minced onion
1 Tbs. chopped parsley

Wash the mushrooms and remove the stems. Chop the stems and mix them well with the remaining ingredients. Stuff the filling into the raw mushroom caps and chill.

Makes 8 servings, 55 calories each.

TUNA PÂTÉ

1 package (8 oz.) low-fat cream
  cheese
3 Tbs. chili sauce
3 Tbs. minced fresh parsley

1 Tbs. minced scallions or
  onion
2 cans (6½ oz. each) water-
  packed tuna, drained

In a food processor, using the steel blade, blend all of the ingredients until smooth. Pack into a 4-cup round-bottom bowl. Cover and chill several hours. Unmold onto a bed of lettuce.

Makes 3½ cups, 17 calories per Tbs.

STUFFED EGGS

1 doz. hard-cooked eggs halved
  lengthwise
¼ cup low-fat mayonnaise

2 tsp. Dijon-style mustard (or to
  taste)
½ tsp. Worcestershire sauce

Remove the yolks and in a bowl mash them with the remaining ingredients. Season to taste. Spoon the mixture into the whites or use a pastry bag, fitted with a decorative tip. Sprinkle with paprika, if desired, or garnish with sprigs of parsley, pimiento strips, or thinly sliced pitted olives.

Makes 24 servings, 45 calories each ungarnished, or 50 calories each garnished.

MEATBALLS CHABLIS

½ cup fine bread crumbs
¼ cup Chablis or other dry
  white wine
1 lb. lean beef round, ground
1 egg, slightly beaten

½ tsp. salt or seasoned salt
¼ tsp. freshly ground black
  pepper
2 Tbs. chopped parsley
1 Tbs. minced onion

Preheat the broiler.

Combine all of the ingredients and mix well. Shape into 1-inch balls. Broil on the highest rack until the meatballs are browned. Turn; brown the other side. Serve on picks.

Makes 25 meatballs, 35 calories each.

CURRIED BEEF BALLS WITH FRUIT

1 egg, lightly beaten
⅔ cup skim milk
1½ tsp. salt
2 tsp. curry powder

1 cup loosely packed soft bread
  crumbs
¼ cup onion, finely chopped
1½ lb. lean ground beef round

In a bowl combine the egg, milk, spices, bread crumbs, and onion, blend well, and add the beef, mixing well.

Shape into 1-inch balls and brown them evenly in a single layer on a broiler pan under a preheated broiler.

Arrange on party picks with cubes of pineapple, unpeeled apple, or pear chunks, dipped in lemon to prevent browning. Provide bowls of imported soy sauce or yogurt for dipping.

Makes 32 balls, 45 calories each.

PINEAPPLE-PEPPER HAWAIIAN PORK BALLS

2 lb. lean ground pork from the
  leg
5 Tbs. soy sauce
1 tsp. ground ginger
1 clove garlic, minced (optional)
1 egg, beaten, or 2 egg whites
  or ¼ cup no-cholesterol
  substitute

2 Tbs. cornstarch
2 cans (1 lb. each) juice-packed
  pineapple chunks, undrained
3 Tbs. honey
2 green bell peppers, seeded
  and diced
1 red bell pepper, seeded and
  diced

In a bowl combine the pork with 2 Tbs. of the soy sauce, the ginger, garlic, and egg. Shape into 1½-inch meatballs and brown them evenly in a single layer on a broiler pan under a preheated broiler.

In a saucepan stir the cornstarch into the pineapple and cook the mixture, stirring, until it bubbles.

Add all the ingredients, cover, and simmer for 4 to 5 minutes. Pour into chafing dish and keep warm.

Makes 36 balls, about 60 calories each.

VEAL BALLS BOLOGNESE

2 lb. lean ground veal shoulder
 or 1 lb. lean ground veal and
 1 lb. ground raw turkey,
 combined
1 cup high-protein cereal,
 crushed
1 cup minced onion
½ cup minced celery
½ cup shredded carrots
½ cup dry red wine

2 eggs or 4 egg whites or ½ cup
 liquid no-cholesterol
 substitute
1 tsp. salt or garlic salt
¼ tsp. coarse-ground pepper
1 can (6 oz.) tomato paste
1 can (10 oz.) fat-skimmed beef
 broth, undiluted
¼ cup dry red wine
1 tsp. basil

Preheat the oven to moderate, 350 degrees.

In a bowl combine the first 9 ingredients. Shape into 24 tiny meatballs, using a 1-inch melon baller.

Brown them evenly in a single layer on a broiling pan under a preheated broiler.

Combine the remaining ingredients in a casserole, mix well, and add the meatballs. Cover and bake for 30 minutes.

Makes 24 balls, 80 calories each (including sauce), or 75 calories each with egg white. Using veal-turkey mixture adds about 10 calories to each serving.

RUSSIAN VEAL BALLS

1 lb. lean ground veal shoulder

1 cup low-calorie Russian salad
 dressing

Preheat the broiler.

In a bowl toss the veal lightly with half the dressing. Shape into tiny meatballs, using a 1-inch melon baller.

Roll each meatball lightly in the remaining dressing.

Brown the balls in a single layer on a nonstick baking sheet sprayed with cooking spray, under the broiler, 3 to 5 minutes on each side.

Spear with party picks and serve immediately.

Makes 25 or 30 servings, 35 calories each.

VEAL BALLS STROGANOFF

2 lb. lean ground veal
1 onion, minced
2 Tbs. Worcestershire sauce
Salt and pepper
2 Tbs. prepared brown mustard
1 Tbs. cornstarch

1 can (10 oz.) onion soup,
skimmed of fat
1 cup dairy sour cream or sour
dressing
1 Tbs. minced fresh parsley

In a bowl combine the veal, onion, Worcestershire sauce, and salt and pepper to taste. Shape into small 1-inch meatballs and spread lightly with mustard. Brown them evenly in a single layer on a broiler pan under a preheated broiler.

Combine the cornstarch and onion soup in a saucepan, heat to boiling, and stir in the sour cream. Heat the mixture through. Add the meatballs and parsley. Pour into a chafing dish and keep warm.

Makes 36 balls, 50 calories each.

VARIATION

Substitute plain low-fat yogurt for the sour cream; 45 calories per ball.

GYPSY TURKEY

2 boned turkey thighs, cut into
1-inch cubes
1 Tbs. salad oil
2 onions, chopped

1 can (16 oz.) tomato purée
Garlic salt and pepper
2 tsp. paprika
1 tsp. caraway seeds

Brown the turkey in the oil in a heavy Dutch oven or a large non-stick skillet. Discard the oil.

Stir in the remaining ingredients and simmer the mixture for 1¼ hours, or until the turkey is tender. (Serve with noodles if desired, 100 calories per half cup.)

Makes 10 servings, 305 calories each.

PINEAPPLE-GLAZED ROAST LEG OF LAMB

5 lb. leg of lamb	2 tsp. dried mint or marjoram
1 clove garlic, minced (optional)	Salt, or garlic salt, and pepper
1 can (6 oz.) pineapple juice concentrate, defrosted, undiluted	

Preheat the oven to moderately low, 325 degrees.

Place the lamb on a rack in a roasting pan and insert a meat thermometer in the thickest part, not touching the bone. Roast, uncovered, no water added, for 1½ hours.

Drain the fat from the pan. In a bowl combine the remaining ingredients and pour over the lamb. Bake it, basting often, until the thermometer reads 140 degrees (rare) or 160 degrees (medium). (Lamb is best served pink in the middle.) Remove lamb to a cutting board and let it stand for 15 minutes before carving. Skim the fat from the pan juices and serve as a sauce.

Makes 12 servings, 270 calories each.

OVEN-FRIED TURKEY

½ cup flour	¼ tsp. poultry seasoning (optional)
2 tsp. paprika	
2 tsp. salt or seasoned salt	1 small (about 4 to 5 lb.) turkey,
¼ tsp. pepper	cut into serving pieces

Preheat the oven to very hot, 450 degrees.

Combine the flour and seasonings in a paper bag. Add 2 or 3 pieces of the turkey at a time and shake to coat them evenly.

Arrange the turkey skin side down in a nonstick roasting pan sprayed with cooking spray and brown it on both sides for 20 to 30 minutes, until the skin is crisp. Use tongs for turning.

When the turkey is brown, reduce the heat to 350 degrees. Cover the pan tightly and cook slowly for 1 hour or more until tender. (The turkey is done when the thickest parts are fork-tender.) Uncover for the last 10 minutes to recrisp the skin.

Makes 10 servings, 345 calories each.

GLAZED BAKED HAM

3 to 5 lb. fully cooked cured
    ham
Whole cloves
    1 can (8 oz.) juice-packed
    pineapple rings
    1 can (6 oz.) frozen cider
    concentrate, defrosted,
    undiluted

1 tsp. dry mustard or 2 tsp.
    prepared
½ tsp. pumpkin pie spice
    (optional)

Preheat the oven to moderately low, 325 degrees.

Arrange the ham fat side up on a rack in a roasting pan. Insert a meat thermometer in the thickest part, not touching the bone, and bake, uncovered, no water added, for 50 minutes. Remove and discard the fat in the pan.

Trim the ham of skin and fat, score the surface in a diamond pattern, and decorate it with the cloves and pineapple rings (reserve the juice).

In a bowl combine the remaining ingredients, including the reserved pineapple juice, and mix well. Pour over ham, return it to the oven, and bake it, basting it often, until thermometer reads 140 degrees.

Remove ham to a cutting board and let it stand for 15 minutes before carving. Skim the fat from the pan juices and use as a sauce.

Makes 12 servings, 290 calories each, plus 25 calories for each pineapple ring.

16

Sweets

WHAT Mother Nature didn't anticipate when she gave us a sweet tooth was that humans would figure out a way to separate the pure calories (sugar) from healthy foods like beets, corn, and cane and turn them into a white powder to sprinkle all over everything else! While a sweet tooth is natural, the craving for sugar is man-made.

In a sense sugar is actually an "artificial sweetener" that's used to make other foods taste much sweeter than anything in nature. Our perception of sweetness becomes so blunted by excess sugar that naturally sweet foods no longer taste sweet, or sweet enough. Even more harmful, excess sugar can derange our metabolism. Sugar can cause a sharp drop in the body's blood sugar level. Low blood sugar causes a nervous, hungry sensation that can only be alleviated by another fix of sugar-rich food. That's one way the "junk-food junkie" is born.

You can break an excess sugar habit by retracing the steps by which it was learned, gradually using less and less sugar, relying more on the natural sweetness of fruit and fruit ingredients. Remember, there is no need for sugar in human nutrition!

Other Sweeteners

What about honey, molasses, maple syrup, "raw" sugar, and fruit sugar (fructose)?

Despite their "natural" image, these sweeteners aren't very different, calorically and nutritionally, from ordinary white table sugar. The tiny traces of vitamins and minerals in honey and natural syrups are slight compared with their caloric count.

FRUCTOSE   Fructose, or "fruit sugar," is the latest fad sweetener being promoted in health food stores. While some of the claims made for it are exaggerated—or downright misleading—fruit sugar does have some interesting calorie advantages if used properly.

Fructose is simply another kind of sugar. It's called fruit sugar because it's the same type of sugar that's found in fruit. But the "fruit sugar" sold in health food stores is *not* refined from fruit; it's manufactured from cheap cornstarch treated with enzymes. Like white sugar, fructose is a refined sweetener that contains nothing but empty calories—no bulk or fiber, no vitamins or minerals, no protein—just calories and carbohydrates, pure and simple. Both white sugar and fruit sugar have the same calorie count: 16 per teaspoon. But fruit sugar can be a definite calorie saver if you use it in place of white sugar, because fruit sugar *can be* sweeter than white sugar.

The actual sweetening power depends on how it's used and what it's used with. Fruit sugar offers no added sweetness—no calorie advantage in most cakes, cookies, and other baked goods. On the other hand, fruit sugar can have as much as double the sweetening power of table sugar when used as a sweetener in chilled fruit desserts.

Here are some basic facts about using fructose. *It has almost double the sweetening power of ordinary sugar when combined with acid ingredients (fruits and juices) in drinks or desserts served chilled or frozen.* That makes it a natural for lemonade, iced tea with lemon, fruit punches, yogurt mixtures, homemade frozen yogurts, sherbets and fruit-flavored ice milks, gelatin desserts, and fruit molds. Fructose is good for sprinkling on grapefruit or cold cereal with fruit; for homemade pickles, relishes, and chutneys; for salad dressings.

Fructose loses some of its sweetening power at progressively higher temperatures. So hot foods or drinks with no acid or fruit ingredients would not be appreciably sweeter if fructose were substituted for sucrose. There's not much point in paying a premium price for fruit sugar if you plan to stir it into coffee, hot chocolate, or make it into pound cake.

Fructose has a synergistic effect on noncaloric sugar substitutes. When saccharin and fructose are combined they magnify each other. In other words, together they are sweeter than equivalent amounts of either one would be by itself. "Light" cooks who want the most sweetness for the fewest calories—without a bitter aftertaste—can use this fact to advantage. In chilled lemonade, a quarter-grain of saccharin and a teaspoon of fructose will taste like almost five teaspoons of sugar.

Fructose is marketed in granulated, liquid, and pill form. Granulated fructose looks exactly like ordinary white table sugar, but it's much more susceptible to heat and humidity. Left uncovered, it will cake like brown sugar. On hot, humid summer days it can actually seem to melt! Once opened, it should be stored in an airtight container and kept in a cool, dark, dry place.

Individual single-serving packets minimize the caking and melting problem, but can be tricky to use in recipes. They may not contain a level teaspoon. Most packets that I've seen contain only three-quarters of a teaspoon—and are labeled "equivalent in sweetening power" to one teaspoon of sugar. However, as we've already pointed out, that depends on how you use it.

Fructose is *not* a no-calorie "sugar substitute" and shouldn't be used by patients on sugar-free diets without medical advice. Health claims for fructose should be taken with a grain of salt, so to speak. The only sweetener for which any nutritional claims are valid is fruit.

Many of the recipes that follow use fruit and fruit ingredients as a primary sweetener.

Quick Breads, Cakes, and Pies

BANANA NUT BREAD

2 very ripe bananas, mashed	1 Tbs. baking powder
1 jar (7¾oz.) junior babyfood apricots with tapioca	¼ tsp. salt
	¼ tsp. cinnamon
2 eggs	¼ cup raisins
1¾ cups cake flour	3 Tbs. chopped walnuts

Preheat the oven to moderate, 350 degrees.

In a bowl combine the bananas, apricots, and eggs and add the dry ingredients, mixing thoroughly.

Bake the bread in a nonstick loaf pan sprayed with cooking spray for 1 hour and 15 minutes.

Makes twelve ⅔-inch slices, 130 calories each.

ORANGE CAKE

5 Tbs. granulated sugar
3 Tbs. free-pouring brown sugar
⅔ cup diet margarine
1 egg
1¼ cups flour
2 tsp. baking powder
½ tsp. baking soda
5 Tbs. golden raisins

½ tsp. pumpkin pie spice or ¼ tsp. cinnamon plus pinch of nutmeg, cloves, and allspice
1 tsp. vanilla
3 Tbs. undiluted orange juice concentrate, defrosted
2 Tbs. water
2 Tbs. chopped walnuts

Preheat the oven to moderate, 350 degrees.

Combine the sugars, margarine, and egg in an electric mixer bowl. Beat for 2 minutes on high speed.

In a bowl stir the flour, baking powder, and soda together and add to the batter. Add the remaining ingredients, except the nuts. Beat for 1 minute at low speed.

Pour the batter into an 8-inch nonstick round or square cake pan sprayed with cooking spray and sprinkle with the walnuts.

Bake the cake for 25 to 30 minutes, until it is golden.

Makes 9 servings, 200 calories each.

VARIATION

Replace the granulated sugar with 2 Tbs. fructose and reduce raisins to 2 Tbs. Omit the nuts. Totals 165 calories per serving.

CARROT CAKE

⅔ cup sugar
1 cup flour
1 tsp. baking soda
1 tsp. cinnamon
½ tsp. salt

1 tsp. vanilla
⅓ cup vegetable oil
2 eggs
1½ cups grated carrots

Preheat the oven to moderate, 350 degrees.

Combine the dry ingredients and add the vanilla, oil, and eggs, beating until well combined.

Add the grated carrots.

Bake the cake in a 9-inch round nonstick pan for about 45 minutes, or until a toothpick inserted in the center comes out clean.

Makes 10 servings, 180 calories each.

STRAWBERRY SHORTCAKE

1½ cups flour
2 Tbs. sugar
2 tsp. baking powder
¼ tsp. baking soda
¼ tsp. salt
3 Tbs. butter or margarine, softened

1 cup plain low-fat yogurt
1 qt. strawberries, sliced and sweetened to taste if necessary with 1 to 2 tsp. sugar or fructose (or equivalent noncalorie sweetener)

Preheat the oven to very hot, 450 degrees.

In a large bowl sift together the flour, sugar, baking powder, soda, and salt. Cut in the butter. Stir in the yogurt until the dough sticks together.

Drop heaping tablespoonfuls of the dough onto a nonstick baking sheet sprayed with cooking spray. (There will be 8 portions.)

Bake for 10 to 15 minutes.

To serve, split shortcakes and spoon strawberries into the middle and on top.

Makes 8 servings, 175 calories each, or 191 to 207 calories if strawberries are sweetened.

COTTAGE CHEESE CORNBREAD

1 cup yellow cornmeal
¾ cup skim milk
½ cup creamed cottage cheese
    or 99% fat-free cottage cheese
1 egg or 2 egg whites or ¼ cup
    of defrosted no-cholesterol
    substitute

1 tsp. salt
1 tsp. baking powder
½ tsp. baking soda
1 Tbs. sugar (optional)

Preheat the oven to moderately high, 425 degrees.
In a bowl combine the ingredients well.
Bake the bread in an 8-inch nonstick cake pan sprayed with cooking spray for 20 to 25 minutes.
Cut the bread into 16 wedges or squares.

Makes 16 servings, 45 calories each.

VARIATION

Omitting the sugar and using egg whites or no-cholesterol substitute and fat-free cottage cheese makes 35 calories per serving.

YOGURT CAKE

3 Tbs. butter
8 Tbs. sugar
1 egg
1 tsp. vanilla
1 cup sifted cake flour

½ tsp. baking soda
¼ tsp. salt
¼ cup skim milk
¼ cup plain low-fat yogurt

Preheat the oven to moderate, 350 degrees.
Cream the butter and sugar together in a bowl until the mixture is light and fluffy. Beat in the egg and vanilla.
In a bowl sift the flour, soda, and salt together and add to butter mixture alternating with milk and yogurt.
Bake in an 8-inch round or square nonstick baking pan well sprayed with cooking spray for 30 to 35 minutes. Let cool completely. Serve topped with sliced fresh fruit.

Makes 8 servings, 145 calories each (cake only).

BRAN GINGERBREAD

5 Tbs. diet margarine	1 tsp. baking powder
5 Tbs. sugar	½ tsp. baking soda
⅓ cup molasses	½ tsp. salt
1 egg	¾ tsp. ginger
⅔ cup whole bran	½ tsp. cinnamon
1¼ cups sifted flour	⅔ cup boiling water

Preheat the oven to moderate, 350 degrees.

In a bowl beat the margarine, sugar, molasses, and egg until light and fluffy. Stir in the bran and let stand for 5 minutes.

Sift the remaining dry ingredients together and beat into the bran mixture.

Add the water and beat until smooth.

Bake the bread in an 8- or 9-inch nonstick cake pan for 25 to 30 minutes. Serve warm or cool.

Makes twelve 1½-inch squares, 120 calories each.

LIGHT CAKE

4 eggs, separated	2½ tsp. vanilla extract
2 egg whites	1¾ cups cake flour
½ tsp. cream of tartar	1 cup plus 2 Tbs. confectioners'
½ cup diet margarine, at room	sugar
temperature	2 tsp. baking powder
½ tsp. orange or almond	
flavoring	

Preheat the oven to moderately low, 325 degrees.

In a mixer bowl combine the 6 egg whites and the cream of tartar and beat until stiff peaks form. Set aside.

In another mixer bowl combine the margarine, egg yolks, orange or almond flavoring, and the vanilla extract. Beat until fluffy. Combine the flour, sugar, and baking powder; sift them together into the egg yolk mixture. Beat 2 minutes.

Gently but thoroughly fold the beaten egg whites into the egg yolk batter. Spoon the batter into a nonstick 9-inch tube pan. Bake for 1 hour. Invert the cake pan over a large soda or wine bottle to cool. Cool thoroughly before removing the cake from the pan. (Slice in half horizontally to fill with fruit, or frost, if desired.)

Makes 20 servings, 100 calories each (cake only).

LIGHT-AND-EASY PIECRUST

2 Tbs. diet margarine, at room temperature	¼ tsp. salt
½ cup flour	1 Tbs. salad oil

Combine all the ingredients in a bowl and mix lightly until the pastry forms a ball.

Flatten pastry on a sheet of wax paper. Cover and chill before rolling out.

Roll pastry out on a well-floured board with a floured rolling pin. Fit in into an 8-inch nonstick pie pan sprayed with cooking spray. Trim and discard the overhang.

Makes 1 crust, 435 calories.

VARIATIONS

Double Crust: Double the ingredients in the single-crust recipe.

Before chilling, divide dough into 2 balls, one slightly larger than the other. Use the larger ball for the bottom crust.

Lattice Crust: Follow the double-crust recipe.

Line the bottom of the pie pan with crust. Roll the top crust out and cut it into half-inch strips, length varying from diameter of pan down. Crisscross the strips over a filling, working from the center out, forming open squares and weaving the strips alternately over and under one another. Discard any leftover pastry.

LIGHT-AND-EASY GRAHAM CRACKER CRUST

1 Tbs. butter	¾ cup graham cracker crumbs
2 Tbs. diet margarine, at room temperature	

If using whole graham crackers, process them in a blender or food processor until crushed into fine crumbs. Otherwise, place a few at a time in a plastic bag and roll over the bag with a rolling pin, until the crackers are crushed into crumbs.

Use a pastry knife or a fork to mix the butter and margarine, by hand, into the crumbs. Or blend the butter and margarine into the crushed crumbs in a food processor, using the steel blade.

Empty the crumb mixture into a nonstick 8- or 9-inch pie pan and with a spoon or a small rubber spatula spread the mixture evenly around the bottom and up the sides of the pie pan. If another same-size pie pan is available, use it to help form the mixture in the first pie pan: insert the second pie pan over the filling in the first pie pan and press firmly.

Chill the unfilled crust thoroughly before filling. Or prebake in a preheated moderate 350-degree oven 6 to 8 minutes. (Watch carefully to prevent burning. Cool before filling.) A baked pie shell will be firmer; an unbaked pie shell will be adequate if the filling is firm.

Makes 1 crust, 530 calories.

HAWAIIAN APPLE PIE

8-inch single frozen piecrust, defrosted	2 tsp. vanilla
1 can (20 oz.) pie-sliced apples (not pie filling)	1 tsp. cinnamon or apple pie spice
1 can (20-oz.) juice-packed crushed pineapple	2½ Tbs. cornstarch
	⅓ cup fructose, or honey
	Pinch of salt

Preheat the oven to hot, 400 degrees.

Allow the piecrust to defrost slowly at room temperature. Transfer the pastry to a larger 9- or 10-inch deep-dish pie plate by gently folding the pastry in half, then in quarters. Unfold, then press and stretch to fit, using your fingertips.

Combine remaining ingredients and spoon into the pie shell. Cover the filling with a round of foil cut to fit or invert the aluminum pie pan from the frozen piecrust over the filling. Bake 35 minutes, until the crust is golden and the filling is thick.

Makes 10 servings, 160 calories each with fructose, or 170 calories each with honey (25 calories less per serving if Light-and-Easy Piecrust is used).

CREAM CHEESECAKE

2 Tbs. butter or margarine, softened	1½ Tbs. flour
¾ cup graham cracker crumbs	¾ tsp. grated orange or lemon rind or a pinch of bottled rind
12 oz. (1½ packages) low-calorie cream cheese	2 tsp. vanilla
¼ cup honey	3 eggs
3 tbs. sugar	1 egg yolk
	2 Tbs. orange juice

Preheat the oven to low, 250 degrees.

Lightly spread the bottom and sides of an 8-inch springform pan with butter or margarine, sprinkle with the crumbs, and press them into place. Chill in the refrigerator.

Blend the remaining ingredients in a blender until smooth. Pour into the pan.

Bake the cake for 1 hour.

Turn off the heat, open the door partly, and let the cake remain in the oven for 1 more hour. Refrigerate

Makes 12 servings, 150 calories each.

BLENDER CHEESECAKE

1 envelope unflavored gelatin
¼ cup water
2 cups skim milk
1 package (8 oz.) low-fat cream
  cheese
1 4-serving envelope instant
  vanilla pudding mix

3 Tbs. fruit sugar (optional)
2 tsp. lemon juice
1 tsp. grated lemon rind
¼ tsp. salt
Ready-to-fill graham cracker
  piecrust

Sprinkle gelatin on cold water in a small saucepan and set aside to soften.

Blend the milk and cream cheese in a blender until smooth. Meanwhile, heat the gelatin mixture over low heat until the gelatin granules melt. Add to the blender and blend until smooth. Add the pudding mix, fruit sugar, lemon juice, rind, and salt and blend until smooth. Spoon into 8- or 9-inch pie pan and chill until set.

Makes 10 servings, 170 calories each with commercial ready-to-fill graham cracker pie shell; 155 calories with homemade Light-and-Easy Graham Cracker Crust. Fruit sugar adds 15 calories per serving.

FRUIT-FILLED GERMAN CHEESECAKE

3 egg yolks
4 egg whites
Pinch of salt
1½ cups (12 oz.) pot cheese

⅓ cup low-fat vanilla yogurt
1 tsp. grated lemon rind
9 Tbs. sugar
Fruit for filling

Preheat the oven to moderate, 350 degrees.

Put the egg yolks into the blender.

Beat the egg whites with a pinch of salt in a metal mixing bowl until stiff peaks form.

Add the remaining ingredients, except the fruit, to the blender and blend until smooth. Pour the mixture into the whites and gently but thoroughly fold them together.

Bake the cake in a 9-inch nonstick square or round cake pan for 40 to 50 minutes, until a knife inserted in the center comes out clean. Cool in the pan.

Fill with slightly sweetened sliced fresh fruit or Nectarine Filling, page 213.

Makes 8 servings, 125 calories each (without fruit).

STRAWBERRY CHEESECAKE

²/₃ cup graham cracker crumbs
2 tbs. butter or margarine, softened
1 cup boiling water
1 4-serving envelope strawberry gelatin dessert mix

3 cups 99% fat-free cottage cheese
5 Tbs. sugar
1 cup thinly sliced fresh strawberries

Combine the crumbs with butter or margarine and press the mixture firmly in the bottom of an 8-inch springform pan. Chill in refrigerator.

In a heatproof bowl stir the water into gelatin until it dissolves. Cool in the refrigerator until lukewarm.

Blend the cheese and sugar in a blender until smooth. Add the gelatin mixture, a little at a time, and blend on low speed until smooth.

Spoon into the crust and arrange the berries on top. Refrigerate until firm.

Makes 8 servings, 190 calories each.

VARIATION

Substitute diet margarine for the butter and use low-calorie gelatin mix; 140 calories each serving.

SPICY APPLE-CIDER PIE

1 Light-and-Easy Piecrust (see
  page 207)
1 orange, peeled and diced
3 oz. cider concentrate,
  defrosted
1 can (20 oz.) unsweetened pie-
  sliced apples, drained, or 1½
  lb. apples, cored and sliced

¾ cup raisins
Pinch of salt
1 tsp. pumpkin pie spice or ½
  tsp. cinnamon plus a pinch of
  ginger, nutmeg, and cloves
3 Tbs. cornstarch

Preheat the oven to moderately high, 425 degrees.

Prepare piecrust and line a nonstick 8-inch pie pan with it.

In a bowl combine the orange with the cider concentrate, apples, raisins, salt, and spices. Stir in the cornstarch and mix well. Spoon into the pie pan.

Cover the filling with a circle of foil, cut to fit, or an inverted pie pan, to protect it from drying out. Bake the pie for 30 to 40 minutes, until the mixture is set. Serve slightly warm.

Makes 8 servings, 165 calories each.

BLENDER PUMPKIN CHEESE PIE

1 cup canned unsweetened
  pumpkin (not pie filling)
1½ cups low-fat large-curd
  creamed cottage cheese
3 eggs
1 Tbs. brandy or rum flavoring

1½ tsp. pumpkin pie spice
Pinch of salt
9 Tbs. brown sugar
1 8-inch ready-to-fill graham
  cracker crust

Preheat the oven to low, 275 degrees.

Blend the ingredients in a blender on high speed until smooth.

Pour into the shell. Bake for 1 hour or more, until set. Chill before serving.

Makes 8 servings, 215 calories each with commercial ready-to-fill graham cracker pie shell, or 190 calories each with Light-and-Easy Graham Cracker Crust.

PINEAPPLE CHEESE PIE

⅔ cup fine graham cracker
    crumbs
2 Tbs. butter or margarine,
    softened
1 package (8 oz.) low-calorie
    cream cheese, softened
2 eggs
4 Tbs. sugar

1 Tbs. flour
¼ tsp. salt
1 tsp. vanilla
1 tsp. grated orange rind
¼ cup orange juice
1 can (12 oz.) juice-packed
    pineapple tidbits
1 tsp. unflavored gelatin

Preheat the oven to moderate, 350 degrees.

In a bowl combine the crumbs and butter or margarine and mix well. Press evenly over bottom of 9-inch pie pan.

Beat the cream cheese in a blender until smooth. Add the eggs and beat until smooth. Add the sugar, flour, salt, vanilla, orange rind, and juice and beat until smooth. Pour into the crust.

Bake the pie for about 20 to 30 minutes, until the filling is set. Chill.

For the topping, drain the pineapple and reserve the juice. In a saucepan soften the gelatin in the juice over low heat until it is dissolved. Cool until it begins to thicken.

Arrange the pineapple on the filling and pour the gelatin mixture over it. Chill until firm.

Makes 8 servings, 185 calories each.

NECTARINE FILLING

3 unpeeled nectarines, pitted
    and thinly sliced
1 can (6 oz.) unsweetened
    apple or white grape juice

1½ tsp. arrowroot or cornstarch
3 Tbs. sugar

Arrange the nectarines in overlapping circles in the crust.

Combine the remaining ingredients in a saucepan and cook, stirring, until the sauce thickens.

Pour over the nectarines. Chill the pie.

Makes 8 servings, 60 calories each; 185 calories each serving cheesecake and filling.

FRESH FRUIT PIE FILLING

1½ tsp. unflavored gelatin
½ cup cold water
3 cups sliced fresh strawberries, peaches, or blueberries or other fresh fruit, except pineapple

½ cup jelly (strawberry, peach, or grape)
1 Light-and-Easy Graham Cracker Crust

In a small bowl soften the gelatin in ¼ cup water. Combine ½ cup fruit, the remaining water, and the jelly in a saucepan. Cook over low heat, stirring, to boiling. Remove from the heat and add the softened gelatin, stirring until it dissolves.

Refrigerate the mixture just until slightly syrupy and stir in the remaining fruit. Spoon into ready-to-fill graham cracker crust and chill until set.

Makes 8 servings, 85 calories each (filling only).

VARIATION

Substitute low-sugar jelly, 60 calories each.

FROZEN YOGURT PUMPKIN PIE

1½ cups canned unsweetened pumpkin (not pie filling)
¼ cup skim milk
½ tsp. cinnamon
1 tsp. pumpkin pie spice

3 Tbs. honey
1 qt. low-fat vanilla frozen yogurt, softened slightly
8 cinnamon graham crackers, crushed into crumbs

Combine the pumpkin, milk, spices, and honey in a large bowl. Gently cut the yogurt in, only until the mixture is marbled.

Spread the mixture in a pie pan and sprinkle it with the crumbs. Wrap with foil and freeze.

Let soften briefly before cutting into wedges.

Makes 10 servings, 135 calories each.

Fruit Desserts

APPLE SNACKS

4 envelopes unflavored gelatin
2 cups unsweetened applesauce

1 can (6 oz.) undiluted apple
juice concentrate, defrosted
¼ tsp. cinnamon

In a small saucepan sprinkle the gelatin over ½ cup applesauce, stir thoroughly, and let it soften for 1 minute. Then heat over low heat until the gelatin dissolves.

Stir in the remaining ingredients.

Pour the mixture into 9-inch square pan and chill until firm. Cut into squares to serve.

Makes 72 one-inch squares, 110 calories each.

APPLE CRACKER BETTY

7 round milk lunch crackers
1 can (20 oz.) pie-sliced apples, undrained
4 Tbs. easy-pouring brown sugar
2 Tbs. granulated white sugar
¼ tsp. cinnamon

6 Tbs. raisins
1 cup 99% fat-free cottage cheese
1 egg
½ tsp. vanilla
½ cup skim milk

Preheat the oven to moderate, 350 degrees.

Arrange the crackers in a single layer in an 8-inch nonstick cake pan.

In a bowl combine the apples with the sugars, cinnamon, and raisins and spoon the mixture over the crackers.

In a blender blend the cottage cheese, egg, vanilla, and milk until smooth and pour over the apples.

Bake for 1 hour. Serve warm or chilled.

Makes 8 servings, 170 calories each.

VARIATION

Omit the brown sugar and replace the white sugar with honey, 150 calories per serving.

APPLE-CHEDDAR BAKE

1 can (20 oz.) pie-sliced apples
(not pie filling), drained, or
1½ lb. apples, cored and
sliced
3 Tbs. honey
2 tsp. lemon juice

1 Tbs. cornstarch
½ tsp. apple pie spice or ¼ tsp.
cinnamon and nutmeg
Dash of salt
½ cup shredded extra-sharp
cheddar cheese

Preheat the oven to moderate, 350 degrees.

Stir all the ingredients, except the cheese, together in a nonstick baking dish. Bake, uncovered, for 25 minutes.

Top with the cheese and bake just until it melts. Serve warm.

Makes 8 servings, 85 calories each.

CRÊPES

3 eggs, beaten, or ¾ cup no-
cholesterol substitute
½ cup skim milk

½ cup pancake mix
¼ tsp. cinnamon (optional)

In a bowl combine the eggs, milk, pancake mix, and cinnamon, if desired, and beat until smooth.

Heat a nonstick small 6-inch skillet or crêpe maker over moderate heat, pour in 1 Tbs. batter, and immediately rotate the pan to coat the bottom evenly. Cook until the batter is set, for 1 to 2 minutes. Lift edges, turn, and cook until set. Do not allow the crêpe to dry out. Remove and fill as desired or fold in quarters and top with sauce.

Makes 6 crêpes, 90 calories each, or 70 calories each with no-cholesterol substitute.

VARIATIONS

Crêpes may be filled with cottage cheese or ricotta flavored to taste with vanilla and topped with sliced fresh fruit.

Cold crêpes may also be filled with Yogurt Ambrosia, p. 217; fresh fruit and No-Cook "Custard," p. 221; Orange Chiffon Pudding, p. 224; Pineapple-Cheese Dessert, p. 223. Or top with Cherry Sauce, p. 226, or Strawberry Romanoff Sauce, p. 227.

THICK BANANA SHAKE

½ very ripe banana
1 tsp. sugar
Few drops of vanilla

1 cup ice cubes
½ cup skim milk
3 Tbs. instant nonfat dry milk

In a blender blend all the ingredients on high speed until ice is dissolved. Serve immediately

Makes 1 serving, 185 calories.

VARIATION

Omit the sugar and replace the skim milk with cold water; 125 calories.

BERRY SHAKE

1 cup frozen strawberries,
    unsweetened
1 cup skim milk
5 Tbs. instant nonfat dry milk
1 cup ice cubes

1 Tbs. sugar or 2 teaspoons
    fruit sugar
½ tsp. vanilla
Pinch of salt

In a blender blend all the ingredients until smooth.

Makes 2 servings, 245 calories each.

VARIATION

Substitute 1½ tsp. honey or fructose for the sugar; 240 calories with honey, or 235 calories with fructose.

YOGURT AMBROSIA

2 oranges, peeled and sectioned
1 unpeeled red apple, diced
1 banana, sliced

1 unpeeled pear, diced
6 tsp. flaked coconut
1 cup low-fat vanilla yogurt

In a bowl combine the oranges, apple, banana, pear, and sweetened coconut and chill. Just before serving, toss with the yogurt.

Makes 6 servings, 115 calories each.

FRUIT YOGURT

1 envelope unflavored gelatin
¼ cup chilled fruit juice, except
   fresh or frozen pineapple
2 cups peeled, diced, or sliced
   ripe fresh fruit, except
   pineapple

4 cups low-fat vanilla yogurt

In a small saucepan sprinkle the gelatin over the juice and let it soften for 1 minute.

Blend the fruit and yogurt in a blender until smooth.

Over low heat heat the gelatin just until it melts and add it to the yogurt mixture. Blend until smooth.

Freeze the mixture in an ice-cream maker according to the manufacturer's directions.

Without an ice-cream maker: pour the mixture into a shallow pan and freeze it for 1 hour or more, until is is slushy.

Break up the mixture in a large mixing bowl. Quickly beat smooth with electric mixture and return it to the freezer.

When partially refrozen quickly beat again. Spoon into a covered container and freeze until firm. Transfer to the refrigerator for about 20 minutes before serving to soften slightly.

Makes 12 servings, 100 calories each.

ORANGE "CANDY"

7 envelopes unflavored gelatin
1 can (12 oz.) undiluted orange
   juice concentrate, defrosted

¾ cup boiling water
½ cup golden raisins

In a small saucepan sprinkle the gelatin over ½ cup of the concentrate, let it soften for 1 minute, and add boiling water. Heat over low heat until the gelatin dissolves.

Remove the pan from the heat and stir in the remaining concentrate and raisins. Pour into an 8-inch square nonstick cake pan and chill until firm. Cut into 1-inch squares. Store, covered, in the refrigerator.

Makes 64 squares, 17 calories each.

PEARS POACHED IN PORT

1 cup port
1 cup water
5 Tbs. sugar or 3 Tbs. fruit
  sugar

¼ tsp. cinnamon
8 firm ripe pears, pared

Combine the port, water, sugar, and cinnamon in a large saucepan or skillet. Bring the liquid to boiling, stirring, until the sugar dissolves.

Add the pears and cook, covered, turning the fruit occasionally, for 8 to 10 minutes.

When barely tender, remove the fruit with a slotted spoon.

Boil down the syrup, uncovered, until it is reduced to 1 cup. Pour over the pears and serve them at room temperature.

Makes 8 servings, 135 calories each.

Puddings and Mousses

GOLDEN BREAD PUDDING

4 slices stale or toasted high-
  fiber bread, diced
½ cup golden raisins
½ tsp. pumpkin pie spice or ⅛
  tsp. cinnamon, nutmeg, clove,
  and ginger

3 eggs
4 Tbs. fructose
1½ cups orange juice
1 tsp. grated orange peel
1½ tsp. vanilla

Preheat the oven to moderate, 350 degrees.

Combine the bread with the raisins in a loaf pan, sprinkle with the spice, and mix well.

Blend the remaining ingredients in a blender or in a food processor with the steel blade.

Pour the mixture over the bread. Set the loaf pan in a larger pan partly filled with boiling water, and bake it for 35 to 45 minutes, until a knife inserted in the center comes out clean.

Makes 6 servings, 170 calories each.

DEVIL'S BREAD PUDDING

4 slices high-fiber bread, cubed	2 tsp. vanilla
½ cup raisins or currants	3 envelopes low-calorie hot
2 cups cold water	cocoa mix
3 eggs, separated	1 cup hot coffee
6 Tbs. brown sugar	¼ tsp. salt

Preheat the oven to moderate, 350 degrees.

In a large bowl stir together the bread and raisins.

Combine the water, egg yolks, sugar, vanilla, and cocoa mix in a blender, in a mixer bowl, or in a food processor with the steel blade. Beat on high speed until well mixed.

Slowly add the coffee, beating.

Stir into the bread-raisin mixture.

With an electric mixer beat the egg whites and salt together until the eggs are stiff.

Gently fold the whites into the bread mixture and pour the mixture into a nonstick casserole sprayed with cooking spray. Set it in a larger pan partly filled with boiling water and bake it for 1 hour, or until set.

Makes 6 servings, 200 calories each.

MATZOH KUGEL

2 matzohs	2 unpeeled red apples, finely
Water	diced
½ cup skim milk	6 Tbs. raisins
4 eggs, beaten	¼ tsp. salt
1 can (8 oz.) juice-packed	⅛ tsp. cinnamon
crushed pineapple, undrained	½ tsp. vanilla

Preheat the oven to moderate, 350 degrees.

In a bowl soak the matzohs in water. Squeeze them out.

In a bowl combine the matzohs with the remaining ingredients and mix well.

In a nonstick pan sprayed with vegetable spray bake the mixture, uncovered, for about 45 minutes, until set. Serve warm.

Makes 6 servings, 175 calories each.

LIGHT ONE-EGG "CUSTARD"

3 cups skim milk
1 egg
1 package (8 oz.) low-fat cream
   cheese, cut in chunks
10 Tbs. sugar or 8 Tbs. fructose
1 Tbs. vanilla
1 tsp. grated lemon rind
   (optional)

¼ tsp. salt
1 envelope unflavored gelatin
2 Tbs. cornstarch
4 Tbs. raisins (optional)
Cinnamon or nutmeg (optional)

Preheat the oven to moderately low, 325 degrees.

Combine the ingredients, except the raisins, cinnamon, or nutmeg, in a blender and blend until smooth.

Stir in the raisins. Pour the mixture into a casserole and sprinkle it with cinnamon or nutmeg. Bake the casserole for 1 hour. Cool completely, then refrigerate for several hours, Serve chilled.

Makes 10 servings, 135 calories each; with raisins, 145 calories per serving; with fructose, 125 calories per serving.

NO-COOK "CUSTARD"

3 eggs
2 Tbs. unflavored gelatin
½ cup boiling water
¼ tsp. salt

⅔ cup dry skim milk powder
1 Tbs. vanilla
9 Tbs. sugar
2 cups ice cubes

Blend the eggs and gelatin in a blender. Let soften for 1 minute.

Add the water and blend until the gelatin dissolves.

Add the remaining ingredients, except the ice cubes, and blend until smooth.

Add the ice cubes and blend until it is dissolved and the mixture is thick. Serve immediately.

Makes 6 servings, 165 calories each.

VARIATION

Reduce skim milk powder to ½ cup and replace sugar with ¼ cup honey. Makes 125 calories each serving.

BLENDER CHOCOLATE MOUSSE

1 envelope unflavored gelatin
3 Tbs. cold water
¾ cup boiling water
4 single-serving envelopes Lite
cocoa mix

Pinch of salt
1 tsp. vanilla
2 cups ice cubes

Sprinkle the gelatin on the cold water in a blender. Let soften for 1 minute.

Add the boiling water and blend on high speed until the gelatin dissolves.

Add the remaining ingredients, except the ice cubes, and blend until smooth.

Add the ice cubes, a few at a time, and blend until they dissolve. Serve immediately.

Makes 4 servings, 80 calories each.

LEMON-BLUEBERRY MOUSSE

1½ cups boiling water
2 4-serving envelopes lemon
gelatin dessert mix, regular or
low-calorie

1 cup ice cubes and water
1 cup plain low-fat yogurt
1 pt. fresh blueberries

In a blender blend the boiling water with the gelatin until the gelatin dissolves.

Fill a 1-cup measure with ice cubes and add cold water to the top.

Pour the ice cubes and water into gelatin mixture and blend until the ice melts. Blend in the yogurt.

Chill the mixture for 20 to 30 minutes until syrupy and fold in the blueberries. Chill for several hours, until set.

Makes 8 servings, 120 calories each with regular gelatin, or 50 calories each with low-calorie gelatin.

ORANGE-PINEAPPLE PUDDING

1¼ cups water
2 Tbs. cornstarch
1 can (6 oz.) undiluted
pineapple juice concentrate,
defrosted

2 oranges, peeled and diced

In a saucepan cook the water and cornstarch, stirring, until the mixture is thick. Stir in the pineapple juice concentrate and oranges.
Chill for several hours in dessert cups.

Makes 4 servings, 150 calories each.

PINEAPPLE-CHEESE DESSERT

1½ cups (12 oz.) uncreamed low-
fat cottage cheese
1 can (8 oz.) juice-packed
crushed pineapple, drained

¼ cup golden raisins
¼ tsp. vanilla
Pinch of cinnamon

Combine the ingredients and refrigerate.

Makes 4 servings, 130 calores each.

EGGLESS YOGURT "CUSTARD"

1 envelope unflavored gelatin
1¼ cups skim milk
6 Tbs. sugar

½ tsp. vanilla
1 cup plain low-fat yogurt
Cinnamon, nutmeg, or fresh fruit

Sprinkle the gelatin over the milk in a saucepan and let soften for 1 minute. Add sugar and cook over low heat, stirring, until the gelatin completely dissolves. Remove from heat and add the vanilla.
Chill until partially set and fold in the yogurt.
Chill until firm (in a decorative mold, if desired).
Serve with cinnamon or nutmeg or top with fresh fruit.

Makes 5 servings, 110 calories each for "custard" only.

ORANGE CHIFFON PUDDING OR PIE FILLING

2 envelopes unflavored gelatin
6 Tbs. sugar
1 cup water
1 can (6 oz.) frozen orange
    juice concentrate, defrosted

2 cups plain low-fat yogurt
2 egg whites

Combine the gelatin and 4 Tbs. sugar in a saucepan, add the water, and let the gelatin soften for 1 minute. Heat, stirring, until it dissolves completely.

In a bowl mix the orange concentrate with the yogurt, stir in the gelatin mixture, and chill until partially set.

In a bowl, beat egg whites until stiff. Gradually beat in the remaining sugar, then fold in the orange mixture.

Chill several hours until firm.

Makes 9 servings, 110 calories each.

Frostings and Dessert Sauces

LIGHT AND CREAMY FROSTING BASE

1 container (15 oz.) part-skim
    ricotta cheese
Pinch of salt
3 or 4 Tbs. undiluted fruit juice
    concentrate, defrosted, or
    other liquid

Flavorings and sweeteners, as desired

In a mixer bowl or in a food processor with the steel blade, or in a blender, whip the ricotta and salt until smooth and thick.

Flavor, sweeten, and thin to spreading consistency by whipping in fruit juice, coffee, or other liquids and flavorings to taste (fruit juice, cider, applesauce, liqueurs, rum, brandy, skim milk, honey, maple syrup, fructose, liquid sugar substitute).

Spread on sponge cake or angel food cake and chill the cake in the refrigerator.

Makes enough to frost 2 layers, 16 servings. A 15-ounce container of part-skim ricotta contains about 626 calories. Four tablespoons of undiluted orange juice concentrate adds 112 calories. Orange frosting to serve 16 is about 45 calories each serving.

WHIPPED FRUIT FROSTING

½ tsp. unflavored gelatin
½ cup fruit juice
1 cup whipping cream

1 tsp. vanilla
1 cup low-fat fruit-flavored
    yogurt, except pineapple

Sprinkle the gelatin over the fruit juice in a small saucepan. Let soften for 1 minute and heat, stirring, until it dissolves. Cool.

In a bowl beat the cream until soft peaks form. Fold in the vanilla and yogurt. Fold in the gelatin mixture. Chill until the mixture thickens to spreading consistency.

Fill and frost a 2-layer 8- or 9-inch cake. Chill the cake until serving time.

Makes 9 servings, 125 calories each (frosting only).

PINEAPPLE FROSTING

1 envelope unflavored gelatin
1 can (20 oz.) juice-packed
    crushed pineapple, including
    juice

½ cup boiling water
2 Tbs. honey

Let the gelatin soften for 1 minute in 3 Tbs. pineapple juice (from the can) in a blender.

Pour the boiling water over the gelatin and blend on high speed until the gelatin thoroughly dissolves.

Add the honey and blend on high speed.

Refrigerate the frosting for several hours, until it sets.

Makes 2 cups of frosting, enough to ice two layers, or 9 servings, 50 calories each (frosting only).

LIGHT SUGAR ICING

½ package (4 oz.) low-fat cream
  cheese, at room temperature
1 tsp. vanilla

2 or 3 tsp. boiling water
2½ cups confectioners' sugar

In a bowl whip the cream cheese, vanilla, and water until soft.
Beat in the sugar, a little at a time, until fluffy.

Makes enough for 1 layer; 9 servings, 125 calories each (icing only).

VARIATIONS

Light Chocolate Icing: Reduce sugar to 2¼ cups and add 3 Tbs. plain unsweetened cocoa; 120 calories per serving.

Fruit-flavored Frosting: Substitute 1 to 2 Tbs. undiluted fruit juice concentrate, defrosted, for the water; 125 calories per serving.

Coffee Frosting: Combine the boiling water with 1 tsp. instant coffee. Add vanilla and cream cheese and beat until soft. Then beat in sugar; 125 calories per serving.

Lemon Frosting: Substitute 4 tsp. lemon juice for the water and vanilla; 125 calories per serving.

Peppermint Frosting: Substitute ½ tsp. peppermint extract for the vanilla; 125 calories per serving.

CHERRY SAUCE

1 can (1 lb.) water-packed
  pitted sour red cherries
¼ cup sugar

1 Tbs. cornstarch
½ cup cherry juice (from can)
¼ tsp. almond extract

Drain the cherries, reserving ½ cup of juice. Combine the sugar and cornstarch in a saucepan. Gradually stir in the juice and cook, over medium heat, stirring constantly, until thickened.

Remove from the heat. Stir in the almond extract and cherries. Chill.

Makes 5 servings, about 100 calories each.

STRAWBERRY ROMANOFF SAUCE

1 container (6 oz.) undiluted
   orange juice concentrate,
   defrosted

2 cups fresh or frozen whole
   unsweetened strawberries
2 Tbs. orange liqueur (optional)

Combine the ingredients in a blender and blend with quick on-off motions just until coarsely chopped.

Makes 10 servings, 45 calories each, 55 with liqueur.

THE
Light and Easy
DIET

14 DAYS OF DELICIOUS DINING ON

ONLY 1200 TO 1500 CALORIES

In this section are two weeks of low-calorie menus designed to show how painless it can be to slim down as a "light and easy" cook. This is *not* intended as a "14-day diet" in the usual sense: it's *not* a crash program that you "go on" and then "go off" when you reach your "goal." Your real goal isn't just to get slim, but to *stay* that way. To stay slim requires developing nutritious, non-fattening cooking and eating habits you can live with for the rest of your life.

These low-calorie menus range between 1200 and 1500 calories a day. Virtually every overweight person can lose weight at a safe and comfortable rate at that range. Most people will find it unwise and self-defeating to try to lose weight on less; it's difficult to satisfy minimum daily nutritional requirements on fewer than 1200 calories, and it's almost impossible to avoid hunger and fatigue.

By following my menu suggestions you *won't* be hungry or lacking in energy. My "Light and Easy" menus and recipes are light only in calories, but rich in nutritious, bulky, appetite-satisfying foods.

Check with your doctor before you begin any extended weight-loss plan. This is *especially* important if you are more than 20 percent over-weight, if you have—or suspect you have—high blood pressure, heart disease, diabetes, high cholesterol or triglycerides, food allergies, digestive disorders, or any other health problem that imposes special eating requirements. Children, teen-agers, pregnant women, nursing mothers, and elderly people should *never* diet without medical advice.

Before you begin, equip yourself with the following:

- A reliable bathroom scale, for daily morning weigh-ins
- A food or postal scale and measuring cups and spoons, to take the guesswork out of portion sizes
- A notebook for keeping track of your daily food intake, and recording your weight loss
- A reliable calorie guide. I suggest the "blue book" you can buy from the government printing office. Send a check or money order for $5.15 to the Superintendent of Documents, U.S. Government Printing Office, Washington, D.C. 20402, and ask for the "blue book" by its correct title: *The Nutritive Value of American Foods in Common Units, Agriculture Handbook No. 456*. Several detailed calorie guidebooks are also available at bookstores.

Getting Started

Read through the menus and decide how you want to use them. You may want to begin by following the menus exactly, at least until you are familiar with calorie counts and confident in your ability to make equivalent substitutions. More than likely, however, you will want to make some modifications in the suggested menus, in keeping with your own food preferences and the availability of ingredients. The goal to work toward is the ability to map out personalized menus of nutritious, appetite-appeasing foods that can keep you happily well-fed the rest of your life!

Some points to keep in mind:

- It is not necessary to follow the daily menus in the same order in which they are given. You may, if you prefer, start with Day 2, followed by Day 7 (or any other order that's convenient).
- If you plan a meat dinner one night, try to have a poultry or seafood dinner the next.
- Although each day's food is listed in the conventional breakfast-lunch-dinner format, it's not necessary—or even desirable—to limit your daily eating pattern to three meals a day. You may find it preferable to save part of your breakfast—fruit, for example—for a mid-morning snack. You may wish to postpone dessert for later in the

evening. You can have your main meal at midday and eat "lunch" in the evening as a light supper (an arrangement that's nutritionally desirable if your schedule permits it). Several small meals a day are preferable to "three squares." The important factor is the total calories consumed all day.

- While you may divide your daily food intake into more than three meals a day, it's definitely *not* advisable to consume fewer than three meals. Skipping breakfast or lunch is self-defeating because it promotes overeating later in the day . . . the bottom line is that *more* calories are consumed!

- Since the point is to dine pleasurably, it's not necessary to eat any food you intensely dislike, or any food you're allergic to. If you can't eat fish, for example, you may substitute a poultry recipe of equivalent calorie count. Pork and ham recipes may be replaced by beef or veal.

- On the other hand, try to keep an open mind about trying new foods and combinations. On this (or any) diet plan, it's important to be flexible and open to change. Don't reject or replace a food or recipe just because it's unfamiliar. Among those with weight problems, one of the contributing characteristics is a restricted set of preferences for a few familiar (and fattening) foods. A rigid list of likes and dislikes leaves you with few alternatives when high-calorie foods are ruled out. Psych yourself into being a free-spirited adventurer where new foods and flavors are concerned. The joy of discovery is one of the pleasures of becoming a light and easy cook!

- Above all, avoid the temptation to pick a few favorite menus or recipes and repeat them day after day. Not only is this boring, it defeats the nutritional benefits of a diet that's based on a wide choice of foods. The more variety you build into your menus, the less chance there is of shortchanging yourself of needed vitamins and minerals.

Some Guidelines for Making Substitutions

Fruit: Citrus fruits of similar calorie counts are interchangeable. For example: a grapefruit half (40 calories) for a small orange (45 calories). Apples and pears are interchangeable, but the skin should be eaten because of its high-fiber content.

A half cup of strawberries (unsweetened) can also replace citrus fruit because its vitamin C content is similar. Yellow fruits—apricots, papaya, mango, peaches, nectarines, and cantaloupe—are all high in vitamin A, so you can interchange calorically similar amounts with each other. (For example: one peach or two apricots.) Cantaloupe is a particularly useful fruit—high in both vitamin C and vitamin A—yet low in calories and delicious. Fruits that are high in natural sugar can substitute for each other in calorically equal amounts: bananas, watermelon, grapes, sweet cherries, and pineapple. It is suggested that you eat fruit rather than drink fruit juices because whole fruit contains natural pectin and fiber (appetite-appeasing bulk). Fresh fruits are best, but frozen or canned (unsweetened) fruit may be substituted. Dried fruits should be substituted unit-for-unit. In other words, one raisin equals one grape; two dried apricot halves equal one fresh apricot.

Vegetables: Cooked vegetables can be eaten raw, or vice versa, if that's your preference. Calorically equivalent amounts of high vitamin A vegetables can substitute for each other. These include asparagus, beet and turnip tops, broccoli, carrots, collard greens, kale, spinach, and squash. (Peas, winter squash, and sweet potatoes are also high in vitamin A but higher in calories.) High vitamin C vegetables are interchangeable in calorically similar quantities; these include broccoli, brussels sprouts, cabbage, collards, cauliflower, kale, and peppers. Starchy vegetables can substitute for each other (or for other starchy foods like pasta or bread); these include sweet and white potatoes, corn, peas, and winter squash. Some vegetables are so low-calorie for their bulk that you can eat them freely without limiting the quantity (because the more of them you eat the less appetite you will have for other foods). Vegetables in this category include green beans, cabbage, celery, cucumber, endive, mushrooms, parsley, radishes, and spinach. A big salad before the main course is an effective de-appetizer!

Dairy Foods: You'll note that the suggested menus list 16 ounces (two cups) of non-fat milk daily, to be consumed anytime during the day. Milk can be used as a beverage, to lighten coffee or tea, in cereals, or as an ingredient in cooking. If you can't digest milk, substitute calorically equivalent amounts of plain low-fat yogurt or low-fat cottage cheese. Two cups non-fat milk are approximately equal in calories to 1⅓ cups commercial plain low-fat yogurt or 1 cup (8 ounces) of low-fat cottage cheese.

Meat, Poultry, and Seafood: The red meats used in light and easy cooking are the leanest cuts of beef, lamb, pork, and ham . . . primarily those cut from the leg and trimmed of fat. Most cuts of veal are also lean. These meats can substitute for each other in calorically similar quantities. Young frying chickens and young turkeys are nutritionally similar and are interchangeable. Most fish and seafood is relatively low-fat and can be interchanged. (Bluefish, salmon, butterfish, trout, and mackerel are higher in calories but even those so-called "fat" fish are relatively low-calorie compared with steaks and chops.) Avoid seafood canned in oil. Liver and other glandular meats are especially low in calories and rich in iron and B-vitamins.

Cereal and Grain Foods: Calorically equal amounts of breads, cereals, rice, grains, and pasta can replace each other. For the most nutrition and appetite satisfaction, it is better to choose whole grain rather than "white" cereal foods—whole grain breakfast cereals, brown rice, breads, and pasta made from whole wheat or high-protein flours. Avoid products made with added sugar or fat. Try to fit these foods into your menus in a way that doesn't call for added sugar or fat in the form of butter or high-calorie toppings.

Fat and High-Fat Foods: should be minimized. Avoid oil, shortening, butter, or margarine as an added ingredient or in frying. Despite the emphasis on low-fat ingredients, this is not a fat-free diet; many foods, even the leanest, contain some fat. Even low-fat products contain fat. The following products are high-fat and should be avoided or minimized: hard cheeses, nuts, peanut butter, salad dressings, mayonnaise, most chips, dips, spreads, crackers, and snack foods. Diet margarines, diet cheeses and spreads, commercial low-fat salad dressings are "low-fat" only in relation to regular products, so be cautious in their use. Avoid exceeding the amounts called for in menus and recipes.

Sugar and High Sugar Foods: There is no need for sugar in the diet; sugar is pure calories and nothing else. Small amounts of sugar are used in some dessert recipes, and for those who would find it difficult to do without some sweetener, it has been listed as optional in the menus. However, you'll save calories and speed weight loss if you eliminate sugar completely or use a non-caloric substitute instead. While attempting to lose weight, it's suggested that the total daily intake of sugar from all sources be limited to two tablespoons, or under 100 calories' worth. The maximum amount of optional sugar listed in the daily calorie counts is about one tablespoon; most of the dessert recipes contain no more than one tablespoon of sugar (or its caloric equivalent) per serving. Any food, drink, sweetener, syrup, spread, or snack that is primarily sugar can make up this 100-calorie limit, for example: regular soda, honey, regular pancake syrups, jams, jellies, preserves. You can cut sugar calories somewhat with low-sugar jams and syrups. But remember, they're low-sugar only in relation to the regular product. Keep in mind also that some sugar-free products are *not* low-calorie. Some are sweetened with fructose, sorbitol, or mannitol . . . sweeteners with calorie counts similar to sugar. And some "dietetic" cakes, candies, and ice creams have a high fat content, and a calorie count equal to (and sometimes more than) conventional products!

Beer, Wine, and Hard Liquor: Like sugar, alcohol is pure calories with no redeeming nutritive value. However, a small glass of very dry wine or light beer is listed as optional because a drink before dinner (or with it) is a part of dining for many people. Obviously, you'll cut calories and speed weight loss if you can do without. Learn to substitute mineral water, iced tea, or diet soda instead. If cutting down is easier than doing without, substitute a wine glass of light beer for wine . . . or combine an ounce of wine with sparkling water as a "spritzer."

Wines aren't labeled for calorie counts, but they are labeled with alcohol content. You'll save the most calories by choosing the driest wines with the lowest percentages of alcohol, some Italian and Portuguese wines, for example. "Light beers" do have their calorie counts listed on the labels.

When you cook with alcoholic beverages, the alcohol calories evaporate, leaving only flavor and the calories found in the carbohydrate (sugar) content. Since there is no carbohydrate in hard liquor, no calories remain when you "flame" fruit or other foods with brandy, rum, or whiskey (or vodka, but vodka has no flavor so there's little point in using it!). Liqueurs have a considerable amount of sugar, so the sugar calories will remain after flaming. The sweeter the wine, the more calories that remain after cooking. Alcoholic beverages used in uncooked desserts will not lose any calories, obviously.

Herbs, Spices, Seasonings, Condiments: While they aren't really calorie-free, herbs and spices are so strongly flavored and used in such small amounts that they really needn't be counted. Other strongly flavored ingredients that are relatively low-calorie are soy sauce, prepared mustard, horseradish, hot pepper and pepper sauce, garlic, vanilla extract, and bottled flavorings. But mayonnaise, tartar sauce, sweet pickle relish, chutneys, and various sandwich spreads are high in either fat or sugar (or both) and must be limited or avoided. Though low-calorie, soy, Worcestershire, and similar steak sauces are high in salt. Salt, seasoned salt, MSG, powdered broths, and bouillons needn't be counted calorically. Though salt and salty seasonings can go a long way toward making low-calorie, low-fat foods flavorful, some people need to avoid these high-sodium ingredients. If you have a water retention problem, you will have to add high-sodium ingredients to the list of foods to be avoided. It's important to follow your doctor's advice on sodium intake.

Cholesterol, Triglycerides, and Saturated fat: Naturally you'll want to follow your doctor's advice if you are on any sort of regimen aimed at lowering your cholesterol or triglyceride levels. Most of the recipes in this book are low in all kinds of fat. But some low-calorie foods *are* relatively high in cholesterol and may need to be avoided or minimized by those with special diet needs. Follow your doctor's counsel about the use of eggs, dairy products, shellfish, liver, fats, and oils. Many of the recipes in this book that call for eggs can be made—and have been tested—with liquid cholesterol-free egg substitutes.

After the Fourteen Days Are Up

· Begin planning your own daily 1200- to 1500-calorie menus, following the same framework. Write out your menus in advance. Use a calorie guide (and calculator, if necessary) to help you devise each day's eating pattern within the 1200- to 1500-calorie range.
· Continue to weigh yourself every morning before breakfast, and keep a record.

If You Stop Losing Weight

· Keep in mind that a "plateau" of no apparent weight loss on the scale is perfectly normal . . . in fact, inevitable. Even though the scale doesn't show it, you *are* continuing to lose fat. Be patient and the scale will again begin to register a loss within a few days.

If a Plateau Lasts More Than Two Weeks

· You may be retaining water. Cut down on salt and salty foods as much as possible.
· If the plateau still continues, eliminate the evening dessert or any other recipe that uses refined sugar (or prepare it with a sugar substitute).
· Recheck portion sizes and calorie math. Are you consuming more calories than you think?

When You Reach Your Desired Weight

· Add an additional 100 calories to your daily menu. If, at the end of the first week your scale continues to show a weight loss, add another 100 calories in the second week. Continue adding calories in 100-calorie increments until your weight stabilizes.

If You Regain More Than Three Pounds

· Immediately return to the 1200- to 1500-calorie eating pattern and stay on it *until* your scale shows your desired weight and remains there for one week. By careful charting of your daily calorie intake and morning weight, you will find the correct daily calorie average to maintain your figure at your desired weight, a calorie goal that's uniquely appropriate for your height, build, age, life-style, and metabolism. Daily weigh-ins will alert you to future weight problems before they develop.

Day 1

BREAKFAST	APPROXIMATE CALORIES*	
1 eating orange, seeded and diced	65	
2 slices high-fiber bread, toasted with 2 tsp.		
diet margarine or	100	
1 tsp. butter or regular margarine	35	
Coffee or tea		
Optional: 1 tsp. sugar		20
16 oz. non-fat milk (anytime during day)	180	

* Rounded off to nearest 5

		APPROXIMATE CALORIES *

LUNCH

Salade Niçoise (page 128)	255	
Optional: 2 sesame-seeded breadsticks		20
Iced coffee or tea (with lemon, *optional*)		
Optional: 1 tsp. sugar		20
1 peach or nectarine or ½ cup canned, juice-packed slices	35	

SNACK

Optional: small banana		80

DINNER

Spinach salad (3 cups spinach, torn)	40	
with 2 Tbs. low-cal commercial French dressing,	60	
and 2 tsp. bacon bits	30	
Optional: 3 oz. dry white wine		60
Oven-Fried Chicken (page 48)	175	
Oriental Stir-Fried Zucchini (page 123)	55	
or Oriental Vegetable Medley (page 123)		+30
French Potatoes and Mushrooms (page 140)	65	
or Parsleyed Potatoes (page 140)		+10
½ cup frozen low-fat yogurt or ice milk	100	
with Strawberry Romanoff Sauce (page 227)	45	
Coffee or tea		
Optional: 1 tsp. sugar		20
TOTAL	1240	*1500* †

* Rounded off to nearest 5
† With optionals

Day 2

	APPROXIMATE
BREAKFAST ON THE TRAIN OR AT THE DESK	CALORIES*

1 tangerine or small eating orange	40	
3 fig bars or Fig Newtons (preferably whole wheat)	75	
Coffee or tea		
Optional: 1 tsp. sugar		20
16 oz. non-fat milk (anytime during day)	180	

LUNCH

Ham and Mushroom Frittata (page 162)	275	
Green beans cooked in broth	25	
1 slice cracked wheat bread with 1 tsp. diet margarine or	65	
½ tsp. butter or regular margarine	20	
Coffee or tea		
Optional: 1 tsp. sugar		20
½ cup grapes	35	

DINNER

Large salad: 3 cups shredded lettuce, green pepper, onion	30	
with 2 Tbs. low-fat dressing	60	
Mexicali Chiliburger Skillet (page 33)	230	
Small ear corn or ½ cup corn kernels	70	
with 1 tsp. diet margarine or ½ tsp. butter or margarine	20	
Optional: 8 oz. light beer		70
1 nectarine or Nectarine-filled Cheesecake (pages 210 and 213)	90	+100
Coffee or tea		
Optional: 1 tsp. sugar		20
TOTAL	1215	1445 †

* Rounded off to nearest 5
† With optionals

Day 3

	APPROXIMATE CALORIES*	
BREAKFAST		
4 High-Fiber "Pancakes" (page 163) or		
2 slices High-Fiber Toast (page 164)	200	
with 3 Tbs. Light Honey Syrup (page 166)	75	
Coffee or tea		
Optional: 1 tsp. sugar		20
16 oz. non-fat milk (anytime during day)	180	
EAT-OUT LUNCH		
Lunch-counter sandwich with 2 pieces of bread	130	
and 2 oz. lean roast beef or "boiled" ham	120	
plus catsup or mustard, dill pickles, lettuce	50	
Iced coffee, tea, diet soda, or mineral water,		
with lemon or lime	5	
SNACK		
Optional: ½ cantaloupe		60
DINNER		
Garlic-Broiled Fish Fillets (page 76)	140	
Broccoli au Gratin (page 113)	85	
Barley Romano (page 143)	120	
Minted Cucumber Slices (page 127) or sliced		
tomatoes	35	
Optional: 3 oz. dry white wine		60
Yogurt Cake (page 205) topped with	145	
Optional: 5 Tbs. juice-packed crushed		
pineapple		40
Coffee or tea		
Optional: 1 tsp. sugar		20
TOTAL	1285	*1485* †

* Rounded off to nearest 5
† With optionals

Day 4

	APPROXIMATE CALORIES*	
BREAKFAST		
1 cup cooked oatmeal	150	
with 2 Tbs. raisins	60	
Coffee or tea		
Optional: 1 tsp. sugar		20
16 oz. non-fat milk (anytime during day)	180	
MID-MORNING SNACK		
Optional: Berry Shake (page 217) using 1 cup milk allowance		40
LUNCH		
Light Reuben Sandwich (page 177)	265	
Green pepper rings or dill pickle slices	15	
Optional: 8 oz. light beer		70
Coffee, tea, diet soda, or mineral water		
Optional: 1 tsp. sugar		20
DINNER		
Large tossed green salad (3 cups mixed raw vegetables)	30	
with 2 Tbs. low-calorie Italian dressing	60	
Veal Chops Neapolitan (page 36)	320	
Optional: 1 bread stick		20
Coffee or tea		
Optional: 1 tsp. sugar		20
Cream Cheesecake (page 209)	185	
TOTAL	1265	1455 †

* Rounded off to nearest 5
† With optionals

Day 5

	APPROXIMATE CALORIES*	
BREAKFAST		
1 cup "Special K" or other unsweetened cereal	75	
½ cup blueberries (or sliced strawberries)	45	
16 oz. non-fat milk (anytime during day)	180	
Optional: 1 tsp. sugar		20
Coffee or tea		
LUNCH		
Meal-Size Turkey Zucchini Soup (page 106)	200	
1 slice Banana Nut Bread (page 202)	130	
1 tsp. diet margarine or ½ tsp. butter or regular margarine	20	
6 apricot halves, fresh, dried, or canned (unsweetened)	55	
Coffee or tea		
Optional: 1 tsp. sugar		20
DINNER		
Raw vegetable sticks with yogurt dip	100	
Greek Spaghetti and Meatballs with Eggplant Sauce (page 142)	300	
Optional: small pita bread		80
Optional: 3 oz. dry red wine		60
Coffee or tea		
Optional: 1 tsp. sugar		20
Pineapple-Cheese Dessert (page 223)	130	
TOTAL	1235	1435 †

* Rounded off to nearest 5
† With optionals

Day 6

	APPROXIMATE
BREAKFAST	CALORIES *

2-egg omelet or scramble made in a nonstick pan with no fat added or ½ cup liquid no-cholesterol substitute	160	
1 oz. Canadian bacon, browned in nonstick pan with no fat added	50	
½ papaya with lemon juice or ½ cantaloupe	60	+20
Coffee or tea		
Optional: 1 tsp. sugar		20
1 slice whole grain bread or toast with 1 tsp. diet margarine, or	65	
½ tsp. butter or regular margarine	20	
16 oz. non-fat milk (anytime during day)	180	

LUNCH

Luncheon "sundae": ¾ cup low-fat cottage cheese garnished with diced fruit:	150	
1 eating orange, peeled	80	
1 unpeeled apple	65	
Optional: Coffee or tea		
Optional: 1 tsp. sugar		20

DINNER

Waldorf Celery Slaw (page 126)	65	
Ham and Noodle Bake (page 56)	300	
Orange Ginger Beets (page 114)	65	
Optional: 8 oz. light beer or 3 oz. dry wine		70
Optional: Apple-Raisin Muffin (page 170)		75
Coffee or tea		
Optional: 1 tsp. sugar		20
TOTAL	1260	1485 †

* Rounded off to nearest 5
† With optionals

Day 7

	APPROXIMATE CALORIES*
BREAKFAST	
1 toasted English muffin, split, spread	145
with 2 Tbs. (1 oz.) low-fat cream cheese or	
Neufchatel	50
½ grapefruit	40
Coffee or tea	
Optional: 1 tsp. sugar	*20*
16 oz. non-fat milk (anytime during day)	180

LUNCH OUT	
Broiled hamburger on a bun with raw onion,	
pickles, lettuce, tomato	350
Diet soda	

DINNER	
Optional: 3 oz. dry white wine	*60*
Large salad: 3 cups mixed raw vegetables	30
with 2 Tbs. low-calorie Italian dressing	60
Spaghetti with Spinach Pesto Sauce (page 153)	345
½ cup sliced strawberries or	60
Strawberry Shortcake (page 204)	*+115*
Coffee or tea	
Optional: 1 tsp. sugar	*20*
TOTAL	1260 *1475 †*

Day 8

	APPROXIMATE CALORIES*
BREAKFAST IN A HURRY	
Eggnog meal-in-a-glass: combine in blender:	
1 egg	80
1 cup ice-cold non-fat milk, plus	90
2 Tbs. undiluted orange juice concentrate	50

* Rounded off to nearest 5
† With optionals

APPROXIMATE
CALORIES *

COFFEE BREAK

Coffee or tea		
Optional: 1 tsp. sugar		*20*
1 medium banana or 1 slice Raisin Bran Loaf (page 170)	100	
Optional: 1 tsp. low-sugar orange marmalade		*10*
8 oz. additional non-fat milk (anytime during day)	90	

LUNCH

Tomato Stuffed with Chicken-Pineapple Salad (page 128)	140	
1 slice rye toast	65	
with 1 tsp. diet margarine or ½ tsp. butter or regular margarine	20	
Coffee, tea, mineral water, or diet soda		
Optional: 1 tsp. sugar		*20*
1 peach or nectarine or ½ cup unsweetened slices	40	

DINNER

Tossed salad (3 cups raw vegetables)	30	
2 Tbs. low-fat commercial dressing	60	
Optional: 3 oz. dry red wine		*60*
Budget Boeuf Bourguignon (page 86)	190	
½ cup rice or noodles	110	
Dilled Brussels Sprouts (page 112), or green beans	60	
Apple Cracker Betty (page 215)	170	
Coffee or tea		
Optional: 1 tsp. sugar		*20*
TOTAL	1295	*1425* †

* Rounded off to nearest 5
† With optionals

Day 9

	APPROXIMATE CALORIES*	
BREAKFAST		
1 wedge honeydew melon or 1 cup cubed melon	50	
1 bagel, toasted	150	
1 oz. low-fat cream cheese or Neufchatel	50	
Optional: 1 tsp. sugar or low-sugar jam		20
Coffee or tea		
16 oz. non-fat milk (anytime during day)	180	
LUNCH		
Beefburger and Sprouts in Pita Pocket (page 179)	235	
1 tomato, sliced	25	
Iced tea, diet soda, or mineral water		
Fruit Yogurt (page 218)	100	
AFTERNOON SNACK:		
1 apricot	20	
DINNER		
Taco Salad (page 129)	80	
Turkey Chili (page 95)	145	
½ cup rice	110	
Cottage Cheese Cornbread (page 205)	45	
1 tsp. diet margarine or ½ tsp. butter or regular margarine	20	
Optional: 8 oz. light beer		70
Coffee, tea, diet soda, or mineral water		
Optional: 1 tsp. sugar		20
Optional: Carrot Cake (page 204)		180
TOTAL	1210	1500 †

* Rounded off to nearest 5
† With optionals

Day 10

	APPROXIMATE	
BREAKFAST	**CALORIES** *	
Breakfast Banana Split:		
Medium banana	100	
with 2 scoops (¾ cup) low-fat cottage cheese	150	
Topped with ½ cup sliced berries or peaches	30	
Optional: 1 tsp. sugar		20
Coffee or tea		
16 oz. non-fat milk (anytime during day)	180	
LUNCH		
French Bread Pizza (page 180)	195	
Green pepper rings	15	
Diet soda, coffee, or tea		
Optional: 1 tsp. sugar		20
AFTERNOON SNACK		
Optional: Apple or pear		*100*
DINNER		
½ cup sliced tomato	50	
Marinated Round Steak (page 68)	160	
Optional: 3 oz. dry red wine		*60*
Baked potato	100	
with Sour Cream Sauce (page 157)	55	
Steamed Asparagus, 10 spears (page 111) with	30	
Optional: 1 Tbs. low-fat mayonnaise or diet margarine or 1½ tsp. butter or regular margarine		*50*
Frozen Yogurt Pumpkin Pie (page 214)	135	
Coffee or tea		
Optional: 1 tsp. sugar		*20*
TOTAL	1200	*1470* †

* Rounded off to nearest 5
† With optionals

Day 11

	APPROXIMATE	
BREAKFAST	CALORIES*	
1 cup raisin bran cereal	145	
16 oz. non-fat milk (anytime during day)	180	
Coffee or tea		
Optional: 1 tsp. sugar		*20*
SNACK		
Optional: 1 eating orange		*80*
LUNCH		
Italian Supper Salad (page 129)	280	
1 slice Italian or French bread	100	
1 tsp. diet margarine or ½ tsp. butter or regular margarine	20	
Coffee or tea		
Optional: 1 tsp. sugar		*20*
Optional: mineral water or diet soda		
DINNER		
Spinach salad (3 cups, torn) with raw mushrooms and	50	
2 Tbs. low-calorie French dressing	60	
Optional: 3 oz. dry white wine		*60*
Chicken a l'Orange (page 58)	220	
Carrot and Celery Casserole (page 115)	40	
Light-and-Easy Fruited Rice (page 149) or	80	
Brown Rice (page 146)		*+10*
Coffee or tea		
Optional: 1 tsp. sugar		*20*
Chocolate Mousse (page 222)	80	
TOTAL	1255	*1465 †*

* Rounded off to nearest 5
† With optionals

Day 12

	APPROXIMATE
BREAKFAST	CALORIES*

2 slices high-fiber bread, toasted,	100	
spread with 1 oz. low-fat cream cheese or		
Neufchatel and sprinkled with	50	
2 Tbs. raisins or minced dried apricots and		
sprinkled with cinnamon, if desired	60	
Coffee or tea		
Optional: 1 tsp. sugar		20
16 oz. non-fat milk (anytime during day)	180	

LUNCH

Egg Salad (or Cottage Tuna) (page 174)	75	
on 2 slices whole or cracked wheat or high-		
fiber bread	140	
with lettuce, pickles, etc.	10	
Fruit spritz (pages 186–87)	50	
Unpeeled apple or pear	80	

DINNER ON THE PATIO

Optional: dry wine or light beer		70
Steak and Mushroom Skewers (page 66)	190	
Foiled Vegetables (page 82)	40	
Optional: small ear of corn with		70
1 tsp. diet margarine or ½ tsp. butter		20
Picnic Coleslaw (page 82)	50	
Cottage Cheese Potato Salad (page 129)	100	
Shortcake on a Stick (page 83) or ¾ cup ice		
milk	165	
Coffee or tea		
Optional: 1 tsp. sugar		20
TOTAL	1290	*1490* †

---

* Rounded off to nearest 5
† With optionals

Day 13

	APPROXIMATE CALORIES*	
BREAKFAST		
½ ripe mango, papaya, or cantaloupe	75	
Blueberry Cheese Muffin (page 169) or	70	
1 slice Raisin Bran Loaf (page 170)		+10
1 tsp. diet margarine or ½ tsp. butter,		
regular margarine, or low-sugar jam	20	
16 oz. non-fat milk (anytime during day)	180	
Coffee or tea		
Optional: 1 tsp. sugar		20
LUNCH		
Sandwich: ½ serving of Light Meat Loaf (page		
51) or 2 oz. lean roast beef round	100	
2 slices high-fiber bread	100	
1 Tbs. catsup	15	
Cauliflower Bowl (page 126)	35	
1 cup fresh strawberries	55	
Coffee, tea, diet soda, or mineral water		
Optional: 1 tsp. sugar		20
DINNER		
Marinated Mushrooms (page 192)	35	
Optional: 3 oz. dry red wine		60
Liver and Onions (page 38)	225	
Light-and-Easy Oven French Fries (page 138)	75	
Green Beans and Tomato with Basil (page 118)	25	
Orange Cake (page 144)	200	
BEDTIME SNACK		
Optional: Light Hot Chocolate (page 171)		
made with part of non-fat milk allowance,		
plus 1 graham cracker		+100
TOTAL	1210	1420 †

* Rounded off to nearest 5
† With optionals

Day 14

	APPROXIMATE
BREAKFAST	CALORIES*

1 cup wheat flakes	100	
with ¾ cup blueberries, fresh or frozen		
(unsweetened)	45	
16 oz. non-fat milk (anytime during day)	180	
Coffee or tea		
Optional: 1 tsp. sugar		20

LUNCH

Grilled Ham, or Turkey Pastrami, and Cheese		
Sandwich (page 177)	240 (300)	
Dill pickle chips, lettuce	25	
Optional: 8 oz. light beer		70
Coffee or tea		
Optional: 1 tsp. sugar		20

SNACK

2 squares Orange "Candy" (page 218), or		
small tangerine	35	

DINNER

Large salad (3 cups green leafy vegetables)	30	
with 2 Tbs. low-calorie salad dressing	60	
Optional: 3 oz. dry red wine		60
Gypsy One-Pot Veal Goulash (page 92)	310	
1 slice rye bread	65	
with 1 tsp. diet margarine or ½ tsp. butter		
or regular margarine	20	
Orange Chiffon Pudding (page 224)	110	
Optional: coffee or tea		
Optional: 1 tsp. sugar		20
TOTAL	1220	*1410* †
	(1280)	*(1470)* †

* Rounded off to nearest 5
† With optionals

INDEX